TONY LOCK
AGGRESSIVE MASTER OF SPIN

Also by Alan Hill

The Family Fortune – A Saga of Sussex Cricket
A Chain of Spin Wizards
Hedley Verity – Portrait of a Cricketer
Johnny Wardle – Cricket Conjuror
Les Ames
Herbert Sutcliffe – Cricket Maestro
Bill Edrich
Peter May
Jim Laker
The Bedsers – Twinning Triumphs
Brian Close – Cricket's Lionheart
Daring Young Men – The Story of England's
Victorious Tour of Australia and New Zealand 1954/55

TONY LOCK
AGGRESSIVE
MASTER OF SPIN

Alan Hill

The
History
Press

To Betty for sharing the pleasures of our travels across the world and the hospitality of so many kind friends down under.

First published 2008

The History Press Ltd.
The Mill, Brimscombe Port
Stroud, Gloucestershire, GL5 2QG
www.thehistorypress.co.uk

British Library Cataloguing in Publication Data.
A catalogue record for this book is available from the British Library.

ISBN 978 07524 4251 8

Typesetting and origination by The History Press Ltd.
Printed in Great Britain

Contents

Foreword

by Dennis Lillee MBE

Alan Hill could not have thought of a more vibrant subject to write on than G.A.R. 'Lockie', or 'Bo' as his West Australian teammates called him, among other things at times. He was a real mixture of the controversial and the inspirational; his cricket career and life were studded with a cocktail of all of that.

A much-decorated career for England and Surrey was highlighted by being an integral member of the England Ashes-winning side of 1953 that heralded a relatively brief but golden era of Test success for England, as well as being a vital member of the all-powerful Surrey teams of the 1950s. In both of those teams, of course, Lockie was paired with perhaps his more famous spinning partner, Jim Laker.

With such a combative, confronting personality combined with the legacy of a doubtful bowling action that brought him under the close scrutiny of the game's authorities – ultimately leading to a significant change of action to remain an effective force in cricket – meant that controversy and Lock were never far apart. I understand that administrators and Lockie were not necessarily always on the friendliest of terms, a scenario that I can personally relate to!

Lockie, however, was never afraid of a challenge – adapting as he did to that necessary change – and was to later write the Australian chapter of his cricket career in conditions that on face value were very foreign to his left-arm finger-spin craft and former lifestyle.

A shock omission from an MCC team selected to tour Australia in 1962, a disappointed and disillusioned Tony Lock was in just the right frame of mind to give a positive answer to a telephone call from Les Truman, the WACA secretary of the time, to play for Western Australia in the 1962/63 Australian summer. An initial one-year stint was to extend to eight seasons and led to uplifting all of his family to make their lives in Western Australia – a place where Lockie called home until his death in March 1995.

For those eight Australian summers, Lockie wore the black and gold with great distinction and for much of that time as its captain. He continued the great work of his predecessor, the late Barry Shepherd, and handed a blueprint of success to those leaders that followed in John Inverarity, Rod Marsh, Kim Hughes, Graeme Wood, Geoff Marsh and Tom Moody, duly helping to convert the once Cinderella State in Sheffield Shield cricket into the Australian domestic-cricket powerhouse for three decades between 1967 and 1997.

Lockie performed remarkably under Australian conditions, with his clever variations and native cunning that 'conned' even the best of the Australian players of the time who he could count among his 326 first-class wickets for Western Australia. He was the ultimate professional and an uncompromising but respected leader who led from the front by performance, and did not accept weaklings or those that were not fully committed to the team cause.

Yet, just as equally, in his own gruff manner, he was awfully supportive and instructive to any young players who he considered had the talent and the attitude to realise their true potential in the game. Lockie had a great knack of getting the best out of the players who played with and under him; it was my good fortune to play under Lockie in my introduction to first-class cricket. Perhaps some part of my own personality and aggression may have gelled with him as he was always very supportive towards me.

I salute Lockie for some happy personal memories and for the positive influence that he had on my own early career. He left a lasting legacy for me in having given me the less-than affectionate nickname of 'FOT', during one hot summer's day in the field, a handle that still sticks with me today among my contemporary teammates and opponents.

Love him or otherwise, Tony Lock was one of the great cricket personalities of his era.

Introduction

The remarkable life of an enduring cricketer placed him in the halls of fame in two hemispheres. Tony Lock, in the words of his Surrey junior, Micky Stewart, was the most inspirational of all the players he had encountered in his own long association with the game. Yet, at the same time, he regrets that Surrey did not see the best of his former colleague in terms of bowling purity. The years of controversy in which Lock destructively ruled at Kennington Oval were disavowed in a return to the orthodox bowling of his youth in Western Australia. His reinvention as a bowler occurred after he had viewed himself on film in a private showing during the tour of New Zealand in 1959. 'If I'd known I was throwing I wouldn't have bowled like that,' was a belated exclamation of remorse.

Pat Pocock, as a younger county player, says: 'The extraordinary thing about Tony is that when he "threw" he was an Underwood type of bowler – by far the best bad-wicket bowler in the world. He then became the best hard-wicket bowler in the manner of Bishan Bedi.'

The zest and fervour which Lock projected as a cricketer was given full rein when he assumed the role of captain, first at Leicester after leaving Surrey, and then in Perth. The rekindling of his talents in Australia and the adjustment to the slower style brought him a late harvest of wickets. He led Western Australia to a Sheffield Shield triumph over Victoria in the torrid heat at Melbourne in February 1968. Dennis Lillee, who has kindly provided the foreword to my book, was one of his young disciples in Perth. 'Lockie taught me the need for a hold-no-quarter approach to playing the game. I had a lot of that in my make-up but to see my captain with the same attributes endorsing this was very important to a young player like myself.'

The intensity of Lock's cricket always signalled him as a man to watch. As one Oval partisan remembered, it was all 'edge-of-the-seat stuff,' Lock possessed a charisma which would have charmed and enthralled another generation just as much as it did his devotees at Kennington Oval and in Western Australia.

Jackie Birkenshaw played under Lock and his successor, Raymond Illingworth, at Leicester. He remembers that each of them had tremendous self-belief. 'Lockie was the showman and led by example. He never allowed a game to drift and tried to make things happen. We watched him tumbling and diving around on the field. You could not help but be infected by his enthusiasm.'

The headlines in Surrey's seven championship years in the 1950s were often dominated by the spinning exploits of Lock and his partner, Jim Laker. It was an alliance culled from fierce personal rivalry but their names were twinned in cricket lore in a way more usually associated with opening batsmen or opening bowlers. Peter Walker, the former Glamorgan and England all-rounder, remembers the perils of facing the pair on the uncovered wickets of the time. 'They induced a kind of fear; there was always the danger of receiving an unplayable ball.'

Lock, at seventeen the youngest player to represent the county in 1946, rose to eminence in a lenient regime. He was the first genuine slow left-arm bowler to play for Surrey. This distinction was soon revealed as a false dawn when he exchanged the hailed orthodoxy for a more violent mode of attack. After two winters spent working at a Croydon indoor school he emerged with a lower trajectory that produced waspish spin at around medium pace. The ball veered crazily from the leg stump to hit the top of the off and often leapt shoulder high.

Jim Parks, in Sussex, was one witness of the newly arrived vicious executioner. 'As a youngster, Lockie had a nice straight arm and was a bowler with flight. Suddenly, the arm bent a little and he became absolutely lethal. He had an enormous drag, too, and he hurled the ball at you from about twenty yards. I scored a few runs against him but you had to fight when the wicket was doing a bit. It was quite a contest.'

Tony Lock won renown in three distinct phases as a cricketer. Contemporaries have said that there has never been a more aggressive spin bowler. His vintage years with Surrey were in the mid-1950s.

He twice headed the national averages; he took 212 wickets in 1957, the last bowler to reach this milestone in a season. He is ninth in the list of all-time wicket-takers, with 2,844 wickets at 19.23 runs each. He was not to be underestimated as a batsman, as he is the only player to score 10,000 runs without a century.

All of my conversations have yielded abiding memories of Lock as a magician in the field, either in his favoured backward short-leg position, or pulling off breathtaking catches off his own bowling. Neville Cardus recalled Lock holding 'quite sinful catches, catches which were not there until his rapid, hungry eyesight created them.' Micky Stewart said: 'The spectacular ones, the sudden full-length dives were the easy ones. His best were when he took the rockets close in, without anyone noticing.' Lock's brilliance as a close fieldsman brought him 831 catches, a career tally only exceeded by Frank Woolley and W.G. Grace.

Geoff Havercroft, the former secretary of the West Australian Cricket Association, first recommended the concept of this book to me. He has since been an able and diligent collaborator and researcher, and also used his good offices to arrange interviews with John Inverarity, the former WA captain, and Dennis Lillee, the current president at the WACA, during my visit to Perth in December 2006. I am most grateful to him for this service and also for undertaking interviews with Ian Brayshaw, Tony Mann and Graham McKenzie, other contemporaries of Lock. It was also good to meet two Surrey exiles again, Peter Loader and Ron Tindall, and be entertained and enlightened with their memories. Among immediate family and close friends I am also indebted to Lock's sons, Richard and Graeme; his brother, Bryan; Nova Hearn, the cousin of his wife, Audrey Lock; Alan Wainscoat and the late Julia White, who offered splendid hospitality and recollections of her long-standing friendship with a great cricketer during a stay at her home in Pembrokeshire.

In England, Roger Packham, the historian, has given invaluable and much appreciated help and guidance in relating the events of Lock's boyhood – and in drawing up profiles of his cricket mentors, headmaster Leonard Moulding and Sir Henry Leveson Gower, the former Surrey president and squire in the picturesque Surrey village of Limpsfield in the lee of the North Downs. Other contributors to the early years were Derek Horn, a fellow pupil at Limpsfield School, Sir Oliver Popplewell and John Banfield, both former Surrey Colts. Sir Oliver pointed me in the right direction when he said that Lock was the best he had seen for a boy of his age.

The remembrances of a great cricketer have been given further impetus in conversations with Surrey and England contemporaries. My book on Lock completes a quartet of studies – it follows Peter May, Jim Laker and the Bedsers – in the Surrey canon. So, this has been an opportunity to revisit the best of times in company with Sir Alec Bedser, Arthur McIntyre, Micky Stewart, Raman Subba Row, Pat Pocock, David Sydenham, Richard Jefferson, David Allen, Trevor Bailey, Doug Insole, Donald Carr, Peter Walker, Peter Richardson, Jim Parks and Tom Graveney. Yorkshire contemporaries, Brian Close, Ted Lester, Bob Appleyard and Raymond Illingworth, have also recalled the courage of a vaunted rival. Illingworth recalled, with some amusement, the keen rivalry between Lock and his arch rival for England honours in Yorkshire, Johnny Wardle. There was also praise from him for a bowler who was always a threat, 'even when we were chasing a small target.'

Michael Turner, the former Leicestershire secretary, was another splendid host with cherished memories of his former captain at Grace Road. He, along with Lock's off-spinning partner, Jack Birkenshaw, remembers the impact on the county's fortunes in the mid-1960s. One of the most amazing aspects of Lock's late-flowering career was that he was commuting between two countries 12,000 miles apart. The transformation in the fortunes at Leicester and in Western Australia raised the status of hitherto struggling cricket camps. One writer noted the portentous arrival of the veteran at Leicester: 'Lock's effect on the county was electrifying, the players were swept along by his leadership and came to believe, for the first time in Leicestershire's history, that they were capable of beating any other county.' He carried the county from the lower depths of the championship to second place to Yorkshire in his last season in 1967.

I must also thank archivists and librarians: David Studham, at the Melbourne Cricket Club; Sylvia Michael at Leicester; Jo Miller at the Oval; David Robertson at Canterbury and Rob Boddie at Hove for their support on a marathon project. David Bennett, the graphologist, has given character impressions based on Lock's handwriting. Alf Batchelder, the Australian cricket historian, has provided illustration items and referred me to notes on the Sheffield Shield in his book, *Pavilions in the Park*. As always, my researches have been lightened by the courteous assistance of the British Newspaper Library staff at Colindale, London. Paul Dyson has brought his statistical expertise to the task of providing a detailed analysis of Lock's career.

Tony Lock was the prince of showmen and the epitome of ebullience on the cricket field. A celebratory roll accompanied the taking of each and every wicket. He placed a severe strain on his vocal chords in his appeals. They reverberated loudly down the Harleyford Road at Kennington. It was said of him that when he appealed at the Oval, someone else was given out at Lord's. There is a strong view that he was responsible for the current vogue of hugs and kisses in the modern game. It is not unfounded. He was always an affectionate man beneath the stern and forbidding façade.

Alan Hill
August 2008

ONE

From School to County

'I shall never forget how good Tony Lock was even at that young age.'
– Sir Oliver Popplewell

The proud parent could not contain his glee. One Croydon opponent remembered the joy of Fred Lock on a summer's day at Limpsfield in July 1929. The tumble of words was an extravagant gesture of pride at the birth of a great cricketer. In the years ahead it would be sealed as a prophetic announcement. 'Fred rushed up to me and excitedly said: "We had a son yesterday, and he's going to play for England."'

Tony Lock, as the son of a domestic chauffeur and local cricket celebrity, grew up in the snug cluster of Surrey villages close to the north-west Kent border. Cricket at Limpsfield was played on the common, part of a swathe of ancient heath land which is so characteristic of this serene countryside. The village still retains its medieval character despite modern amenities; the centuries-old dwellings perch together as old friends that climb up the steep high street. The twelfth-century St Peter's parish church, where both Lock and his elder brother, Bryan, were choirboys, nestles proudly in the lee of the North Downs.

Tucked at the bottom of the cricket field, little more than a six-hit away, is the church school, its tall windows and high ceilings betraying its Victorian origins. This is where headmaster Leonard Moulding held sway as a disciplinarian, running the school almost like a military academy for nearly thirty years. One former pupil, Derek Horn, remembers Moulding as a big man who dominated the classroom and regularly carried a cane in his hand to admonish offending children. 'I think the other teachers as well as the children were in awe of him.'

One item in the school logbook in September 1941 cites the twelve-year-old Tony Lock as receiving punishment for misbehaviour. Punishment at the school was graded to fit the crime, the most severe for actions of outright insolence. The young Tony received the special attention of the headmaster for his offence. The ominous wording, 'inflicted by', specifies Moulding and that it was his cane that administered 'six strokes on the hand and two on the seat.'

The religious assemblies held in a room adjoining the main school were followed by another instance of military-style discipline by Moulding. His pupils were constantly reminded that he had served as a physical training instructor in the Army during the First World War. At the end of the morning devotions, he would shepherd the children with the brisk tapping of his cane into a 'left-right' march back to the classroom. Playtime at the school was summarily ended with a blast on a whistle. This was a signal that everyone should keep still before the instruction to line up and form a 'crocodile' for an ordered return to lessons. 'It was a kind of square-bashing for children,' remembers Derek Horn.

None of the children was excluded from the Friday games day. Moulding selected two teams comprising his best players and another team called 'the scraps'. A particularly testing exercise was fielding using a cricket cradle. 'We were only little boys but our headmaster had no scruples. He threw the ball as hard as he could into the cradle,' says Horn. It was a discipline designed to sharpen the reflexes. Only the most alert could cling on to the ball as it careered violently at differing angles from the slatted box. It was an early lesson for Tony Lock in achieving mastery as a fieldsman.

There was a strong patriotic atmosphere at the school in the final days of Britain's imperial rule of the world. Commemorative days were zealously observed and the Empire Day celebrations were endowed with a special fervour. Leonard Moulding devised an elaborate programme, including the school's annual sports day. There was a guest speaker, usually a prominent military dignitary, the ceremony of saluting the flag, an exhibition of school work, prize-giving on a dais beside the British Legion Club and concluding with teas for parents and children.

Leonard Moulding, despite his magisterial manner, was regarded as a man who ran a good school. He made sure as he presided over the classes that none of his pupils left without knowing how to read or write. He was particularly praised for the care he displayed during the years of the Second World War. One obituary on his death at the age of seventy-six in September 1965 commented: 'As headmaster he will be remembered for the constant watch which he kept on the pupils' welfare during the air raids.'

Limpsfield was a village under siege at the height of the German bombardment. From late August 1940 it suffered raids both by day and night. 'We were on a direct line for attacks on London,' recalls Derek Horn. 'During the day it was the turn of fighter planes in aerial battles above us. It wasn't exactly hellfire corner but it was pretty busy and frightening for a time.'

For the children of the village this involved rapid escapes to the air-raid shelters positioned on the perimeter of the cricket field. Most schooldays were interrupted by raid alerts and there were times when pupils were detained in shelters for entire mornings or afternoons. An exasperated Moulding wrote in the school logbook in October 1940: 'There were five air-raid warnings today. Times were: 9.00 a.m. to 9.40, 9.50 to 10.55, 12.03 p.m. to 12.40, 1.20 to 2.20, and 3.05 to 3.33. Fifty-five children absent in the morning and seventy-seven in the afternoon.' The shelters that once helped to guard Limpsfield children during the horrors of the Blitz have been reconstructed in association with the National Trust and are now used for history studies by another generation. Tony Lock grew to adolescence in the austere and grim years of the 1940s, although he did have the blessing of influential benefactors in his progress as a cricketer. Parental support was unfailing and he also came under the vigilant scrutiny of headmaster Leonard Moulding and the distinguished squire of Limpsfield, Henry Dudley Gresham Leveson Gower.

Leveson Gower (pronounced 'Loosen Gore') held high rank in English cricket for almost six decades. He was one of a Limpsfield family of a dozen brothers and known as 'Shrimp' among his associates because of his small stature. He was an Oxford blue at the turn of the twentieth century and led the university to a dramatic win by four wickets over Cambridge at Lord's in 1896. One Oxford contemporary, Sir Foster Cunliffe, wrote of his captain: 'We possessed in him the ideal Varsity captain. I have never played under such a leader and the team that finds one is indeed fortunate.'

Leveson Gower captained England in his only three Tests on the tour of South Africa in 1909/10. He represented Surrey from 1895 to 1920 and was the county captain for three years. He achieved equal if not greater renown as an administrator, including a long spell as a Test selector and service on both MCC and Surrey committees.

The dignitary of Titsey Place at Limpsfield did, in the natural order of things, establish a bond of sympathy with Leonard Moulding, a representative of the professional class and a shrewd cricket observer. Moulding was a veteran of the Limpsfield Club, representing them for over thirty years, as well as captain in the years leading up to the war. His liaison – a common undertaking – with Leveson Gower was one that would have great significance for an aspiring and enthusiastic pupil.

The parental pleasure of Fred Lock was heightened by their interest in his son. He was himself renowned as a fast bowler throughout East Surrey and West Kent. On his death in 1959 the Lock family inherited two mounted cricket balls. One was inscribed and marked his achievement in taking 9-15 for Limpsfield against Croydon in August 1923. This preceded the first references to him in the club records of 1924 and 1925, both against Oxted. He failed to score in the first game which Oxted won but not before his colleague Moulding had taken seven wickets in a closely contested match. Next season, in the return fixture between the local rivals, the tables were turned. Limpsfield were the victors and Fred Lock hit 30 and took 4-24. *The Westerham Herald* reported: 'On a bumpy pitch some brilliant hitting by F. Lock enabled Limpsfield to pass Oxted's total with six wickets down.'

It was highly possible that the ambitions that Fred Lock vested in his son, Tony, might have been realised by the father himself but for the demands of the recessionary years of the 1920s. As a signal of his all-round talents, he was offered terms by Surrey. He declined what must have been a tempting proposition. The hailed cricketer was mindful of his domestic responsibilities at a time when first-class cricket was hardly a financial sinecure. Instead he pursued a livelihood as chauffeur to the Sankey family in Blue House Lane in Limpsfield. Later, following the death of his employer, he set up in business as a painter and decorator.

Bereavements stalked the Lock family. Fred served in the Queen's Royal West Kent Regiment in the First World War. He came through unscathed but had to suffer the mental scars of the death of his twin brother in the conflict. Family researches recently carried out by a granddaughter have brought to light another casualty – the death of another brother in the war. There was a bereavement of more immediate concern to Tony and his brother, Bryan. Tony was only eleven when his mother died in early 1941, aged just fifty-one. It was a cruel blow and the widowed father sought to alleviate the loss by careful ministry of his children. Always protective, Fred regularly escorted Tony on his forays in junior cricket.

Limpsfield – and its neighbouring village Oxted – have played hosts to many distinguished cricketers. Clapham-born Neville Knox, who played in two Tests for England in 1907 and was for a brief time the equal of any fast bowler in the country, was among the luminaries who represented Oxted between first-class engagements. Before the First World War, when less county cricket was played, it was relatively easy for amateurs like Knox to move between county and club. Henry Leveson Gower accepted the Oxted captaincy in 1896 on 'the understanding I am likely to be away a great deal playing for Surrey.'

Another of the itinerant amateurs at Oxted was E.R.T. (Errol) Holmes. Holmes was invited to captain the club in 1928. He had scored a century for Oxford in the Varsity match the previous year and would later captain Surrey both before and after the Second World War. Fred Lock was his opponent on one derby occasion. He was never fazed by reputations and, in Holmes's first recorded match for Oxted, he dismissed the university centurion for nought.

The rivalry between Oxted and Limpsfield produced the fiercest of local derbies. It was never keener than in the series of encounters in the 1940s, the formative years of Tony Lock. The fixture had originated in 1892 and Oxted held sway for many seasons in the inter-war period. Twelve years had elapsed before Limpsfield recorded their first victory in 1934. They were set a target of 106 in two and a half hours.

'The Oxted bowling was very steady and the fielding remarkably keen and but for a splendid innings by L.A. Moulding it is extremely doubtful whether Limpsfield would have got the runs,' reported *The Westerham Herald*.

The intensity of these games was illustrated in another anecdote featuring Moulding, the Limpsfield captain. Oxted had been dismissed for a small total but as a counter they had in their ranks a formidable opening bowler, Bob Collyer Hamlin. Hamlin was swiftly on the offensive; his third ball struck Moulding over the heart. There was intense concern among the surrounding huddle of players as the stricken captain received attention. Moulding was sufficiently recovered to take guard again. The unabashed bowler sent down another stinging delivery. The batsman staggered once more at the impact of the blow.

There was now one ball remaining and it must have seemed to the embattled Moulding that the over would never end. As he recovered for the second time, the stentorian voice of Percy Widney, the village postman, echoed from his bench in front of the British Legion Club. 'Hit the bugger again, Bob,' went up his cry.

Leonard Moulding, a splendid coach by all accounts, spent many hours discussing the merits of Tony Lock as he monitored the progress of the boy. Cross-country running was among Tony's sporting accomplishments but cricket was always the first priority. Moulding recognised from the outset that his pupil was endowed with natural ability. One delightful photograph in a family album shows him at the age of six, accoutred for cricket, wearing pads and holding a bat. As a boy he tested his growing strength and reflexes by throwing and catching a ball.

Tony first played for St Peter's Church school team at the age of eleven and took over the captaincy in his last two summers at school. His weekend cricket at Limpsfield was restricted to Saturdays because it was common ground and became a public recreation area on Sunday. It did not mean a break in cricket; he simply transferred his allegiance to Oxted on the Sabbath. Claude Whitworth, the former Surrey Colt, recalled playing against Tony at Oxted. Fred Lock was the club umpire and his neutrality might have been affected when his son was bowling. It was a tricky assignment for him as well as opponents. Perhaps there was just a suspicion of bias in his response to the appeals of his son – 'How was that, Dad?'

There was a special bonus for Tony of good net wickets at Limpsfield because the common was also the home of the local club. It was an extensive playing area without boundary fences and included parts of the eighth and nine holes of the nearby golf club as well as a vast acreage of common land.

A career in cricket was always Tony's goal but between times, after leaving school, he was apprenticed to a local cabinet-maker. It was a short-lived venture as he related; he was dismissed for daydreaming about cricket and leaving an ugly scar on the glass top of a dressing table that he was smoothing with pumice stone!

Bryan Lock remembers greater concentration during the hours of diligent practice carried out in a field adjacent to their home. 'Father always keenly encouraged Tony in his cricket ambitions,' he says. The practices included the time-honoured quest for accuracy in bowling at a single wicket. The quickening mastery of Tony in this basic tenet is shown by the tribute of Bryan: 'Although he was nearly four years younger than me, I always found difficulty in facing his bowling.' Bryan, by his own admission, was less conscientious in his practices and was thus denied parental encouragement.

The elder brother, like his father, designated his cricket as a leisure pursuit. He did, however, play club cricket into his late sixties. Before moving to Hampshire he was a member at Oxted, which celebrated its centenary in 1990. Bryan remembers Oxted as a lovely ground, the 'magnificent jewel in the centre of the village', in the words of another witness. Guy Bennett, the Rector of Oxted, coupled his tribute with a glance in the direction of St Mary's Church in the village. 'If you want to conjure up a picture of a traditional English village there is no better scene than a game of cricket on a village green with a parish church (preferably with a solid Norman tower) as the background.' The Oxted ground is situated in Master Park adjacent to the Hoskins Arms hotel, both named after the local squire, Captain Hoskins Master. The Hoskins Masters, father and son, were custodians of this country retreat and generous benefactors to the village club for over seventy years.

Summers at Oxted have been graced by benefit matches for Surrey players on wickets acknowledged as among the best in the county. The seasons in their turn brought the celebrations of the annual fête, travelling fairs, circuses and donkey derbies. An idyllic setting did lead to indiscriminate use of the ground. The intrusions were brought into question at one club dinner when the public were warned that Master Park was not designed for perambulator walks, racing tracks, or in the evening, a courting track. The Oxted secretary at the time said that choir boys were the worst offenders; they went to church and sang 'We plough the fields and scatter', and then went on the field and did it.

By the time that Tony Lock came under his patronage, Henry Leveson Gower, who would later be knighted for his services to cricket, had assumed the presidency of Surrey. Through his good offices – and the recommendation of Leonard Moulding – Tony, as a fourteen-year-old, first played for the Surrey Colts against Kenley on 29 April 1944. The Colts won by 112 runs. Tony did not bat and watched his future county colleague Dave Fletcher score 89 out of a total of 182. There was just time for Tony to enjoy his first bowl in the county's junior ranks. He took 1-10 in eight overs.

Prolonged success as a bowler rewarded the Surrey recruit in his debut season in 1944. Fletcher vied with his colleague, scoring a century, while Lock took 7-37 in a victory by seven wickets over Dorking. In successive matches against King's College, Wimbledon and Epsom he captured 13 wickets for 26 runs. Greeting these feats was a percipient note in the *Surrey Yearbook*. 'G.A.R. Lock (left-arm slow) although only fifteen, will be an asset to the side in the future.' Lock later recalled: 'At that stage, I was bowling slow, and earned my wickets mostly by flight. This was something that came naturally to me, part of the ball sense I possessed. I did not genuinely spin the ball then.'

Sir Oliver Popplewell, then a fellow Surrey Colt, enthuses about Lock in those apprentice days. 'I shall never forget how good he was for a boy of his age. Tony was, for all the time I knew him, an orthodox left-hand bowler whose enthusiasm was enormous and much encouraged by his energetic father who followed him to every game. His fielding even as a boy was of the highest quality. His talents at the age of sixteen were self-evident.'

Tony's youthful exploits also won favour with the Surrey Colts manager, Mr G.S. Bungay, the fixtures manager and the sole selector who attended every match. At the end of the war Surrey asked him to recommend his four best colts. Henry Leveson Gower had also been keeping a watch on the county prospects. Lock, from his home village, aroused his particular interest. Leveson Gower telephoned Bungay one day to confirm his hopes for the boy. The sequel to the call was Tony's introduction to the Oval.

In a letter to the county club Bungay wrote: 'I have put Lock in because he bowls so well for a boy of sixteen although I am rather dubious of slow left-arm bowlers at the Oval.' This was a pointed reference to the heartbreaks facing bowlers on the featherbed wickets prevailing before the war. Lock thus gained the distinction of being the first genuine slow left-arm bowler to represent Surrey.

Bungay's other choices were Dave Fletcher, Claude Whitworth and Peter Wingate. Whitworth, as an all-rounder, was considered to have tremendous potential. He was outstanding in 1945, the season in which Lock blossomed as a cricketer. Whitworth also impressed Andrew Sandham, the Surrey coach, and Laurie Fishlock, the county veteran.

The stylish youngster starred in a match against a Lord's eleven as late as 1949, scoring 82 against opposition which included Gubby Allen, Charles Palmer, Jim Sims and Ian Peebles. There were also first-team outings as a member of strong Surrey teams in matches against Sussex and the Australian Services elevens in 1945. In that season Whitworth dominated the Colts batting averages with 314 runs at an average of 67.80, and Lock was the leading bowler with 42 wickets at 10.14 runs apiece.

Lock, in the end, was the only one of the boys to accept the offer of a contract worth £3 10s a week at the Oval. He was the first to be given a contract without the formality of a trial. Whitworth, with a coveted promotion within his grasp, declined the offer. His reason was the disparity between cricket and his earnings elsewhere. The *Surrey Yearbook* dryly noted: 'Cricket as a profession had no appeal for him.'

In 1947 Lock was a member of the Surrey Second XI which finished as runner-up to Yorkshire in the Minor Counties Championship. Surrey, under the captaincy of the Hon. R.R. Blades, won nine games, including three by an innings and two by ten wickets, and lost only one championship match in addition to defeat in the deciding challenge game against Yorkshire. Geoff Whittaker, Tom Clark and Bernie Constable were the mainstays of a strong batting side. The accurate fast bowling of Stuart Surridge and Peter Westerman was complemented by the spin attack of John McMahon (34 wickets at 12.44) and Lock (42 wickets at 17.42).

Jim Laker, a senior Surrey colleague, remembered Lock as a 'tall, slim and enthusiastic youngster, with a head full of ginger hair, and a quiff falling down over his ears.' Laker and Lock were paired for the first time in a second XI game at Bristol. On a sandy pitch the ball spun at right angles. 'Monty Cranfield tore through us with nine wickets which seemed to suggest that I was due for a hatful.' In Gloucestershire's reply, Laker pursed his lips in annoyance as four straightforward catches slipped through the hands of his short-leg fieldsman. The culprit was Lock. 'I looked at the crestfallen Tony and said to our skipper: "Do the kid a favour and stick him on the boundary. He will never be a short leg as long as he plays the game."' It was a comment that Lock never forgot and he relished reminding his senior of the gaffe in the years ahead.

An auspicious season for Lock in the Surrey seconds had been preceded by his first-team debut, eight days after his seventeenth birthday in July 1946. He was the youngest player to represent Surrey and the opponents were Kent at the Oval. Lock batted at no. 11 and watched Arthur McIntyre and Whittaker hit centuries. He bowled ten overs, conceding 24 runs, and took the first of his catches for Surrey to dismiss Arthur Phebey off the bowling of Alf Gover.

Lock recalled that Phebey essayed a hook and mishit the ball which spiralled in the air towards square leg. 'I saw it leave the bat but then, to my horror, lost it in the dark background of the flats that encircled the Oval. The next thing I knew was that the ball was dropping three yards to my right. I frantically darted a couple of paces, and then dived the rest of the way.'

Describing this early example of his agility in the field, Lock then plunged, as he said, into a 'two-point' landing on his right shoulder and the back of his neck. 'Fortunately, I managed to shoot out an arm and scoop it beneath the ball and the ground. I held on for dear life.' Gover looked across and smiled approvingly. 'Well done, young 'un,' he said.

Lock was given one more first-team appearance – against the touring South Africans in 1947 – before his call-up for National Service in the Royal Artillery the following year. Early in his services training he began to suffer problems affecting his right knee. The strenuous 'square-bashing' exercises at Bodmin in Cornwall probably contributed to a worrying injury. Both cartilages in the knee were removed in an operation at Truro Hospital.

In later years teammates and opponents alike would marvel at Lock's courage, beset, as he was, by the gruelling strain of the knee handicap. The preparations for a day's play, involving extensive bandaging of the affected limb, would have overcome a less dauntless man. The Lock 'hobble' became a familiar sight at the Oval. It vied with the stumbling, nautical walk of his England colleague, Denis Compton, whose own knee troubles at one stage produced near apoplexy among the Test selectors and his cricket admirers.

Bryan Lock has referred to his brother's subsequent discharge from the Army on medical grounds. The elder Lock believes that although the problem restricted mobility it may also have influenced Tony's excellent fielding close to the wicket. Athleticism was required here, too, but he was usually spared the gallops in the outfield.

There were proud days to bolster Lock's morale in the Army during 1948. He took 6-48 in the Combined Services' victory by 66 runs over Glamorgan, the ultimate county champions, at Pontypridd. *Wisden* praised the 'clever left-hand spin bowling of Gunner Lock, the young Surrey professional.' At Lord's in August, the Army beat the Royal Navy by eight wickets. Lock's three wickets included that of writer P.B.H. May, his future Surrey and England captain. May fell for just six runs to a catch by Major General A.T.H Cassels off the bowling of Lock. The senior officer might well have reversed the usual order of things in saluting the bowler for bringing about the downfall of a prolific scorer.

On his return to the Oval in 1949 Lock confirmed his ascendancy over his spinning rival, John McMahon. 'At the age of twenty Lock revealed considerable promise as a slow left-arm bowler and consequently McMahon could not retain his place,' commented *Wisden*. McMahon, a South Australian and a vigorous personality, was Lock's senior by twelve years. He had been capped by Surrey in the previous year. The arrival of his successor usurped his authority and he left the Oval for Somerset in 1954.

Peter Loader, another Surrey colleague, amusingly recalls the episode of McMahon's departure. 'Our great friend, "Digger" was very successful as a finger-spinner and, if required, as a wrist-spinner, too. Suddenly, Lockie came on the scene and blew him away with the beautiful legal action.' McMahon thereupon went to see the Surrey secretary, Brian Castor. 'Lockie's taken over,' he said. 'I'm no further use to this club.'

Castor looked quizzically through his monocle at the player. 'My dear chap, do settle down. Whatever is the matter? Why do you want to leave Surrey?' McMahon replied: 'It's for the same reason as when you left Essex to come here.' The interview ended abruptly with Castor reaching for a shelf and hurling a book at him. 'Well, at least it was *Wisden*,' added McMahon. Castor's monocle used to bristle with menace, as in this encounter, at any wrongdoing. The Australian's effrontery fell into a similar category as that of one misguided supporter who chose to wear a richly decorated Hawaiian tee shirt in the Long Room at the Oval. 'You, sir,' thundered Castor, 'the Battersea funfair is somewhere down the road.'

The heralds welcoming Tony Lock to the Oval in the late 1940s included Alec Bedser. 'Lockie,' remembers Sir Alec, 'had a good brain and was an intelligent cricketer.' He had watched, with interest, the progress of the youngster after his demobilisation. His memory is of a 'fine slow bowler with a good use of flight.' A telling example of this sleight of hand was Lock's dismissal of Denis Compton – a prized scalp for a newcomer – who was stumped by McIntyre in Eddie Watts's benefit match against Middlesex at the Oval in 1949.

Micky Stewart, a future Surrey colleague, recalls watching Lock on his visits to the Oval as a schoolboy member. 'Tony had a long, smooth and rhythmical approach to the wicket and purveyed plenty of flight with not a great deal of spin.' The latter remark was reinforced in critical views in public prints. They informed Lock that he had a challenge to overcome. It preyed on his mind. *The Cricketer* correspondent praised a developing bowler. 'He makes full use of the crease and keeps an immaculate length. If he can acquire more spin he will be in the top rank.' The qualification was reiterated in *Wisden*. 'Lock, the young slow left-hander, maintained his promise but unless he imparts more spin to his leg-break will not reach the pinnacle.'

Surrey kept faith with Lock; he was capped, belatedly in his view, in 1950. The delay almost conspired to end the Oval association. In his autobiography, *For Surrey and England*, Lock revealed that he had seriously considered an offer from another county. It promised financial security and comfortable accommodation. 'Looking back on it all I realise I would have acted very hastily had I accepted the offer,' wrote Lock. Buoyant as a newly capped player, Lock took 72 wickets to help Surrey, under the captaincy of Michael Barton, share the championship with Lancashire. It was a closely fought contest with the Red Rose County, lasting until the final stages of the season. Surrey were able to exult in breaking a famine. They headed the championship for the first time since 1914.

The storm clouds were hovering over Lock's bowling but he was able to point with pride to reports of his first-class fielding close to the wicket. Leslie Smith, in his survey 'Round the Counties' in *The Cricketer* in 1952, was among his growing legion of admirers. 'Surrey seem to have discovered a worthy successor to J.W. Hitch, who apart from his great-hearted bowling before and after the First World War, earned the reputation of being one of the best short-legs of his day.

'In recent matches G.A.R. Lock has held a number of brilliant catches in that position. His three in succession off E.A. Bedser's off-breaks helped Surrey beat the Indians and he also shone in the match at Cheltenham. The short-leg catch he held to dismiss Emmett was remarkable, for the ball travelled with such force that it knocked Lock off his feet. Shortly afterwards he held one almost as good to get rid of Graveney.'

The Cricketer correspondent was now writing at a time when voices were starting to be raised about Lock's bowling. He did, however, prefer not to sully his eulogy. 'Lock has shown splendid form with his slow left-arm bowling. He maintains a tantalising length, turns the ball even on pitches which give him little help, and he makes good use of his faster delivery.'

The threat to Lock's aspirations was looming closer in 1950. For two years Lock had marvelled at the bowling skills of his new spin partner, Jim Laker, at the Oval. He was guided in his attempts to achieve enhanced spin by Laker. They quietly spent some time working on a new grip, very similar to one that Laker himself employed. In 1951 Lock was appointed as winter coach at Allders indoor school in Croydon. Over two winters he worked for six days a week giving lessons and improving his own technique.

The repercussions of this seemingly innocuous and apparently beneficial remedial work plunged Lock into deep controversy. John Banfield, a former Surrey Colt, believes that the ensuing criticism stemmed from Lock having encountered wickets providing little purchase for spin. 'Lockie was perhaps trying too hard because he always gave his all.' Sir Oliver Popplewell also strongly suspects that Lock's deviation from an orthodox style was the consequence of pressures being brought to bear on him at the Oval.

The die was cast, for better or worse, in the bowling experiments conducted at the Croydon school. It was a dramatic transformation and one that provoked disbelief among Lock's senior colleagues back at the Oval. Trevor Bailey, the Essex and England all-rounder, had first watched Lock at Southend in the summer of 1949. He would later echo the general astonishment: 'Nobody could have foreseen that a slow, graceful left-hander with an almost classical style and good flight would develop into a medium-paced spinner with a flat trajectory who, in certain conditions, could be virtually unplayable.'

The stigma of guilt would throw a long shadow over a great bowler and tarnish his achievements in an illustrious decade.

TWO

Armed for Aggression

'He was now the ultimate destroyer. On anything approaching a spinners' pitch his break was staggering. His quicker ball came through at a wicked pace.'

– John Arlott

An assembly of incredulous Surrey players watched Tony Lock unfurl his new action at the Oval in April 1951. There were gasps of amazement, with united voices expressing the general refrain: 'he'll never get away with it.' None of the players present at the practice sessions were aware of Lock's assignment at the Croydon indoor school during the previous winter. 'The net wickets, due to rain, were far from satisfactory,' recalled Jim Laker. 'As Tony ran in and let the ball go, at near medium pace, he made it turn and kick.' Jack Parker, the veteran on the receiving end, roared in reply: 'Lockie, you threw that bloody thing.'

Envy at the mounting eminence of Laker, seven and a half years Lock's senior, might have been at the core of the drastic change. Their rivalry, even in their great years as a pair, was always fuelled by intense competition. It did, however, seem like a betrayal of the orthodox talents that had enabled Lock to bridge the gap between school and county cricket in the remarkably short span of three years. It was an eye-opener for all and sundry. Lock had abandoned the style of the traditional slow left-arm spinner – the deception through the air, the line of his delivery at off stump or just outside, bowling to a packed off-side field.

Before the change Laker's greater experience had been reflected in the disparity in their bowling analyses. Lock took 74 wickets compared with Laker's 166 in 1950. Two years later Lock's action may have been questionable but the results were emphatic. He edged ahead of Laker with 131 wickets to his partner's 125. The county novice, unschooled in helpful conditions, had now controversially found the answer.

The sessions in the basement school at Allders department store had converted the 'flight and guile' bowler into a vicious executioner. The netting above the coaching area was lower than conventional nets and so restricted Lock's flighting of the ball. He was forced to flatten his trajectory.

Lock himself recalled: 'Though I was not conscious of it at the time, my arm dropped a little in the delivery of the ball. The low-slung beam supporting the roof curbed the trajectory of the flight and I started to bowl a little quicker. I also found that by "digging" the ball into the wicket I was able to secure more spin.'

Two other Surrey colleagues, Peter Loader and Raman Subba Row, also attended the Croydon school. Loader remembers the restricted headroom which obstructed Lock's endeavours to gain more spin in his experiments. The unfortunate legacy was that his colleague did start to bowl illegally. 'It wasn't every ball, this was the problem, just his quicker ball,' says Loader. Subba Row also recalls that it was difficult to bowl properly with so little room at the top. 'I think that's where he started to fire them in.'

Sir Alec Bedser tends to undermine the theory advanced by the former Surrey players that Lock was the victim of the low-slung nets at Croydon. In his view, Lock may have been constrained but the major factor was that his pupils were putting bat to ball with some vigour off his bowling. In his frustration at the impertinence, the coach stepped up his pace to check them.

Jim Laker, in his later reminiscences, said that he was never quite sure that Lock's delivery was illegal. It was, though, perilously close to the mark and he would certainly have been banned in present times. Laker further explained: 'There has never been anything illegal about bowling with a bent or crooked arm, provided that it remains that way until after the ball is released. It contravenes the rules only when the arm is straightened prior to delivery, which then constitutes a jerk or a throw.' He said that Lock's quicker deliveries fell into the latter category but stoutly resisted the opinions of others that his partner was an out-and-out thrower.

Ted Dexter, one of Lock's later England captains, maintained that the problem about bending the arm was that the variation of speed was much more easily disguised because there was not the same evident effort with the body. The effect was merely achieved from the elbow. Dexter remembers his first meeting, as a Cambridge University freshman, with Lock in 1956. These were times when it was possible to talk freely with umpires.

One such conversation occurred in the match against Surrey at Fenner's. Having, as he says, gained the sanctuary of non-striker's end, he asked Frank Lee, the former Somerset opening batsman, if he had just been on the receiving end of Lock's quicker ball. 'Quicker ball!' exclaimed the umpire. 'You'll spot the quicker ball when you get one from Lockie, don't worry about that!'

The general consensus in the Surrey dressing-room was that if Lock was not called for throwing why should they complain. Jim Laker summed up the prevailing mood: 'Apart from leg-pulling about how well he would throw the javelin, we did not want to discourage Tony in his new enthusiastic approach to the game. We did not want to undermine his confidence. So many bowlers over the years had got away with throwing or jerking the ball that we decided that we were not going to act as jury. It was up to the umpires to decide.'

The more vocal of observers outside the Oval felt that Surrey had a duty to the game to remedy matters and put their house in order. Sir Alec Bedser latterly has responded to the urgings of those critics when Lock was selected for England. 'Why should he have changed? It was down to the selectors not to pick him.' Sir Alec does, though, present his own charge that Lock continued to throw for the next five years. 'He possibly could not have made the ball jump and turn without bowling as fast as he did.'

By 1952 Lock was quite literally a new bowler. The high action had disappeared in the school practices. John Arlott commented: 'He was now the ultimate destroyer as a spin bowler. He could wrest turn from the deadest of pitches: on anything approaching a spinner's pitch his break was staggering. His quicker balls came through at a wicked pace.'

Jim Laker remembered Lock's faster ball, which some people conservatively estimated accounted for 25 per cent of his wickets. 'It would burst through a batsman's defence before he could pick up his bat from the blockhole.' Ted Lester recalls the amazement of his Yorkshire colleague, Vic Wilson, in one confrontation at the Oval. 'It was like Tyson at his fastest. Vic hadn't got a very high back-lift. He hadn't got his bat up before the middle stump was ripped out of the ground.'

Doug Insole, playing for the Rest of England against Surrey, was another victim of this devastating delivery. The Rest were chasing the runs against the clock and, after a shaky start, Insole was beginning to accelerate. Lock thereupon wheeled in and, with his fast throw, spread-eagled the wickets. Insole stood there in disbelief and turned to the umpire to query his dismissal. 'How am I out then? Was I run out or bowled out?'

Raman Subba Row, even with the benefit of prior knowledge as a Surrey teammate, was overthrown by Lock in a festival match at Hastings. 'I knew what was going to happen. The ball whistled through and knocked my stumps all over the place.' Another version, involving Fred Trueman, very nearly resulted in serious facial damage. 'I was facing Lockie on a drying wicket at the Oval. He pitched the ball about the line of the leg stump. It lifted and turned and somehow, as I tried to take evasive action, I found myself standing on my toes. The ball just flicked my chin before hitting Arthur McIntyre on the shoulder and going over Peter May at slip for four byes.

'In the pavilion afterwards I realised that he could have broken my jaw. There are many international bowlers whom I would rather have faced than Tony in this period.'

Behind the scenes there were influential men at Lord's keenly aware of the criticism. More than three decades on, Gubby Allen, who was one of the England selectors to pick Lock, recalled a secret mission to examine the Surrey bowler in action in Kent. Joining Allen on this outing was Les Ames, a fellow selector. Allen recalled: 'Les and I walked round the ground and looked at him from every possible angle. What we both said: "He looks peculiar but we don't think he throws the ball." That was our absolute, sincere belief. I would not have picked Lock if I had thought he threw.'

Lock must also have satisfied Norman Yardley, the chairman of the selectors in 1952, and Leonard Hutton, the England captain, who had batted against him in the week before he made his England debut against India at Manchester. Around this time, Hutton was questioned on Lock's action: 'Don't you think Tony's action is a little peculiar?' He replied: 'Yes, but he'll win the Ashes for us next year.' Hutton's response, unwitting or not, carried a broad hint of collusion in selectorial attitudes. Lock's name was clearly already pencilled in as the potential match-winner in the forthcoming series against Australia in Coronation Year.

Lock had barely had time to relish his considerable part in the innings victory over India at Manchester before he was arraigned as a thrower against the same opponents at the Oval. He was called by the square-leg umpire, Fred Price, the former Middlesex and England wicket-keeper. Price no-balled Lock in one over, and twice in another.

An angry Oval crowd kept yelling 'no-ball' at the umpire, who stopped play and lay on the grass until the noise subsided. It required a strident appeal by Surrey secretary Brian Castor over the loudspeaker to quell the barrackers.

Peter May, who had just come down from Cambridge, was Lock's captain for the first time against the Indians. He asked Price for an explanation of his decision. 'We were all amazed. Fred was in no doubt that Tony had thrown his faster ball.' It was the first time that Lock's action had officially been regarded as questionable. 'Why,' said Tony, 'should one umpire no-ball me when all the other umpires have allowed me to go on bowling as I please?' He considered that Price should have had the courtesy to give him a prior warning.

Lock said the shout of 'no-ball' came completely out of the blue. 'I would not have felt nearly as upset if Fred had advised me that he considered my action was unfair and that I should alter it. I was bowling slowly at the time and, quite frankly, was astonished that my delivery should be questioned.' The 'howls of disapproval' from the Oval partisans were remembered by Lock in later years. 'There's a card on my mantel-piece every Christmas now from Fred, and every Christmas there's one of my mine on his mantelpiece. But my idea of a nightmare would still be to hear his voice yelping, above the background muttering of the Vauxhall End, "no-ball."'

Peter May later conceded that the alarms sounded by Lock disturbed Price and other officials. 'Lock obviously troubled certain umpires with his quicker ball, which was doubtful at times. But the tendency at that time was to sweep such unpleasantness under the carpet.'

The no-ball calls were not, however, entirely unexpected. In the case of Lock's quicker ball – the fast yorker – half the umpires said, in private conversation, that he threw it but they were afraid to do anything about it. In the winter of 1952 a writer in *The Cricketer* also commented on the throwing incidents at the Oval. 'Unhappily there is one disquieting feature about this young bowler. In his endeavour to impart more spin and to bowl a faster ball he has raised doubts about the legitimacy of his action ... opinions will vary about the fairness or otherwise of a bowler's action. It is to be hoped that Lock will be able to eliminate any element of doubt about his delivery without in any way spoiling his skill as a slow left-arm bowler.'

Bob Appleyard, the former Yorkshire and England bowler, offers a typically reflective viewpoint on his fellow spinner. 'Tony became known as a thrower but he only threw certain ones. The more he sought to spin the more his elbow came into it.' Appleyard speaks of an inexorable progress in the transition. 'It had grown into his action, moving from straight to bent, because he was putting in that extra effort to get more out of the pitch.' The success in the reformed style, he believes, could have encouraged Lock to bowl at greater pace. In time it would have become the norm. 'That can happen and become progressively worse until it is part of your armoury.' The venom was even more pronounced on wet wickets. Bowling more quickly in these conditions it enabled his Surrey rival to make the ball 'dig in and bite'. 'Tony would, by this method, get something out of the pitch whereas Jim (Laker) was just spinning through and not getting as much turn.'

Appleyard, in summary, believes that it would not have been too difficult for Lock to bowl in an orthodox manner if he had cut out the quick throw. 'He was getting away with it until it got to a stage when it became more noticeable and he was successful with it.'

Raymond Illingworth, another Yorkshire rival, confirms the commonly held view that Lock was totally unplayable on a wet wicket. 'Even when faced with a small target, you were never safe against him.' Illingworth remembers that others likened Lock to Derek Underwood, who bowled at a similar pace. The difference, in his view, was that Lock was a genuine spinner of a ball even though he bowled it quickly.

The spin might have been reduced if he had not thrown. 'Lockie could get turn even on a dry pitch. The only way to play him was to get on the back foot and attempt to cut him. But when he was pitching leg and middle that wasn't the easiest thing to do.'

Trevor Bailey, a former England colleague, was one of the critics espousing reservations (except when he was on the same side) about the legitimacy of Lock's action. He thought the blame lay with the county rather than with the umpires. 'They did not want to become embroiled in controversy, especially as the England selectors had decided his action was legal.' Bailey said that his own reaction, as a batsman, was to treat Lock as a spinner with a bent arm. 'Tony's fast ball, which was yards quicker than any I've seen from slow or medium-paced bowlers, should have been outlawed from the start.'

Doug Insole, as a former Test selector, maintains that the fact television coverage in the 1950s was in its infancy should be regarded as a mitigating factor in this examination. 'It was a big issue then, not so much now, because there is far more overall coverage.' Insole says that the chief problem was Lock's faster ball; the other deliveries weren't anything like as obvious. Ian Johnson, the Australian off-spinner, did arouse similar concern with his 'vaguely dodgy' action. Insole poses the question of the actuality of Lock's faster ball. 'Once you've been on the receiving end it is lodged in your mind. You're always looking for it.'

Insole speaks from experience as a player who wasn't mesmerised by Lock (or Laker for that matter); he scored heavily against Surrey during his career with Essex. 'I used to try and give Lockie the old heave-ho at times. He didn't like that at all. He thought it was humiliating and tended to bowl quicker and quicker. That was fine by me; it allowed me to cut him. Tony reacted to denigratory treatment by a batsman extremely vigorously.'

There was, in the decade under review, an extreme reluctance to indict a bowler by persistently no-balling him and umpires were loath to take this measure. Insole remembers this as a time when there was a much greater bond between umpires, many of whom were former first-class players, and cricketers. 'All were known and liked by players who realised that they had a difficult job to do. Players tried to help officials. There was far more honesty in accepting decisions, "walking"'and picking up or not picking catches. While not a game for philanthropists, there was a general feeling "we're all in this together, boys!"'

The 1950s passed by without outright censure of Tony Lock. The player most frustrated by the transgression was his arch rival, Johnny Wardle, the Yorkshire left-armer who considered that he was being unfairly deprived of England caps. 'If Johnny had an Achilles heel, it was Tony Lock. He shouldn't have shown it,' commented one Yorkshire observer. 'Come on lads,' Wardle would call out in a beseeching voice. 'Just watch that bastard throwing it out there.'

After his retirement from the first-class game, Wardle, remembering his own disillusionment as a Test cricketer, wrote: 'Lock used to impart tremendous spin with his jerk and never had to resort to flight to get anyone out. Some people are sympathetic and say bowlers will be put out of the game. I contend that they should not be in cricket keeping legitimate bowlers out of the game. Others remark that the slow bowler does not do any harm so why worry about them. My answer is that he gets wickets to which he is not entitled because of his peculiar method of delivering the ball.'

Wardle strongly resented cheating in any form and the bias towards Lock only increased his aggravation. It was, as Jim Laker said, a marvellous prospect to see Wardle or Lock bowling to each other. Tony was the bowler when Johnny came out to bat in his benefit match against Surrey at Bradford in 1957. The field spread out for the single, traditionally 'given' to the beneficiary on these occasions. Lock bowled the usual long hop. Wardle hit it away and jokingly pretended to set off for a second run. As he did so, Lock dived at full stretch for the ball. Laker said he was sure that he would cheerfully have run Wardle out, given half the chance.

Raymond Illingworth also remembers how the feud yielded so many wonderful contests and provoked great hilarity in the Yorkshire dressing-room. 'Wardle won most of his personal duels with Lockie. We would kill ourselves laughing at these times because we knew what would happen with them. Johnny would take much delight in teasing Lockie with his chinamen and googlies.'

On one occasion at Bramall Lane, Sheffield, Yorkshire had collapsed to 80/7 against the fiery bowling of Alec Bedser and Loader. It was a signal for a renewal of the rivalry between Lock and Wardle. As Wardle came to the crease, Lock was immediately summoned to bowl to him on a damp pitch. Any terrors which might have resided in the wicket were quelled by whirlwind hitting. 'Johnny got only around 30 or 40 but he struck Tony three times for six on to the top of the football stand,' recalls Illingworth. 'They were massive hits and a tremendous carry from the pavilion end at the Lane.'

Doug Insole believes that most of the antipathy between the two bowlers lay on Wardle's side because Lock was in possession of the England place. He applauds Lock's forbearance and exemplary conduct, when he might well have been resentful at having to play second fiddle to Wardle during the Yorkshireman's finest hours in South Africa in 1956/57. The relationship between the two men was just as wary when they were opposed in Lancashire League cricket in the 1960s. In one match with Ramsbottom, Lock dismissed his rivals, Rishton, for 72. During the tea interval Tommy Welsh, the Rishton chairman, complimented him on his fine bowling. 'Yes, I did well,' replied Tony. 'But this bugger (pointing to Johnny) will bowl us out for even less.' His prophecy was fulfilled but this was an instance when he made clear the respect he had for Wardle as a rival.

Insole vehemently disagrees with those who contend that Wardle was as good an orthodox slow left-arm bowler as Lock. Wardle was rarely allowed to bowl his wrist spin – his stock-in-trade – in Yorkshire; in this department, says Insole, he was supreme, quite magnificent. Wardle's command of this beguiling art compared with Shane Warne in modern times. Sir Alec Bedser, with vast experience of both bowlers, awards the palm to Wardle on good wickets, generally available in Test cricket.

Trevor Bailey, however, insists that during the period of their competition, Lock had the winning hand as a *fast* left-arm bowler, especially on wet wickets. 'On a pitch giving assistance, particularly in England when the wickets were uncovered, Lock was far more of a menace.'

On the harder wickets overseas, says Bailey, Wardle was a more likely prospect because of his more thoughtful approach to bowling. 'Tony would still think he could bowl them out by pitching leg-stump and hitting off. And that didn't happen.' Bailey reckons that, overseas, when batsmen realised that Lock was just a medium-pacer, his opponents did not find him a difficult proposition. The only exception to this was when the wicket was bad and the ball travelled through 'very straight and very quickly.' 'I would have preferred to play against Lock rather than Wardle on perfect wickets overseas. In England it would probably have been a different matter.'

Tony Lock was selected along with his Yorkshire adversary, Fred Trueman, later to become a good friend, for the MCC tour of the West Indies in 1953/54. This was a tour marred by political disturbances, riots at grounds and contentious umpiring decisions. Leonard Hutton, their captain, would later say that the West Indies made heavy demands on young players and 'were not an ideal place to send immature young players.' The principal dilemma – and not just for the alleged 'problem boys', Lock and Trueman – lay in the stories being circulated from island to island and magnified to ludicrous proportions. There was an immense pressure to succeed and in this, the decline of the British Empire, the touring party was not helped by the reluctance of the white population in the Caribbean to come to terms with the changes that were about to engulf them.

The rumpus rose to a deafening pitch during the third Test at Georgetown in pre-independent British Guiana. Extra police had to be brought to the Bourda ground in an area only recently under strain through political demonstrations. They were recruited to protect the Indian umpire, 'Badge' Menzies, who was also the home groundsman. Angry spectators had thrown hundreds of bottles and broken beer crates on to the field.

The dissension arose after Menzies had given a run-out decision against Clifford McWatt, the local hero. 'It was like setting a spark to a gunpowder barrel,' reported one observer, Peter Ditton. Alex Bannister, another witness of the hooliganism, said the hysteria was really attributable to the cheapness of rum and Guianese betting habits. 'It also sprang from the practice of clapping in anticipation of an individual century, or when a partnership was in striking distance of a similar total.'

McWatt and the injured John Holt, batting with a runner, had stepped into the breach after West Indies had lost seven wickets for 139 runs, following England's total of 435. Peter May, as the fieldsman on the leg-side boundary, was the unwitting cause of the disarray. The West Indians' stand had reached 98 when McWatt, having taken one run, foolishly attempted another to hoist the century partnership. May's throw, fast and true, ran him out by at least two yards.

The spectre of illegality again reared to undermine Lock in the West Indies. George Headley, the great West Indian batsman, then aged forty-four, was one of Lock's victims in his last Test, the first of the 1953/54 series, at Kingston, Jamaica. A fund had been organised by local enthusiasts to bring back Headley, the hero of pre-war days, to play for his country once again. He had made 16 in the first innings score of 417, and when he came in for the second innings his side were far in the lead, but at that moment had lost four wickets for 90 runs.

Headley got off the mark with a single and then faced Lock's faster ball. It was said that he had only got about halfway through his generous and rather flourishing pick-up when the wickets went down with a crash. Hutton recalled: 'His stumps were spread-eagled by Lock's faster ball which, not surprisingly, he did not see. A faster ball from an alleged slow bowler would be hard to imagine.'

Jim Swanton related the incident in his book, *West Indian Adventure*. 'The legitimacy of Lock's faster ball has been a matter for contention since he was no-balled at the Oval by Fred Price two years ago. It was a matter of more than abstract discussion in Lock's next over after Headley's departure, for he bowled another fast one to Gomez and umpire Perry Burke no-balled him from square leg.' Hutton intervened after the calling and instructed Lock to drop his quicker ball forthwith. The consequence was that his nine wickets in four Tests thereafter were heavily bought at an average of 67.

A fascinating record on film taken by the MCC manager Charles Palmer travels back in time to set the scene. Riot police on horseback exude menace as they patrol one ground in contrast to the leisurely footage of May, Graveney and Compton mingling their strokes on the tree-fringed field. Palmer, as commentator, at one stage remarks that Lock will have to reconsider his bowling action. It prefaces sightings of Lock in both orthodox and unorthodox styles on the tour. While at times – perhaps after Hutton's reprimand – he appears without fault there are glaring instances of an outrageous jerk propelling the ball as if aiming at a coconut shy in a funfair.

A chastened young man was christened 'Shylock' when he was again no-balled for throwing against Barbados at Bridgetown. His guilt was confirmed by the action of two umpires. The square-leg umpire, Harold Walcott, the uncle of the Test player Clyde Walcott, twice called him in three balls. Later in the same day he was called by umpire Jordan, also standing at square leg.

Of the Barbados incidents, Alex Bannister wrote: 'With his faster ball, Lock shattered the stumps of the young left-hander, Sobers. The call did not seem to have been made until Sobers had hurriedly attempted an unsuccessful defensive jab. Sobers walked away not realising he was entitled to stay. Neither he nor Dick Spooner, the MCC wicketkeeper, heard the umpire's call.'

A distraught Lock went over to register his complaint to the captain. Hutton heard him, then walked across to umpire Walcott. He knew better than anyone that he could do nothing about the decision. The short break in play did give time for Lock to simmer down and regain his composure. Hutton then protested to Walcott that the call had come late – most people agreed that it came a split second after the ball had hit the wicket – and Walcott, whose efficiency was seldom questioned, replied: 'I'm sorry.'

Hutton, in his recollections of the tour, said the no-balling of Lock had a big effect on him in the West Indies. 'Being no-balled for throwing three times in one day unsettled him so much that never again on the tour did he try to bowl the fast ball. Consequently the batsmen were not compelled to always be on their guard against it. This clearly minimised their difficulties against Lock and decreased his effectiveness.'

The England captain thought that Lock was no worse a culprit than the West Indian off-break bowler Sonny Ramadhin, or Australia's Ian Johnson, both of whom jerked the ball even if they didn't actually throw it. 'If I were an umpire, I would be very careful about taking action unless I was convinced beyond a shadow of doubt. What may look like a throw from one position can appear to be a perfectly legitimate delivery from another.'

The late Bill Bowes, a wise counsellor of Yorkshire cricket, and Bob Appleyard emphasised the complexities of judgement in their analysis of the situation. Bowes said: 'Lock threw everything although you would probably pass all of them from certain parts of the field. You cannot blame the England selectors for going for Lock when he hadn't been banned for throwing. You had to watch him down the mid-on line to see the offending action.'

Appleyard remembered staying with Don Wilson, the former head coach at Lord's. He had the opportunity to view players at practice from the balcony of the indoor school. 'There, it could be said, many appeared to be throwing. But from a different angle the judgement was nothing like so clear cut.'

Jim Laker welcomed the moves against Lock because he felt that his Surrey partner was too good a bowler to resort to a ball that was suspicious. As a result of his experiences in the West Indies, Lock restricted his use of the quicker ball.

The misadventure in the West Indies was a major setback for Lock. It effectively precluded his selection for Australia in the winter of 1954/55. Fred Trueman was another discard and an even more surprising omission was Jim Laker. That one of England's greatest bowlers of this or any other period should have to wait until his thirty-seventh year before gaining a place on an Australian tour in 1958/59 was an affront to his talents. Bob Appleyard, his replacement, considered his promotion ahead of Laker to be the biggest compliment of his career.

The captaincy of Len Hutton in Australia was, for a long time, under threat. There was strong evidence of opposition to his appointment within the cricket establishment. Accusations were barely veiled and looked askance at his powers of discipline in the leadership on the previous tour of the West Indies. It was thought that, as England's premier batsman, he should be relieved of the extra burden. As John Arlott observed, any indication of an inability to discharge the diplomatic or disciplinary side of his duties could be taken as confirming the inadequacy of a paid player for the post.

Hutton was far from well during the summer of 1954. David Sheppard, with a strong lobby supporting his candidacy, deputised for him in two Tests against Pakistan. The tide did turn in Hutton's favour; his appointment was renewed after he announced his restored health and the historic victory in Australia sealed his status as a great cricketer.

One of the ironies of the situation appertaining four years later was that Tony Lock gained his place as England's first choice left-arm bowler by default. Johnny Wardle, his long-standing rival, surrendered his customary role overseas following a series of controversial articles bearing his name. They dwelt upon what he considered to be a lamentable decision to appoint Ronnie Burnet as Yorkshire captain. He was duly sacked by Yorkshire. An unseemly domestic wrangle spilled over into the pages of the national press and the MCC subsequently withdrew his invitation to tour Australia.

The throwing issue was brought starkly into focus in this series. England – and Lock – were hoist by their own petard. The Australians, Ian Meckiff and Gordon Rorke, unpredictable in line and pace, threw out England in a horrendous masquerade. This was a cricket assault, brutish and forbidding, which had to be outlawed. These throwers could hurt. The culprits were banned from cricket and their tyrannies quickly dissolved. Tony Lock then knew that he was no longer immune in his own impropriety.

THREE

Bowlers on a Bender

'It is the most complex question I have known in cricket, because it is not a matter of fact, but of opinion and interpretation.'
– Sir Donald Bradman

The period of reappraisal for Tony Lock began after the tumble into disgrace in the Caribbean. The crucial reversion to orthodoxy was yet only a future objective; but he did for some time afterwards renounce the faster ball which had so offended his critics. Leslie Smith, in an article in *Wisden*, expressed his pleasure at this decision. 'To Lock's credit he realised his problems and set about remedying them. Twice he changed his action completely and he obviously made a tremendous effort to put himself right.'

John Arlott perhaps best expressed the enormity of the task to satisfy an increasingly vigilant jury. He said that to produce an exact definition of a throw was more a job for a lawyer and an anatomist than a cricketer. The problem of throwing was a cobwebbed skeleton in cricket's cupboard in the 1950s. Yet it was not a new phenomenon: in the 1890s an injunction was issued to first-class umpires to be very strict in their judgement of bowlers' actions. Among the bowlers under scrutiny were the Lancashire and England fast bowler Arthur Mold; Edwin Tyler, the Somerset slow bowler; Fred Geeson, fast-medium from Leicestershire; and Bobby Peel, an outstanding member of Yorkshire's slow left-arm bowling dynasty.

C.B. Fry was another of the 'doubtful' bowlers. He had what was described as an 'eccentric' action. In 1898 Fry was called three times and mockingly referred to by the irreverent umpire as 'C.B. Shy.' Fry writhed in anger but *Wisden* described it as long overdue justice. In the next century the Australian Bert Ironmonger was also the subject of disapproving murmurs. Notwithstanding this, he was judged by Patsy Hendren to be the best slow-medium left-arm bowler of his day. Ironmonger had lost the first finger of his left hand down to the middle joint (said to be the result of a naïve understanding of the workings of a circular saw).

In contrast to his general ungainliness, Ironmonger's run-up was so surprisingly light-footed that he was nicknamed 'Dainty'. He gave the ball such a tweak that it buzzed audibly on its flight. However, a pronounced flexion of his left-arm aroused unspoken criticism among visiting teams in the 1930s and even doubts in Australian minds. One critic, who had made a close study of the subject and watched him bowl all day through glasses, commented: 'Before lunch, Bert threw two balls every over. Between lunch and tea the tally rose to four an over. After tea, when he was tired, he threw the lot.'

Another bowler under the microscope in the 1950s was Sonny Ramadhin, the West Indian. He bowled with his sleeves buttoned at the wrist. The dark hand cradling the ball made it almost impossible to judge the angle of his spin. The suspicions, quietly whispered, cloaked his triumphs against England. John Arlott wrote: 'Ramadhin's finger-spin perplexed almost every batsmen who opposed him. Only the best of technicians, prepared to use quick footwork, achieved anything like a solution.' In an interview with the *Daily Mail* in 1999, Ramadhin confessed that his faster ball was thrown. 'Nowadays, the television cameras would have picked it up immediately. But I got away with it in every grade of cricket for thirty years.'

Writing in *The Cricketer* in 1954, C.B. Fry said: 'The plain difficulty is that in the modern sense nobody has succeeded in framing a satisfactory definition of a throw which umpires are required to no-ball. In point of fact the whole question turns on what is done with the elbow in the action of projecting the ball.

'The present MCC definition is that the ball is fairly delivered if, once the bowler's arm has reached the level of the shoulder in the delivery swing, the elbow joint is not straightened partially or completely from that point until the ball has left his hand. This did not debar a bowler from flexing or rotating the wrist in the delivery swing.'

David Frith, in an article in *Wisden* in 2005, referred to the new ICC directive allowing bowlers to flex their arm during delivery to an extent of fifteen degrees. The modern 1,000-plus-frames-a-second television camera had enabled scientists to calibrate a movement in a bowler's elbow and shoulder joints. 'From this,' wrote Frith 'has sprung the ground-breaking finding that the arm of just about every bowler inadvertently flexes in the act of bowling.'

In one conversation in the 1990s the former Australian all-rounder Alan Davidson maintained that he could name upwards of twenty bowlers, some of them respected names, around the world, guilty of transgressions. The 1998 edition of the *Wisden Book of Cricket Records* more than confirmed this disconcerting analysis when it produced a four-page list of bowlers who had been no-balled for throwing.

Rob Smyth, in another article in *Wisden*, said that the ICC panel investigating the issue had found that almost all the great bowlers in history bent their arms. It had been noted by some sceptics that the new guidelines were uncomfortably close to the fourteen degrees at which Muttiah Muralitharan's doosra – the off-spinner's googly which was banned in 2004 – was measured. 'I think it has been brought in through pressure from Sri Lanka and Murali's supporters,' contended Geoff Boycott. 'It's a sad day for cricket that this pressure can allow Muralitharan to bowl whatever he wants.'

Frith, in his review of the situation, wrote that the introduction of the name of Muralitharan into a cricket discussion could be relied upon to divide any room outside Sri Lanka. He had been sensationally no-balled seven times for throwing in three overs by Darrell Hair in the Boxing Day Test against Australia at Melbourne in 1995/96 and again by Ross Emerson in the following one-day series. The ICC subsequently passed Murali's action after a biomechanical analysis at the University of Western Australia and at the University of Hong Kong. It was concluded that the action created the 'optical illusion of throwing.'

The consensus of expert advice given to the ICC investigating panel in 2005 suggested that fifteen degrees would accommodate any straightening which is purely a consequence of biomechanical forces – such as the hypertension of an elbow joint – and also the point at which the straightening becomes visible. Angus Fraser, the former Middlesex and England bowler and member of the ICC panel, rejected claims that the ruling would legalise throwing. 'All the information and opinion collected, along with the fact that it is impossible to see an arm straighten with the naked eye until it reaches this angle, points to fifteen degrees.'

The recommendation was accepted by the ICC's committee of chief executives meeting in Melbourne in February 2005. Afterwards the ICC's own chief executive, Malcolm Speed, said: 'Try as it might, the sport has never properly come to terms with it. There are emotional reactions from people around the world based on fear and ignorance. The reality is that the new process provides the game with a sensible way forward.'

The pursuit of legality in bowling has bedevilled cricket through the ages. C.B. Fry, in his submission at the turn of the last century, said that nowhere in preceding laws was there any definition of a jerk or a throw. The previous obscure ruling, said Fry, depended entirely on an individual umpire's notion of what the term signified. 'Suppose the bowler's umpire detects a doubt in his mind but the square-leg umpire does not. We then have two judges appointed equal in their powers, directly contradicting one another. What it comes down to is that each umpire is instructed to be judge but if they differ one of them is suddenly whisked away from the bench and treated as a non-operative.'

In 1888, when *Wisden* hailed the proposed formation of the first Cricket Council at Lord's, Charles F. Pardon wrote: 'I have watched for many years with interest, and generally with cordial sympathy, the efforts of Lord Harris to improve conditions under which the great game is played. His crusade against throwing was fully justified, and there is today very much less unfair bowling than was the case a few years ago.'

Pardon expressed the view that the game should be played fairly and honourably and that cricketers should be above suspicion. Prominent umpires had repeatedly told him about the unfairness of bowlers whose style had attracted adverse criticism. The dilemma for them was that they were not sufficiently sure of support to take the initiative in no-balling them.

In 1952 – the year in which Tony Lock was first no-balled – the same position applied, chiefly because, as Norman Preston, the then editor of *Wisden*, maintained: 'No one wants to shoulder the responsibility.' During the summer, Cuan McCarthy, the South African fast bowler, was no-balled for throwing while playing for Cambridge University against Worcestershire. The previous summer McCarthy might also have fallen foul of the esteemed umpire, Frank Chester. He wanted to call McCarthy again in the first Test against South Africa at Trent Bridge. Chester asked two leading members of the MCC Committee if they would support him should he no-ball the South African. One of them, it was said, was Pelham Warner. Their reply was non-committal. Warner merely said: 'These people are our guests.' Chester was not satisfied with the flimsy answer. He thus turned a blind eye on McCarthy in the Test.

Another umpire, Australian Cec Pepper, who had settled in England, was also denied support by the ruling body. Charlie Griffith, the West Indian fast-medium bowler, was unpredictable at times in line and pace. He possessed a peculiar and questionable delivery where the arm emerged suddenly and late from behind his head. His attitude, said one observer, did not immediately bring the term chivalrous to mind. Griffith bowled one vicious bouncer in a match against India, which felled their captain, Nari Contractor, who recovered from the blow but did not play cricket again. Pepper was convinced that Griffith threw but he was quietly asked not to make an issue of the matter. Brian Close, with vivid memories of his duels with the West Indian, said: 'You could almost put one hand in your pocket and play him … and then one would come at you four yards quicker.'

Leslie Smith pursued his claim of worldwide trangressions in the *Wisden* of 1961. 'The spread of throwing in recent years has been alarming,' he said. In 1959, on his visit to the West Indies, he had noted instances of bent elbows among fast and off-break bowlers. One leading umpire in British Guiana had resigned rather than give an assurance that he would no-ball bowlers for throwing. In many parts of the West Indies Smith saw youngsters, many of them schoolboys, exaggerating the bend in their elbows, either to impart spin on an unresponsive turf, or to get added lift to the ball.

There had been a lull in the throwing saga in the early years of the twentieth century. Only one instance was recorded before 1930, but with increasing competition and as the emphasis on winning became paramount, the epidemic spread again in the 1950s. In 1959 English umpires, now with the assured support of the MCC behind them, no-balled three bowlers. Unfortunately the new resolve was badly timed, for it followed shortly after England had lost a series in Australia. It was difficult, as one writer said, to avoid the accusation of retaliation on the part of the English authorities.

In 1960 a further purge resulted in bowlers being called in twelve separate matches, one of them in Australia, and the others in England.

The prosecutions included, in a bizarre sequence of events, the South African fast bowler, Geoff Griffin. He was the first visiting bowler to be called; hitherto the only others to be censured while playing for their countries were Ernest Jones, the Australian, against England at Melbourne in the 1897/98 series and Tony Lock against the West Indies at Kingston, Jamaica, in 1953/54.

Griffin's case assumed frightening proportions. South Africa had gambled in their selection on a bowler with a doubtful action – he had twice been called in his own country. Griffin was doubtless called up to augment the threat of Neil Adcock in the tourists' attack. He was still only twenty-one when he was selected for the first Test at Edgbaston in June. There had been considerable misgivings about his action in the early matches of the tour. He was first no-balled against Nottinghamshire and Hampshire. Against the MCC at Lord's in May, Frank Lee and John Langridge no-balled him three times for throwing. A week later, two more umpires, Tom Bartley and Bill Copson, called him eight times for the same offence against Nottinghamshire.

The sad affair reached its peak when Griffin was selected for the second Test at Lord's. He even managed to take a hat-trick – to become the first South African to achieve the feat and the first from any country at Headquarters. The distinctions would be seen as hollow conquests in the ensuing disarray. Griffin was called eleven times in the Test and, unsurprisingly, did not bowl again on the tour. Altogether seven first-class umpires condemned Griffin's action as unfair. He was no-balled twenty-eight times in four first-class matches, quite apart from his only over of eleven balls and completed under-arm in the exhibition match, which followed England's innings victory shortly after lunch on the fourth day at Lord's.

Retribution had followed swiftly after the downfall of the lauded England team in Australia in 1958/59. A breach in Anglo-Australian relations on the scale of the Bodyline series thirty-six years earlier was only averted by careful diplomacy. The cannonade of throwers included, as the chief culprit, the Victorian left-arm bowler Ian Meckiff. A charming man, 'the honest chucker', in the words of Alf Gover, would become castigated as a social oddity, a man people pointed to as a rebel.

Jack Pollard, the Australian writer, said Meckiff bowled with an arm that had a permanent bend in it and could not be fully straightened. 'He achieved his pace from double-jointed shoulders and from extremely thin wrists.' Originally, Meckiff had made very little use of his front arm but when the chucking controversy raged he started to use it more, lifting it higher. The action of his bowling remained the same but the change in the use of the front arm made some critics believe that he altered his bowling action.

E.M. ('Lyn') Wellings, one of the English press corps, commented: 'Meckiff approaches the wicket in the deliberate manner of a bowler who delivers the ball at medium pace. He runs no faster than did Hedley Verity to bowl his spinners. And yet the ball leaves his hand at express pace.'

The need for diplomacy was paramount in Australia on the 1958/59 tour. Throwing was a disfiguring feature in every state. There were also the 'draggers', well remembered by one English player, Tom Graveney. 'It was absolutely terrifying,' he said. 'We just stood there like rabbits.' They left behind a wake of aggrieved batsmen. 'Having a ball thrown at you from eighteen yards blights the sunniest disposition,' observed Peter May in this sternest examination of his captaincy.

He might then have reflected on ostrich-like attitudes back home, which had brought about this final reckoning. Norman Preston, the editor of *Wisden*, reiterated that the authorities had only themselves to blame for the menace which threatened the very fabric of the game. Peter May ruefully recalled the diminished sensitivity in an unfair situation. 'Those brave umpires who did call offending bowlers were looked upon as publicity-seekers. The tendency was to sweep the unpleasantness under the carpet.'

The quality of mercy was strained during these controversial years. Tony Lock was one of the beneficiaries of a lenient regime. He rose to eminence as one of many sinners in the field. Lock was not alone in this pardon. Tom Graveney, as one batsman of the time, pursued his own claim that he had been on the receiving end of other throwers in county cricket for years. The alarm bells that rang to the dismay of Lock's opponents signalled the dread of the unexpected faster ball. It was a weapon greatly to be feared and it brought rich dividends for a ferocious competitor in his inspirational reign. Surrey and England, untrammelled by official censure, had no trials of conscience and rejoiced with him in his many triumphs.

FOUR

The Vintage Years

'We were a star-studded team that operated as one unit. But if I were forced to name one player who contributed most to our seven championships years my man would be Tony Lock.'
– Micky Stewart

The endurance of an indomitable man was a key element in Surrey's glory years. Tony Lock often waged his sporting warfare with a bloodied finger, the torn flesh then a sacrifice of the spinner's trade. Down the years of their rivalry and comradeship Fred Trueman never deviated in his admiration for a fearless competitor. 'Lockie had a heart as big as a London double-decker bus,' he said. The irrepressible big man had every right to play the thespian. The full-throated and demanding appeals, the arms raised in supplication, held attention as riveting as any melodrama. As they rang out over Harleyford Road at Kennington, one wag remarked: 'When Lockie appeals at the Oval someone else is given out at Lord's.'

It was said of Lock that inside the nomenclature of a slow bowler, itself a questionable category for him, was a fast bowler fighting to get out. No one of that period could match his boundless fury as a spinner. Bill O'Reilly, the Australian leg-spinner of another generation, was aptly nicknamed 'Tiger' and closely paralleled Lock in his disconcerting attack.

Above all, it was the impassioned competitive persona that was Lock's great strength as a team man. For his hero-worshipping supporters, it was the energy of his cricket and inspirational qualities which day after day commended him. Excitement reigned on the terraces whether Lock was bowling, batting or fielding. One correspondent recalled: 'It was, for me, "edge of the seat" stuff; he was a cricketer who made things happen on the field – always proactive, seldom reactive.'

Lock won admiration even among his fiercest rivals in Yorkshire. One of them paid him a handsome compliment. 'Lockie would be the man you want alongside you in the trenches.' One instance of his courage as a batsman, not to be underestimated in a crisis, was the famous game Surrey played against Yorkshire in near darkness at Headingley in 1955. Street lamps were burning brightly after the furious bowling assault by Trueman and Cowan.

One observer commented: 'It was dark enough to make Aunt Edith a menace on the back lawn rather than two Yorkshiremen hell-bent on destruction.' There were no light meters then to ration the dismay of the Surrey batsmen. Peter May said the light was the darkest he could remember as a player in England. The lights on the scoreboard were described as shining like a beacon on the Eddystone lighthouse. Ted Lester, one Yorkshire rival, remembers Lock's heroics on that occasion. 'Fred was bowling a bit quick. Lockie came in as nightwatchman against us. He was staying while in Yorkshire at Fred's home. It didn't affect their rivalry. Fred really let him have it but Lockie stuck it out. There was absolutely no doubt about his courage on that day.'

Surrey lost seven wickets for 27 runs in an hour and forty minutes in the Headingley twilight. Trueman's figures were 3-18 and Cowan's 4-4. The rout was encompassed in alarming conditions when batting survival demanded physical courage in disproportionate relation to technical skill. Lock was a survivor in such circumstances. He was battered from foot to shoulder but he displayed exceptional courage as an unbeaten nightwatchman.

Yorkshire were victors in the end but not before Surrey had staged a spectacular recovery the following morning. The ninth-wicket pair of Lock and Loader added 96 runs, each compiling defiant half-centuries. Loader advanced to 81 in a stand of 53 for the last wicket. Jim Kilburn, the Yorkshire historian, conceded that the spirit in the batting was of 'such stuff as champions are made of … Lock and Loader were fortunate in the origins of their transfiguring stand but they were brave and deserving in the development of it. The hitting was hard but selective; Yorkshire were outmanoeuvred as well as outfought.'

Lock perhaps remembered his duel with Trueman at Headingley, when the pair were opposed again in the traditional late-season match between Yorkshire, the county champions, and the Rest. David Allen, the Gloucestershire off-spinner, recalls: 'I was fielding at mid-on when Fred came in to bat. Lockie said: "I'm going to bounce him."' Allen thought this rather unwise. 'Careful, Lockie,' he whispered. Lock was undeterred and replied: 'I'm faster than he is. He daren't retaliate.'

Pat Pocock, one of Lock's younger colleagues at the Oval, provides another example of the nerveless approach to the game. Lock used to spend every spare moment during play deeply engrossed in his favourite cowboy books. On one occasion Surrey were involved in a run chase against the clock. 'Lockie, batting number eight, put his pads on and then took his ease in the back room with his book,' says Pocock. All the while an intense battle, runs and wickets equally shared, was proceeding out on the Oval, Suddenly, as another wicket fell, the cry went up: 'You're in, Lockie!' 'How many do we need?' he asked, when he re-emerged on the players' balcony. 'Five,' chorused his anxious teammates.

Lock thereupon put down his book, stood up and said: 'Right, I will hit a six.' True to his word, he strode out and nonchalantly, as if it was a net session, struck the first ball he received thrillingly beyond the boundary. Then, with a wave to the crowd, he returned to the pavilion and carried on reading.

Lock, even as a young cricketer, was unfazed by the reputations of bowlers, fast or slow. He bristled with antagonism, relishing his elevation above recognised batsmen towards the close of play. Sam Cook of Gloucestershire, then a veteran spinner but still a wily opponent, had cause to remember Lock's name in one encounter against Surrey at the Oval. Jack Parker was the non-striker and Cook, before proceeding to bowl to the newcomer, asked Parker: 'Who's this lad?' 'Tony Lock,' replied Parker, 'he's quite a promising left-arm bowler.' An amazed Cook could only raise his eyes to the heavens and follow the flight of his first ball to the top of the ladies' pavilion. The exuberance of his strike was accompanied by a hearty expletive from the brash young aggressor.

This was an early demonstration of what Pat Pocock describes as a mad streak in Lock's personality. 'Lockie,' he says, 'had the typical mentality of a top-class rugby player. These are normally quite gentle blokes but act differently in action. That was Lockie. If he had been a rugby player he wouldn't have tried to tackle someone. He would have run straight at them.' Pocock adds that Lock, as a player, had a near kinship with another reckless sporting warrior, Brian Close. Both may have had their irrational moments but they were supreme fighters.

Micky Stewart has dwelt upon the exciting years of Surrey's command in the 1950s and the influential role of Tony Lock. 'We had moulded a winning unit under Stuart Surridge and then Peter May. It was hugely talented and experienced. If I was asked – and I wouldn't really want to answer it – to pick the one player who made the all-round cricket contribution it would have to be Lockie. But nothing revolved around him because there was so much talent in the team.'

Douglas Jardine reflected on the influence of Surridge, which enabled Surrey to assume the ascendancy in 1952. Surridge was aged thirty-four when he acceded to the leadership. He followed Michael Barton, a fine tactician but a gentleman of milder temper. The gain in authority dealt Surrey a winning hand and the first title to be held outright by them since 1914. 'There was a world of a difference between the good, workmanlike stuff served up before Surridge and the dynamic current with which he charged it for the next five years,' said Jardine.

Sir Leonard Hutton endorsed the verdict of others that the Surrey team was powerful enough to bear comparison with the famed Yorkshire team of the 1930s. Hutton was acknowledging the brand of resolution which vied with the inspirational figures of his youth. He also perceived that Surrey's dominance was directly attributable to having four quality bowlers – Alec Bedser, Loader, Laker and Lock – all in harness at one time.

Stuart Surridge, the champion optimist, bullied and cajoled his charges at the Oval. None was immune from the blasts of criticism. He led the team with an iron fist, urging them on with Machiavellian fervour. The tactics did, at times, rile the players. The hair-trigger tempera-ments of Loader and Lock were put under immense strain and they were treated with equal severity. 'He certainly stirred me and Lockie likewise,' says Loader. Ron Tindall, another Surrey teammate, adds: 'We were all terrified of him, he was so aggressive.' Even the players' wives or girlfriends surely knew better than to offend Surridge.

Loader, who shared the new ball with Alec Bedser, enlarges on the intimidating manner of his captain. 'Alec and I normally got so many opponents out very quickly. But if we didn't make a breakthrough in the first three or four overs we were on the receiving end of a verbal broadside.' Surridge would mop his brow and make plain his disgust at their efforts. 'England bowlers!' he would exclaim with a derisory epithet. 'Put your sweaters on.'

The demanding pattern of authority certainly brought results but it almost produced a strike by the disaffected players in one season. 'We had a blazing row with Stewie,' recalls Loader. 'The boys just wouldn't put with it because he was coming over so strong. We threatened to walk off the ground.' Tempers were cooled and in the following match at Gloucester the jokes aroused by one incident probably helped to break the ice between captain and players. 'Someone put the "lap on",' as Loader described it, and Surridge, fielding close to the wicket, received a hefty blow on the head and fell to the ground. Arthur McIntyre took the catch on the rebound. 'Stewie got up; he looked fiercely at me and Lockie and growled his response to the indignity. "You lot can bloody well stop laughing."'

Doug Insole, admittedly outside the reach of the irascible Surridge, remembers him as a great disciplinarian in his management. 'He transformed the team, drove the buggers and swore at them. Lockie used to bowl dripping with anger.' Insole eavesdropped, to his considerable delight, on one vigorous conversation between Surridge and Lock. Eric Bedser was bowling in tandem with Lock in one match against Essex. Insole was at the striker's end and facing Bedser. Surridge and Lock stood shoulder to shoulder in the leg-trap. Between balls their opponent became aware of a fractious exchange of views. 'Stewie was accusing Lock of not being able to spin the ball.' Lock indignantly pointed to his gnarled spinning finger. 'What do you know about it?' he responded. Insole listened to the talk with mounting rapture. He told Surridge: 'I want to get runs off Eric but I'm enjoying your conversation so much that I'd rather stay at this end.'

The late Alf Gover explained the psychology adopted by Surridge. There was invariably a velvet-gloved approach in his dealings with Jim Laker. 'He used to butter-up Jim: "c'mon, I'll give you another short leg."' The accusatory method worked better with Lock. 'I've never seen such [expletive deleted] bowling. What are you supposed to be … doing? Now, c'mon, for God's sake.' Gover added: 'Lockie would shake his head in disbelief at the Gaffer, redouble his efforts and probably take a crucial wicket.'

The man who brought 'heart, body and soul' to the Surrey team resented even more any inactivity, especially when conditions were propitious for his vicious spin. Derek Hodgson remembered Lock's enforced withdrawal from the field against Gloucestershire at Bristol. He left for treatment after having been struck on the head by a violent pull by George Emmett. 'Lock had to be helped off and was sitting in the pavilion, being revived, when he noticed that Eric Bedser, who bowled off-spin, had turned his first delivery a long way. Lock, still groggy, leapt up and insisted on returning to the field.' He peremptorily brushed aside any protests. His eyes gleamed with delight as he resumed his place in the attack. He proceeded to take 6-24 in fifteen balls.

Donald Carr remembered the enormous drive of a bowler in his many conquests. Carr was cast in a different mould to Surridge as a captain. He was a man of more sober complexion, reflective and diplomatic, befitting his later role as an administrator. The Derbyshire captain and Oxford blue was highly regarded as a leader on the county circuit. He was Lock's captain on the MCC tour of Pakistan in 1955/56. Stuart Surridge had issued words of warning before the tour. He told Carr: 'You will have to be beastly with Lockie.' It would have been against Carr's nature to follow this advice. 'My attitude was entirely different. He didn't need driving as far as I was concerned. He liked leading the pack. Tony had the fire and ability and you just gave him encouragement, if it was necessary. That was all that was necessary. He was a good chap and a fine asset to the team.' Lock later repaid the compliments when he said that Carr was the best of his captains.

Peter Loader presents an amusing recollection of his cricket days 'rooming' with Lock on tours with Surrey. Surridge displayed his puritanical side on the question of the accommodation of his team. During one match at Pontypridd, Loader and Lock were allocated a double-bedded room. 'I'm not having my boys sleeping together,' insisted Surridge. A separation had to be effected by using a mattress on the floor. Loader recalls: 'I won the toss for the use of the bed and to make matters worse poor Lockie had gone down with a bout of mumps.' His stricken partner, having forfeited the chance of a comfortable night's sleep, was not amused. 'That's not what I would call teamwork,' he said.

Sir Alec Bedser regarded Stuart Surridge as the last true amateur, an independent spirit who, whatever the odds, always thought Surrey could win. There was a collective spread of endeavour. 'Every day, under Stewie, we tried to make things happen,' says Bedser. One example of his whirlwind captaincy belongs to the championship year of 1953 when Surrey completed their programme by beating Warwickshire by an innings in a day. Members rose in unison to acclaim the team. The last and only time that a first-class match had finished in a day was at the Oval in 1857.

Warwickshire were dismissed for 45 and 52. Bedser took 12 wickets, including 8-18 in the first innings, and Laker performed the hat-trick. Twenty-nine wickets fell in the day. Testifying to the brilliance of the fielding was the fact that not one of the visiting batsmen was bowled. Warwickshire, in their second innings, were all out in seventy minutes, five minutes fewer than in their first innings.

Tony Lock, having now remodelled his action, cut a swathe through county batting. He was remorseless on the uncovered wickets of the time. It was admirably summed up by Freddie Stocks in Nottinghamshire. Surrey had posted a substantial total before dismissing the home side twice very cheaply in one match at Trent Bridge. In his broad Midlands accent Stocks said: 'It seems like a different pitch when thoust are bowling.'

Lock's haul of wickets in 1955 was 216 at 14.39 runs apiece. It was the best season's aggregate of his career. Two years later he lowered the average to 12.02 and headed the national bowling lists, bowling 1,200 overs with 212 wickets. Glamorgan, in May at the Oval, were among his hapless victims in 1955. They lost by an innings and were bowled out twice in three and a half hours for a combined total of 93 runs.

At five to three on a wild, blustery afternoon, the score was 52/2. Half an hour later Glamorgan were dismissed for 62, and at the tea interval they were 25/5 in their second innings. The last four wickets fell for the addition of only six runs, which meant that in 90 minutes, 16 wickets tumbled for 37 runs, ten to Lock and six to Laker. *The Times* described how Lock and Laker made the ball turn and lift 'in the craziest way.' Lock's figures were remarkable even for him: he bowled 31 overs to return match figures of 12-34. He completed the most satisfactory of days with one of his best catches at backward-short leg, off a full-blooded sweep by Hedges. 'He parried it first,' reported *The Times*, 'and then leapt like a salmon to grab it before it was out of reach.'

There was, except on rare occasions, an inevitability about Surrey's rampant progress in the 1950s. Emulating the traditional Roses rivalry were the contests between Surrey and Yorkshire. Raymond Illingworth recalled the expectant hush that preceded play between two great counties. So close were the encounters that they exercised a fascination as compelling as the most intense Test match. Watching the combatants, almost literally on tiptoe, were massed crowds, totalling as many as

60,000. The narrow divide between the teams can perhaps be best judged from the fact that they jointly supplied thirteen players to England in one season. In 1955 the Surrey representatives were May, Barrington, Lock, Alec Bedser, Laker, Loader and McIntyre. Yorkshire contributed six others: Wardle, Appleyard, Trueman, Lowson, Close and Watson.

Yorkshire made Surrey fight hard for their fourth championship in this season of glorious weather. The feat had only twice been accomplished under the same captain. Yorkshire, led by Brian Sellers, were champions in three seasons immediately before the Second World War and for one season afterwards. Alfred Shaw captained Nottinghamshire in their run of four titles from 1883 to 1886.

Surrey, fielding probably the finest team in the club's history, were just as imposing in their rule. They set up a new record for championship points since the system of awarding twelve points for a win and four points for a lead on the first innings was introduced in 1938. Surrey recorded twenty-three victories out of twenty-eight games to total 284 points. Yorkshire, in fierce but unavailing pursuit, won twenty-one games. An aggregate of 268 points beat their previous highest total of 260, achieved in 1939. Significantly, Surrey held their catches, 383 in all, and three players – Surridge, Lock and Stewart – shared 156 of them.

Between 1952 and 1956, the years of Surridge's reign, Surrey were victorious in 86 matches, with winning margins in the championship ranging from 16 to 32 points. Lock, Laker, Alec and Eric Bedser, Loader and Surridge between them took 2,163 wickets, all but two of them with averages of under 20. One Yorkshire player paid his tribute to the inspirational Surridge. 'If we had had Stuart as captain during those five years, we would surely have done just as well.'

The sequence of five victories over Yorkshire in the 1950s included the first double for thirty-six years. Yorkshire squandered an opportunity in Jim Laker's benefit match at the Oval in June 1956. The match was dominated by the bowling of Lock and Appleyard, who each took 9 wickets. It was completed in two days. At the last, Yorkshire, set a modest target of 124 runs, collapsed from 60/2 to 100 all out.

The defeat was replicated in another fluctuating battle in the return fixture at Bramall Lane. Yorkshire gained a first innings lead of 61, a commanding advantage in a low-scoring game. Peter May, top scorer in the match with 68, and Barrington added 94 for the third wicket in Surrey's second innings but Yorkshire's position seemed unassailable when they began the last fresh and breezy morning needing only 67 runs, with eight wickets in hand.

Tony Lock had been held in reserve because Surrey did not consider the pitch ready for his spin. He was not called upon until Yorkshire had laboured to 50/4. A position of stalemate threatened. Lock swiftly bowled Close to give Surrey a faint prospect of victory. In the end, Lock and Loader were almost contemptuous in their mastery. Lock furiously swept aside the Yorkshire tail. His final figures were 5-11 and Surrey, against all expectations, were the victors by 14 runs.

Surrey, urged on by Surridge, could scarcely believe their luck. Opposed by frail batting, they became increasingly convinced of their own invincibility. For an hour and a half, Yorkshire defended like slaves in chains, and then abandoned hope in the madness of a wild counter-attack. Alec Bedser remembered the fusillade of cushions, pitched on to the ground by the disgruntled Sheffield partisans. The adjacent factories fashioned their protest at the impending defeat. Plumes of smoke belched forth as a signal of distress to reinforce the old legend. Micky Stewart recalled: 'After we had taken three or four wickets, the smoke was so dense I thought they'd set the stadium on fire.'

Lock took four hat-tricks in his career and might justifiably have expected another but for a miss by one of Surrey's later recruits, fast bowler David Sydenham. The spilled catch at Southampton occurred after Hampshire had slumped to 126/8. Lock wheeled in to deliver what should have been his hat-trick ball to Danny Livingston. Sydenham recalled the lapse on the deep fine-leg boundary.

He had been invited to speak at an old boys' dinner at Guildford Grammar School. It was his debut as a public speaker and he was nervously rehearsing his lines instead of concentrating on his patrol in the outfield. 'Suddenly, my name was screeched from members of the team bringing me to my senses. I looked up to focus, but not quickly enough, on the ball rapidly descending in my direction.' As the ball dropped like a stone beneath his feet, there were gestures of sympathy from all but the aggrieved bowler. The expectations then, with the ball turning sharply, were that the missed chance would not prove too expensive.

The commiserations became more subdued as the day dragged on and Livingston proceeded to profit from his escape to score a double century. Total silence enveloped Sydenham when he again dropped the

Hampshire batsman on 99 at mid-on. He did manage to have the last word in a painful episode when he took the second new ball. Livingston at last succumbed to a catch by Micky Stewart at deep long-off.

The towering achievements in three matches in the 1950s serve as a vivid memory of Tony Lock in his prime. They were especially apt in the context of the fluctuating struggles between Kent and Surrey at the Rectory Field at Blackheath. The historic heath in the London village links cricket and rugby in its proud sporting traditions. It was where the famed rugby club, the oldest documented in England, hosted the first international – against Wales – in 1881. The origins of cricket on grasslands of the heath, straddling the boundary between the boroughs of Lewisham and Greenwich, go back over 150 years. The inaugural first-class match was played there against Gloucestershire in May 1887. Two years later came the first of the derby matches as part of a sequence of first-class cricket, which did not end until 1971.

The Romans' Watling Street, which crossed the heath, was the stopping point for stagecoaches en-route for north Kent and the Channel ports. It was also a notorious haunt for highwaymen in the seventeenth century. Three centuries later it witnessed pillage almost as distressing for the embattled Kent cricketing stalwarts. Tony Lock plundered his own booty at Rectory Field.

The men of Kent were victims of his cunning in an audacious march to 41 wickets in three matches in two peak years, in 1956 and 1958. They were dominated by his 16-83, including all ten in an innings, at Blackheath in the first year. It remains a record championship analysis by a Surrey player. The tally followed another ten wickets in defeating Kent at the Oval a week earlier in July.

Surrey won by an innings and 173 runs at Blackheath. Tom Clark and Peter May, who was to vie with Lock in his batting mastery against Kent, both hit centuries. Weekend rain gave a fresh impetus to Lock's biting leg-spin. Only Cowdrey, who fell one short of his half-century, and Phebey countered his wizardry. After Stuart Surridge had declared at the start of play on the Monday, he took 6-29 runs in Kent's first innings. By the close Lock was in sight of all ten wickets for the first time. He reached a coveted milestone the following morning when he dismissed the last four batsmen without conceding a run. As a testimony to his accuracy in the rout, he bowled 29.1 overs, including 18 maidens, and had conceded only 54 runs.

There were 'showers and sunshine for the spin twins (Lock and Laker),' reported *Wisden* in the match against Kent at the Oval. Surrey won by eight wickets, the winning run resulting from a boundary overthrow off the last ball of the extra half hour on the second day. Sealing another century by May were the ten wickets of Lock (5-36 and 5-24) and five more to Laker as Kent were bowled out for 98 in their second innings.

Kent narrowly avenged their earlier reverses in a stunning encounter at the Rectory Field in July 1958. They won by just 29 runs with eighteen minutes to spare. Lock's fifteen wickets in the match were unavailing this time but he did hectically put bat to ball in an exciting run chase. Surrey were set a target of 252 to win at 88 an hour. It preceded an assault that never wavered in the interests of safety. May set the tone by hitting the first ball he received from Halfyard for six. He struck 17 fours in scoring 99 in two and a half hours. May and Clark added 51 in twenty minutes and McIntyre followed their lead with six fours in half an hour. Then Lock, with 104 required in an hour, was in a belligerent mood, intent on a grandstand finish. His innings lasted only 37 minutes but it was heady stuff while it lasted. Five successive balls from Halfyard were sent hurtling to the boundary. He hit five more fours in his 57 before being ninth out, venturing once too often to be caught by Evans off Page.

By a cruel twist of fate Lock was denied his fair reward in 1956. The Brylcreem manufacturers had provided an award of a silver cup and £100 for the best bowling performance of the season. For connoisseurs of statistics a remarkable feature of this season was that three bowlers achieved all ten wickets in an innings. Laker's haul for Surrey against the touring Australians headed the list until Ken Smales, another Yorkshire-born off-spinner, took all ten wickets for 66 for Nottinghamshire against Gloucestershire at Stroud.

Early in July, with Laker absent through injury, Lock must have thought that the prize was safe in his keeping. He lowered the run count to 54 against Kent at Blackheath. The unkindest cut of all was the further reduction of one run in Laker's analysis in the extraordinary Test at Old Trafford. It was the last straw for the crestfallen Lock, not only outwitted as a bowler but also forced to surrender riches, which in this, and most other seasons, he would have well and truly earned.

FIVE

The Two of Them

'They were both formidable competitors and induced a kind of fear.
There was always the dread of receiving the unplayable ball.'
– Peter Walker, the former Glamorgan and England all-rounder

'Sometimes,' said Jim Laker, 'it is hard to recall what on earth we had in common.' The pact he sealed in his bowling tryst with Tony Lock was to break the hearts of opposing batsmen. It was a curious and embattled relationship between the two men but really just one other competitive strand in a fiercely demanding situation at the Oval. It was not an environment for the faint-hearted. 'The Surrey team was very loud, there was quite a lot of swearing,' recalled Micky Stewart. He was once asked whether he enjoyed playing in such a highly charged atmosphere. 'It's lovely,' he replied. 'We win all the time.'

Over the eleven years of their partnership Lock and Laker earned each other's respect, but it required the mellowness of middle age before it spilled over into affection. The gulf in years during their playing days was undoubtedly a factor in any estrangement which afflicted them. Lock was seven and a half years Laker's junior. Laker said: 'We were poles apart in many ways; Tony was a country lad who had played in the leisurely atmosphere of the lovely Oxted cricket club. On the other hand, I had emerged from the industrial north, endured the rigours of tough league cricket and been fatherless from the age of two. I had completed five years active service abroad before Tony left school.'

The menace of Laker, as the senior partner, clearly goaded Lock on to his path of violent conquests. He was strongly aware that he had to make his impact boisterously on the field. 'At times,' said Micky Stewart, 'Lockie projected himself differently from his natural self which cut across the grain with some people.' Laker, with maturity on his side, had the degree of refinement which enabled him to mix comfortably in any social environment. Laker's equanimity contrasted sharply with Lock's uncertainty. Stewart adds: 'Lockie did try to cultivate social niceties, but he didn't have the ability. Jim, as the more sophisticated type, made him ill at ease. He might have got up Lockie's nose at times.'

Raman Subba Row, another Surrey colleague, also reflects on two disparate personalities. 'Jim was a more stable person whereas Tony was excitable. There were always plenty of ups and downs with him. He could be nice but he had a varying temperament. You didn't know what department you would be running into on a given day.'

Micky Stewart made the valid point, in cricket terms, that two players at the top would want to improve on each other. 'It was an intense personal rivalry between two different people from entirely different backgrounds.' Trevor Bailey, as a neutral observer, believed that Laker was privately less indulgent about the controversy surrounding Lock's bowling in the 1950s. 'Each of them, of course, were naturally looking to their own laurels. But Jim was slightly cynical about Tony. He was the *bowler* and the bloke at the other end was not a legitimate bowler.' The late David Sheppard remembered one conversation with Laker shortly after Lock had changed his action. 'Lockie is throwing this year,' said Laker. 'If I can turn the ball two inches, he is turning it twice as much.'

Laker, whatever the differences in the phases of their triumphs together, said that he would take a great deal of convincing that he and Lock, as a spinning combination, ever had any serious rivals. In his retirement, he staunchly maintained that Lock had never been accorded the appreciation he deserved. 'He was just about the greatest competitor I ever saw, he never shirked an issue and never failed to give his best. I have seen him bowl a thirty-over spell with knees and ankles strapped up to such an extent that many would not have attempted to walk down the pavilion steps.' In the 1990s, as a lingering testimony to their feats, Lock and Laker shared a runners-up place to Jack Hobbs in a members' poll on the top twenty Surrey players.

The verdict, surely beyond reasonable dispute, acknowledged the accomplishments of the Surrey 'spin twins'. Together they captured

4,788 wickets in first-class cricket, 367 of them in ninety-five Tests. Laker remembered that they were both prodigious spinners of a cricket ball which meant that they could get a modicum of turn on wickets unresponsive to the average bowler. 'Consequently on a helpful pitch,' he added, 'we could increase our pace which cut down the prospect of a batsman getting after us.'

Laker also reflected on the changed angles of their spin and how they each contrived to bowl at those rivals more or less fallible to the trajectories of their respective attacks. 'It is seldom that you find a batsman equally at home against a ball spinning into him a well as the one turning from leg.' Laker recalled that Denis Compton and Doug Insole were both superb players of off spin and that he was spared heavy punishment because Lock was at the other end. In contrast, Len Hutton and Don Kenyon were composed and unflurried against left-hand spin. Yet Laker, with his off-breaks, enjoyed a high success rate against them.

The fruits of an ideal partnership blossomed in these joint endeavours. Laker saluted a remarkable fielding accomplice in a modest footnote. 'It is only fair to say that Tony was of greater help to me than I was to him, due to his brilliance in the leg-trap. I have no idea how many batsmen departed "caught Lock, bowled Laker".' It was rumoured that the compositor in the Oval printing shop kept this line constantly made up.

The untimely death of Jim Laker, at the age of sixty-four in 1986, was marked by a telephone call across the miles to Lock's adopted home in Western Australia. The spokesman from the BBC asked him for a few words of appreciation at this sad time. 'The world may have lost a great cricketer but I have lost a bloody good friend,' said Lock. His memories, as he took in the shattering news, scrolled back to the years of a magnificent collaboration. 'Jim and I were not always the greatest of friends, or for that matter, even friends, for he was a hard man to get to know, very deep and quiet,' wrote Lock in his obituary tribute.

The ice was well and truly broken when they shared a room during the Centenary Test in Melbourne in 1977. Lock recalled their rapport on the cricket field. 'I had the greatest confidence in Jim's ability as a bowler, so I was able to stand very close to a batsman knowing I would not get hit.' A missed chance by Lock was a rare event. 'If it did happen Jim would stand there looking at me, one arm folded across his chest, cupping his chin in the other hand.' It was the mildest of rebukes but Lock instantly knew what the disappointed bowler was thinking.

The dire handicap of split spinning fingers was the bane of the careers of Lock and Laker and others of that era. The seasons of purveying huge spin exacted a fearsome toll. Pat Pocock, a Surrey off-spinner of later years, remembers his own martyrdom as a bowler. 'I used to walk back to my mark with my finger up, as if firing a gun, to prevent the blood from dropping down from the end of my elbow. I used so many potions in an attempt to relieve the burden that my locker resembled a chemist's shop.' Pocock enlisted a medical view on his trauma. He was told: 'You're asking your finger to do something it wasn't designed for. It's like a car brake pad that doesn't wear, an impossible happening.'

The profits of a spinner's trade were delivered at a punishing price. John Arlott commented on the example of Jim Laker and the physical cost entailed in his bowling forays. 'Like most men who spin the ball really hard, he often wore away the skin from the inside of his index finger. If he bowled on, it would harden, a corn would form and then, as it grew too hard, it would tear away, leaving the raw flesh exposed once more.' Stuart Surridge's boundless respect for Laker was heightened by the Yorkshireman's fortitude. 'Jim's power of spin meant that by halfway through a season he had developed a terrible callus. He would pack it with Friars Balsam to try to get some relief.'

Ted Dexter also remembered the daily ritual of emergency treatment pursued by spinners of that era which enabled them to surmount their handicaps. In a less spin-conscious age, a modern generation had themselves given evidence of a declining art. Dexter said that he had been told that they did not suffer from 'spinner's finger'. 'Even after bowling 50 overs in a match they do not have a problem. I doubt, though, whether it is a question of luck. The truth is that they grip the ball too low in their fingers and so do not really spin it.' Pat Pocock found confirmation of this view in one conversation with Shaun Udal, the erstwhile Hampshire off-spinner now of Middlesex. He asked Udal if he and others 'rip' their fingers in play today. The answer came as no surprise. 'No, we don't really spin the ball.'

Laker, in his own appraisal of spin bowling, emphasised the importance of the grip. 'You must force your fingers apart. I know it hurts like hell, but this is a pain which you must ignore.' It was, he said, necessary to press the first finger as far down the seam as possible. Spin was imparted by flicking the first finger upwards and the second finger downwards at the point of delivery. 'My index finger often bleeds when I spin the ball across the seam.'

Micky Stewart remembered how Tony Lock displayed a similar fortitude in the wear and tear of spinning the ball. The problem of a severely damaged finger was close to depriving Lock of a share of the fortunes in England's victory over Australia at the Oval in 1953 to wrest back the Ashes after an interval of twenty-one years. Redoubling his efforts to produce extra spin resulted in the displacement of several layers of skin from the inside of the top joint of the first finger on his left hand. The skin was left exposed and raw and, said Lock, if the wound had penetrated further, he would have been bowling off the bone. 'As it was, it remained open and angry, and I could hardly bear to bathe my finger in cold water.'

There were innumerable remedies suggested by his admirers; one local farmer rather fancifully recommended washing in paraffin oil and then placing the finger in a glass of best bitter ale three times a day. Lock instead turned to advice of specialists, the first of whom softened and trimmed the torn flesh. The finger was then subjected to violet-ray to heal and harden the wound. The next stage was a daily course at St Mary's Hospital, Paddington. He underwent deep-ray treatment in gradually increasing sessions each day up to a maximum of ninety seconds.

Slowly the injury improved to bolster hopes of uninterrupted cricket. Lock had been restricted to eleven championship matches and missed the first three Tests against Australia. Johnny Wardle was his deputy and was on standby at the Oval until the morning of the match when Lock passed a fitness test.

Len Hutton, England's first professional captain, had not been swayed by the criticism of Lock's remodelled action the previous summer. He had asserted then that he had found a match-winner in the Surrey bowler. At the Oval, crowning the Coronation Year in 1953, his prophecy was fulfilled.

The expressions of joy on the palace balcony in June was replicated by the waves of acclaim which greeted the triumphant cricketers on the victory by eight wickets on another balcony at Kennington in August. Lock and Laker paraded their dominance for the first time to cast a spell over the Australian batsmen.

The opportunity to win back the Ashes only came after a superb rearguard action at Lord's where Trevor Bailey and Willie Watson batted most of the last day to save the game. This was one of four draws in the series before the thrilling pageant at the Oval. The excitement aroused by the events led to a swift rearrangement of television schedules. Ronnie Aird, the secretary of the MCC, issued a statement in which he said that, because of the 'enormous public interest', the MCC had decided to allow the BBC to transmit the whole of the final day's play. The decision was forced by the aggravations of the previous day when the state of the game had played havoc with other television programmes. Aird said it was hoped that the MCC response would not curtail attendances at the county games. For those loyal followers there would be the chance to watch a telerecording of the final scenes of the match.

Fascinating coincidences embroider the hems of memory of a special cricketing occasion. Eight years after the First World War, in 1926, the forty-nine-year-old master of spin, Wilfred Rhodes, won back the Ashes with the following bowling analysis: 20-9-44-4. Eight years after the Second World War it was the turn of another left-armer, almost half his age, Tony Lock, to help open the doors to another reclamation of the Ashes. His figures were: 21-9-45-5. The Test match of 1926 was Harold Larwood's first and, in 1953, his fast-bowling successor Fred Trueman made his debut against Australia.

Len Hutton had to overcome the burden of losing the toss in all five Tests in this tumultuous summer. Australia's collapse after the fluctuations, veering to one side and then the other, was judged by many observers to be directly attributable to a masterstroke by the England captain. Bill Bowes, an England bowler of yesteryear and then an esteemed member of the press corps, said that Hutton had noted the potential of spin as early as Saturday afternoon. He realised even then that his spinners, Lock and Laker, could capitalise upon the state of the pitch, whereas Australia did not have such resources at their disposal.

England had gained a precious lead of 31 on the first innings. 'That set the stage for an afternoon of upheaval,' reported *The Times*. 'There is no need to decorate the truth. It was hard reality, an age of exploration and discovery as the expansive crowd sat agog.' The dusty, arid pitch, commented *The Times*, was 'full of practical jokes for those able to induce them.' Hutton allowed Trueman only two overs and Bedser three before introducing the spinners.

Laker, from the Vauxhall End, began the Australian procession in his first over, twice beating and then snaring Hassett, pressed back on his wicket, lbw for ten. One hour later half the Australian team were back in the pavilion. In one astonishing spell of fourteen minutes and sixteen balls, four wickets fell while only two runs were scored. Laker dismissed

Hole and then lured Miller forward and his off-break was edged to short leg where Trueman made a brave and unflinching catch.

Lock, at first straining too hard and with too loose a trajectory, now found his length and an appropriate speed through the air. He bowled the dangerous Harvey and trapped Morris leg before wicket. Four of Australia's best five batsmen had gone and an incredulous crowd was happy.

There was, at the last, a stirring counter-attack by Australia's youth, headed by Ron Archer, the nineteen-year-old from Queensland. Archer hit a six and seven fours in a valiant 49. He and Davidson added 50 in thirty-eight minutes. *The Times* reported: 'Archer held the tattered standard high from the moment he arrived on the scene. He led the answering challenge with brilliant forcing strokeplay.'

Australia went in to tea with their score at 131/6. On the resumption Lock swiftly brought the innings to a close. In four overs he dismissed Davidson, Archer and Langley for two runs. Lindwall hooked him for six and was then missed at slip before launching into a massive strike off Laker. Compton, pressed hard against the pavilion rails, held on to a towering catch.

Laker and Lock decisively shared nine wickets in the innings. *Wisden* praised them both but it was, for Lock, a deserving end to a season of concern and worry. As he nursed his still raw finger, he could take pride in the *Wisden* accolade and his subsequent award as one of the almanack's five Cricketers of the Year. 'England owed much to Lock. He never erred in length or direction. The pitch gave him little help, yet such was his finger spin allied to flighting and change of pace that he took five wickets for 45 runs. Laker was not as accurate but he, too, played a valuable part. He accounted for the dangerous right-handed hitters, Hassett, Miller, Hole and Lindwall.'

One Australian observer, R.S. Whitington, provided a neat and wry footnote on England's spinners and their enterprising captain at the Oval. 'They both walked off in a triumphal procession that Hutton, the man who had the astuteness to leave the fight to them, should have shared. Not even the most dyed-in-the-wool worshipper of amateurism could have denied England's professional captain had led his team like a general.'

The revels of Lock and Laker at the Oval followed a familiar script, notably on Test match days. A venerable ground was the showcase for their skills. The unchanging pattern of the climactic occasions, invariably charged with urgency and suspense, found them in their accustomed roles as match-winners. One cartoon of the period depicted them as gleeful hosts waiting on the doorstep of their lair. Many visiting batsmen had reason to beware the old refrain: 'Ashes to ashes and dust to dust. If Laker doesn't get you, Lockie must!'

In five series against Australia, South Africa, West Indies and New Zealand in the 1950s, Lock and Laker shared 57 wickets at the Oval. Their peak performances together were 15 wickets against South Africa in 1955 and 16 in the rout of the West Indies in 1957 when Lock returned figures of 11-48. The last act of a mesmeric alliance came against the inexperienced New Zealanders in 1958. They were spared further ignominy by rain at the Oval but the ordeal was unrelenting elsewhere in a treacherous summer. Lock took 34 wickets at an average of 7.47 runs in the series and Laker 17 at 10.17 runs apiece.

One of the most intriguing of the final Test cliffhangers occurred in 1955, two years after their deeds in the Ashes-winning year. South Africa were the opponents and England had no illusions about the serious challenge awaiting them. The exceptional brilliance of the Springboks' fielding had aroused admiration in Australia in 1952/53. Under Jack Cheetham's captaincy they set and maintained the highest possible standards of discipline and physical fitness to overturn the odds in sharing the series 2-2.

Early reverses in bitterly cold weather demonstrated the South Africans' unease in such conditions. England won by an innings at Nottingham and less commandingly at Lord's. It required the bowling heroics of Brian Statham to halt a winning advance by South Africa at Headquarters. He returned figures of 7-39 and bowled unchanged throughout the South African second innings. England were heavily indebted to this feat of endurance in gaining victory by 71 runs.

South Africa now staged a wonderful recovery. Buoyant fielding, in alliance with the impressive spin-pace combination of Hugh Tayfield and Test newcomers Trevor Goddard and Peter Heine, confounded England. First, there was a narrow victory by three wickets at Manchester. Then, after winning the toss but losing seven wickets for 98, they gloriously overcame the disadvantage to win by 224 runs and level the series.

The real prospect of winning their first rubber in England was denied South Africa in a thrilling encounter at the Oval. This was a match dominated by the spin of Lock, Laker and Tayfield. The redoubtable Springbok off-spinner had reason to be disappointed by the failures of the batsmen. A remarkable feature of the Oval decider was a marathon spell with few parallels. On the third day he bowled for five hours from half-past twelve to the close, completing 52 overs, including 29 maidens, to take 4-54.

The batting vigil of Peter May, unbeaten on 89, alone prevailed against Tayfield's bowling masterclass. It left the merest chink in the door but it was enough for Lock and Laker to summon their own spinning skills and share nine wickets in England's victory by 92 runs. It brought their contribution to fifteen of the eighteen South African wickets that fell to bowlers in the match.

Jim Laker conceded that the presence of four Test bowlers operating on uncovered wickets was the prime factor in Surrey's long run of success in the 1950s. It was also, thought others, allied to a conspiracy that the Oval wicket was expressly designed for the Surrey bowlers. Doug Insole, as one opponent, maintains: 'There is no doubt that Bert Lock (the groundsman) ensured that "two amazing bowlers" got a wicket that helped them. It is also true that it aided Alec Bedser, with his leg-cutters.' Insole adds that Lock had the ability to produce a wicket to suit bowlers, with their particular skills, which very few groundsmen had been able to do since that time.

Bert Lock was a Devonian recruited by Surrey after the Second World War to perform what must count as one of the miracles of groundsmanship. The cricket acres of Kennington had been prepared as a major prisoner-of-war camp for the Germans who might have been captured during an airborne invasion of London. The hallowed turf had been desecrated by stakes and caged with barbed wire. The camp was never used, although the legend persists that a German bomber pilot bailed out over Kennington and spent the rest of one wartime night at the Oval.

Lock was given the monumental task of restoring the Oval in Surrey's centenary year. The great clear-up began in October 1945. The preliminaries involved the removal of mounds of accumulated debris. Concrete posts were dismantled and holes filled in. Then scythes and sickles were deployed to uncover the cricket square. Lock organised transport and laid 45,000 turves brought from the marshes in Kent.

Alec Bedser is unstinting in his admiration for Lock's stamina over many arduous months. 'Starting at 8 a.m., and working until he could no longer see the pitch, he and his makeshift staff somehow got the ground into playable shape. The practice nets had been gnawed by rats. Bert sat in the east stand, often in freezing winds, repairing the nets to have them ready for the new season in early April 1946. I have often thought of him as an unsung hero.'

The outcome was a pitch dramatically transformed from the days of 'Bosser' Martin, Lock's predecessor, when the wickets were as unyielding as concrete and overwhelmingly in the batsman's favour. In many people's eyes, the new-look Oval contributed greatly to Surrey's reign as champions. As Neville Cardus said: 'If Tony Lock had arrived at the Oval in 1930, with all his great dowry of gifts, we should have heard little of him. He owed much to his namesake, Bert Lock. In fact, Surrey may fairly be said to have won the championship seven years consecutively because of Stuart Surridge's leadership, Jim Laker and the joint Lock coincidence of circumstances.'

Peter May exonerated Bert Lock in defence of his home ground. He said that the Surrey bowlers were incensed at the charges that the pitches were prepared for them. 'These implied a subtlety, a prescience and deviousness that Bert and his staff did not possess.' May recalled that the Surrey team were often assured that a splendid pitch was at their disposal. 'The promise left us rather mystified when we found ourselves, or our opponents, on the rack at 43-7.'

Even more pertinently, Arthur McIntyre stresses that the Oval wicket aided both teams. 'We had to bat on it as well as the opposition.' Micky Stewart was one of the home batsmen confronted with its perils. 'the Oval wasn't the easiest pitch to bat on in the 1950s. It used to break up either before noon on the first day, or before tea on the second day. I fielded for Surrey for three years before we faced a total of 300.'

If the Oval wicket could be preposterous terrain, then there is statistical evidence to deny its overriding value in Surrey's successes. The figures conclusively reveal that Lock and Laker in championship matches obtained more wickets away from the Oval.

Amid the selection debates in the summer of 1954 prior to the tour of Australia, one of the ironies was that, after being omitted from the party, Lock and Laker suddenly found rampant form. In their last ten championship matches, they took 103 wickets between them, Laker securing 59 and Lock 44, both for an average of less than nine runs apiece.

In August, as they established their stranglehold, the Oval wicket was at its most daunting. Worcestershire were overwhelmed by the spin of Lock and Laker. The match started at two o'clock; by quarter to four they had been bowled out for 25, having lost their last seven first-innings wickets for five runs. It was the lowest score since Somerset were bowled out by Gloucestershire, also for 25, in 1947. The Worcestershire total was greater by only one run than the lowest they had ever made, which was against Yorkshire in 1903.

The subsidence continued on the second day at the Oval. By 12.30 on the second day – after only five hours of cricket – the game was over. Worcestershire were dismissed for 40 in their second innings. Surrey, having batted for only 24 overs before the declaration, won by an innings.

'It was, perhaps, the most comprehensive and impressive of all Surrey's victories in recent times,' reported *The Times*. 'It was again inspired by the two spinners whom England have forsaken, Lock and Laker.' Lock's return in the first innings was 5-2. 'His astonishing figures speak for themselves,' added *The Times* report. 'He was accurate and deadly, turning the ball venomously and occasionally making the ball lift as well.'

Stuart Surridge, with a glance at the baleful skies, had quickly assessed that batting was an untenable proposition. He dispensed with unnecessary runs in making the declaration at 92/3. It seemed likely, at one stage with eighty minutes left for play, that Surrey might win in an afternoon and an evening. 'Lock and Laker, after rubbing the new ball in the mud, were again at Worcestershire's throats,' continued *The Times* report. 'They were whipping like rattlesnakes from the pitch, if anything more fiercely than before.'

Peter Richardson, one of the humbled opponents, recalled the farcical conditions. 'We shouldn't have been playing on that wicket.' He remembered the mastery of Peter May, unbeaten on 31 before Surrey's declaration: 'Everyone was in disarray, edging or gloving catches but we never missed the middle of Peter's bat.' Of his own dismissal in Worcestershire's second innings, he said that he attempted to raise his bat out of harm's way on a skittish pitch. 'The ball kept on climbing to such an extent that I was still caught behind off Laker.'

The phenomenal accuracy of Tony Lock earned the appreciation of his captain, Donald Carr, on the MCC tour of Pakistan in 1955/56. 'Lockie was magnificent on the mat,' recalled Carr. 'He pushed the ball through so quickly, quicker than Derek Underwood and almost as fast as Fazal Mahmood.' Fazal, with his taxing leg-cutters, was the fast-medium bowler who had won acclaim in enabling Pakistan to pull off a surprise first Test victory in England in 1954.

Carr remembered his sense of relief when he found that the opposition in Pakistan included several so-called 'chuckers'. 'In one minor game they had this chap who made Lockie look like a straight arm bowler by comparison. It meant, as he said, that he could cast aside any worries about 'our man,' Carr pointedly remarked.

Wisden enthused about Lock as the outstanding personality on the tour of the subcontinent. 'His 81 wickets at a little over ten runs apiece, on such a short tour was a remarkable achievement. He found the pitches completely to his liking and he enjoyed a tour of almost unbroken triumph.' Lock's tally included 11 wickets in the victory over the Governor-General's XI at Karachi. It was in this game that he bowled a sequence of 104 deliveries without conceding a run. Lock was able to retain a slip and a gully (sometimes two) and quite often two short legs as well. Rarely were there less than three men, other than the wicket-keeper, close to the wicket.

Carr remembered the unerring control against the Pakistanis, ten of whom had represented their country in the victory over England at the Oval. 'Lockie, in this first spell on the mat, bowled 17 maiden overs, and had taken three wickets for none before he had his first runs scored off him. Our opponents were good players but the ball was keeping low. hey just pushed and pushed. That's all they could do, such was his pinpoint accuracy.'

Abdul Hafeez Kardar, the Pakistani captain, prevented Lock from establishing a new record of consecutive maiden overs. He pulled the third ball of the eighteenth over to the fine-leg boundary. Two balls later Lock had his revenge when Kardar was superbly caught by Carr at mid-off. He had failed by those two runs to break the record of Horace Hazell, of Somerset, who sent down 105 deliveries without conceding a run. One curiosity of two bowling marathons was that Harold Stephenson, the MCC wicketkeeper, was behind the stumps on both occasions. Lock was able to rejoice in a signal feat. His analysis in the first innings at Karachi was 38 overs, 26 maidens and 5-31.

Lock took two of his four hat-tricks in Pakistan and it might have been four in four balls in the match against the Combined Railways XI at Multan. Carr, at slip, missed the sharp chance as the 'ball sped by my right ear'. 'Lockie wasn't too upset, just amused that the skipper was the culprit. We had a good laugh about it but I'm glad it was me, as captain, who dropped it.'

The innings victory in the then new stadium at Multan, built on the corner of an old Muslim fort, was completed before lunch on the third day. It was decided to complete the entertainment with a soccer challenge match on the cricket field in the afternoon.

Nets were rigged up and the field marked out. Public announcements were made and it was disclosed that the MCC's opponents would be the reigning Pakistani Cup finalists. There was a crowd of 20,000, far exceeding the numbers in the recently completed cricket match. The tourists had several footballers, some of professional status, and felt that they would not be outclassed, even against a team crowned with pride in Pakistan.

The fixture assumed civic importance when the local mayor arrived carrying a large silver cup which was intended, or so it was understood, to be presented to the winning team. 'A couple of hours later,' said Donald Carr, 'after our victory by 2-0 had installed us as champions, the mayor and the trophy had mysteriously disappeared.'

The prizes of cricket were those which concerned Tony Lock. The 'splendid team man' flourished as the experienced leader of the bowling pack in Pakistan. Ron Roberts, in his summary of the tour, enthused about an outstanding individual performance. 'One has come to judge him by the most exacting standards and even by those his form has been excellent. An indefatigable worker, always on the attack, he has now emerged among the top exponents on all wickets.'

Lock's candidature was now assured for more red-letter days with England. How and why did his nerve fail him when he crossed swords with Australia at Manchester in the following summer? The memory of a doleful episode would haunt him for the rest of his career.

SIX

The Old Trafford Mystery

'Two men more in sympathy with each other would have made the Manchester Test a more enjoyable experience.'
– Doug Insole

A triumphal message scrawled on a coal truck at Tilbury bore the words: 'Wot! No Ashes?' to mock the departing Australians in Coronation Year. The pleasures of another memorable summer for England three years later in 1956 were blunted for Tony Lock. Forlorn and dispirited, he was left trailing in the wake of his spinning partner, Jim Laker, on what was for him an infamous Test occasion at Old Trafford. The unprecedented feat of Laker taking 19 wickets, including ten in an innings, mercilessly exposed his failings. The solitary wicket against Australia was the most humbling statistic of his career.

The ascendancy of Laker coincided with England winning three consecutive rubbers against Australia, the first time this had happened for sixty years. The nonchalant Surrey spinner, his appeals always without special pleading, twice took ten wickets in an innings against the Australians in 1956. There was the usual shrug of the shoulders, the sweater unfurled lazily over his back, as he departed the fields of the Oval and Old Trafford.

Altogether Laker took 63 wickets in seven matches, including two for Surrey, against the demoralised tourists. By contrast, his partner, Lock, could not stifle his exasperation as an also-ran in the proceedings. He twice bowled through an Australian innings without taking a wicket. His analyses for Surrey and England totalled: 88-44-169-0.

Arthur Mailey, a great Australian leg-spinner of yesteryear, was a sympathetic observer in the cricket judiciary. He reflected on Lock's plight amid the jubilation which greeted Laker's performance at Old Trafford. 'I believe that Jim's continued and unbroken success had an effect on Tony's bowling. Seeing so many wickets fall at one end, he naturally strove harder to get in on the act.' Mailey correctly assessed the competitive fervour charging Lock's efforts and wryly added that the consequence was that Lock lost something of his normal immaculate control.

Wrestling with his temper over spurned opportunities did scramble Lock's acumen – as a bowler at Manchester – but his wits did not fail him at other times. He vied with Laker in an ominous curtain-raiser to the forthcoming Test series at the Oval in May. The Australians were always struggling to survive against the rampant Laker in the first innings against Surrey. The first instalment of his shoal of wickets was collected in the game. They were gained on a sweltering day and on an unhelpful pitch. He had actually declared himself unfit after a sleepless night helping to nurse his sick daughter, three-year-old Fiona.

Stuart Surridge, the Surrey captain, persuaded him to play and he was equally determined to cajole further exertions after tea on the first day. Laker had then taken four wickets and Surridge brushed aside the protestations of the tired bowler. 'No, Jim,' he said, 'there are more Australian wickets for you in this innings.' Three of them, those of Maddocks, Lindwall and Johnson, were taken without cost in two overs on the resumption. As one observer said, 'Laker cut through them like a grocer's wire through Cheddar cheese.'

Laker bowled unchanged from just before half-past twelve for four hours and twenty minutes. In a spell of 46 overs from the pavilion end, broken only by the lunch and tea intervals, he took 10-88. Not since 1878, when another Surrey man, the left-arm bowler Edward Barratt, did so for the Players, had ten wickets been achieved against the Australians. Barratt conceded only 43 runs in 29 overs out of a total of 77 and his feat was acknowledged by a bonus of £5. Laker's reward was the match ball and a cheque for £50 from the Surrey committee.

Laker did, though, have two slices of luck. Lock, with sharply contrasting figures of 0-100 in 33 overs, should have had one wicket to reward his toils from the less favourable Vauxhall End. Miller miscued a chance to Dennis Cox at deep extra cover where, according to Pat McKelvey, another former Surrey player, Cox always claimed that he thought about the nuances of the situation as the ball plummeted towards him. Cox decided to muff the catch on purpose and make the attempt look as realistic as possible.

So Laker's return ought to have been limited to nine, or even eight since the catch which Swetman took to dismiss the last man, Wilson, was dubious. Laker, referring to Cox's chivalrous gesture, said: 'I was so tired that I just wanted the innings to end. I would certainly have held the catch if it had been mine.'

Surrey gained a lead of 88 runs on the first innings. For a time, it seemed that Lock, now switched to the Pavilion End, might emulate his partner. *The Times* reported: 'At lunch time the writing was clearly on the wall, the victory almost consummated, and there was a chance that to crown everything Lock would do as Laker had done and make a clean sweep of the Australians.' A 'fabulous coincidence' did not materialise because Laker intervened to trap Mackay lbw after Lock had taken the first six wickets.

'As soon as Lock began to bowl straighter and to a fuller length,' wrote Jim Swanton, 'he had the Australians in continual distress. There was venomous spin, a stark Spofforthian hostility and threatening fielding to his own bowling.' Lock's figures for the innings were 7-49; in fact all his wickets were obtained in one spell of 23.1 overs costing 36 runs.

Denys Rowbotham, in the *Manchester Guardian*, considered that the change in Lock's fortunes might have been partly due to Laker suffering a reaction to his efforts in the first innings. 'Lock's blood was up as soon as he saw his first ball rear angrily at Burke. Thereafter all the colour drained from the Australians' cheeks; they wore the haggard look of a cornered foe. From a position of safety at 56 without loss, the Australians collapsed to 107 all out. Surrey won by ten wickets to become the first county to beat an Australian touring side for forty-four years.'

The Times commented on the contrariness of the Australian batting. 'When the ball is coming through truly they are immensely formidable. But when the pitch is playing false they are inept and vulnerable.' The report exonerated the openers, McDonald and Burke, whose watchful defiance carried a lesson for their colleagues. The fall of Burke, caught and bowled by Lock, presaged the rout. 'From then until the end Lock bowled superbly,' continued the report. 'He was aggressive, relentlessly accurate and virtually irresistible.' McDonald, a model of obduracy for two hours, was finally dismissed, edging a vicious, kicking leg-break to Laker at slip. As a postscript to the command of the Surrey spinners at Kennington,

The Times concluded that unless Australia failed to counter the turning ball their chance of regaining the Ashes was a slender prospect.

Australia, in fact, never recovered from their eclipse by spin at the hands of Surrey at the Oval. Their indecision had psychological roots. Preying on their minds was the stranglehold of Lock and Laker on the same ground and the loss of the Ashes in 1953. In their technical dilemmas they became nervous and too often impetuous. Time and time again they were betrayed by the vulnerability of their young batsmen against the sharply turning ball. They were cruelly exposed like blank-faced dunces in the classroom.

'The Australian,' wrote Norman Preston in *Wisden*, 'is mainly a Saturday afternoon cricketer, brought up on hard, true pitches, blazing sunshine and in clear light.' Trevor Bailey confirmed the disparity between the two opposing forces. He emphasised the advantage enjoyed by England players in regularly playing on bad wickets. The supreme accolade, as paid to Len Hutton, was that he was a master in such conditions. 'We have always tended to play better on turning wickets. The Australians did not play on as many and we did.'

The winning salvo by Australia in the second Test at Lord's was a false dawn, soon to be darkened at Leeds and Manchester. In mitigation, the Australians were rendered helpless on spinners' wickets in one of the wettest summers in memory. But even more pertinently, they lacked the menace and craftsmanship of Lock and Laker. In the final Test at the Oval, where they were spared further humiliation by rain, this deficiency was underlined when England had to bat on a treacherous pitch. They were unable to capitalise on the opportunity. The four tosses which Peter May won in the series would not have affected the outcome had the coin dropped the other way. Had Australia batted first on the heavily criticised wickets, the two matches in which England pronounced their superiority with innings victories would conceivably have finished earlier.

Wilf Wooller, the former Glamorgan captain and a Test selector in 1956, recalled the blessings of a fruitful summer and a series in which 'we walked on water'. Selecting is very often a matter of faith in class or pedigree; in this year England were rewarded in the recalls of a distinguished trio. They included the selections of the forty-one-year-old Cyril Washbrook, himself a selector, at Leeds; David Sheppard at Manchester; and Denis Compton at the Oval. After going into the ministry, Sheppard had almost completely severed his connection with first-class cricket; he had played only four innings for Sussex before belying his lack of practice with a century at Old Trafford.

The romantics also found pleasure in the return of the thirty-eight-year-old Denis Compton who scored 94 at the Oval. The bewitching improviser had recently undergone major knee surgery but there was little or no loss in his batting powers. *Wisden* reported: 'Gradually, Compton unfolded all the familiar strokes of his golden days. The special leg sweeps of his own brand and the most delicate of late cuts, as well as the peerless cover drives, took him and England to prosperity.'

England were perched on the abyss, having lost three wickets, those of Richardson, Cowdrey and Oakman, dismissed by Archer for 17 runs on the first morning at Headingley. Wooller remembered the foreboding of the selectors, including his colleague, Les Ames, after the tumble of England wickets in the first hour of the match. 'Les took his selection duties very seriously. By the time we got to Leeds England were in deep trouble. Les was threatening to resign but May and Washbrook saved the day.'

Washbrook, against his own inclination, had been persuaded to make a comeback to Test cricket. 'Surely the situation is not as bad as all that!' was his response to the decision of his fellow selectors. His experience in the heat of battle against Australia was a key factor in the selection. It was considered a better proposition than submitting a younger candidate to the pressures of a crucial match. The surprise move, heavily criticised at the time, would prove to be the turning point in the series.

Australia, after their early successes, swaggered proudly. They might well have capitalised on Archer's opening thrusts had they been able to deploy Keith Miller. Miller, above all players, could swing a game in a trice. He was unable to bowl because of a sore knee. Washbrook, perhaps fortunately, did not have to weather such an assault at the start of his innings.

Wilf Wooller remembered the entry of the 'great Red Rose foe' at Headingley and how Washbrook won over the normally alien Yorkshire crowd. 'It was one of the finest pieces of psychological cricket I've ever seen. Cyril strutted out, his cap at a rakish angle, to join Peter May at the crease.' Archer, eagerly anticipating another scalp, was kept waiting by the veteran. 'Cyril took guard quietly, then he stood back and memorised the field. He then looked down again, checked his guard, and signalled to Archer that he was ready.'

A hush enveloped the ground as Washbrook maintained his calm to play out the first over from the Australian bowler. He was like a musical conductor on the rostrum, willing the vast crowd to respond to his bidding. Suddenly, the Yorkshire partisans were no longer hostile; they recognised that their adversary from across the Pennines was fighting their cause this time. 'The crowd settled down,' said Wooller. 'It was as though he'd given them a bromide. May got his hundred and Cyril just missed his by two runs, hitting across the line.' It was an epic swansong for the Lancashire stalwart. He was associated in a fourth-wicket stand of 187 with May in what would prove to be a match-winning partnership.

Before this happened, Doug Insole remembered the brusque intervention of Tony Lock as he waited for his turn to bat. Five minutes before the close, May's great innings came to an end when he was superbly caught down by his boots by Lindwall at fine leg off Johnson. Insole was officially next man in at number six. Lock had been padded up since six o'clock and he was not going to forfeit his right as nightwatchman. 'When the fourth wicket fell Lockie pushed me to one side and said:"I'm bloody well going out." He always fancied his chances as a batsman.'

The following morning, Lock was so confident against Benaud and Archer as to justify the claim. The mean spirit of his bowling was just as evident in a batting role. The boundaries flowed. He square-cut Benaud for four and then struck out again to send another ball hurtling high over long off. 'He was making it all look simple before he mistimed a back stroke and spooned the ball gently into the covers,' wrote one observer.

The Headingley wicket, reported one correspondent, was already opening its arms to spin on the afternoon of the second day. Doug Insole timed the deterioration even earlier – by the end of the first day. 'It was beginning to crumble then and by the time I went in it was turning square. It had been a perfectly good wicket on the first day.' *The Times* correspondent had had his binoculars trained on the pitch while England were batting. 'It was possible to see bare patches forming on the wicket and puffs of dust flying as the ball pitched'. The knowing souls in the press corps sensed that sooner or later there would be a rout.' Insole said that but for the loss of seven and a half hours' play to rain, involving a complete washout on the Saturday, England would have won the match in two and a half days.

The stage was set for Lock and Laker, with 18 wickets between them, to flourish zestfully on the broken pitch. 'Who would have thought,' said one incredulous supporter, 'when we sat here on Thursday morning, with England 17/3, that we should be here today, cheering victory by an innings.' In one hour after tea on the second day Australia tumbled from 38/1 to 69/6. Miller and Benaud, in defiant company, offered their team a tentative hope of a lifeline. Their seventh wicket stand of 73 was a vain attempt to avert the follow-on. There was the intermission of rain, which poured continuously for thirty-six hours, before the final act of submission on the Monday.

The grim duel on the last day was played out against a bleak backcloth. Smoke rose in ghostly spirals from the red-bricked houses at the Kirkstall Lane end and the flags hung lifelessly from the white masts on the pavilion roof. 'We were told that rain was falling all round Leeds,' wrote Sir Donald Bradman in the *Daily Mail*.

'Watching play in the hazy gloom, a patriotic Australian could not be blamed for believing that it would fall here any minute.' Peter May, the England captain, was also on tenterhooks, fearful that the torrents might engulf his team's hopes. 'The real menace was rain,' he said. 'It chilled me to hear that rumble of thunder down Kirkstall way, half an hour before lunch.'

Beneath the canopy of grey skies and in deteriorating light Lock and Laker were again paired in a concentrated and relentless attack. Miller, this time in tandem with Neil Harvey, fought the rearguard action. 'As the struggle continued, one could not help but note that the Ashes were now right on the dividing line,' ventured one Australian correspondent, R.S. Whitington. Denys Rowbotham, in the *Manchester Guardian*, described the hazards facing the batsmen, repeatedly confounded by quick spin and changing pace. 'Miller was three times rapped on the pads. Finally, with the temper of some caged and wounded animal, he was goaded into a huge pull. The spin beat him and his flailing bat merely rent the air. Then Harvey was all but beaten by Laker's quicker ball. During this time Lock and Laker bowled six maiden overs in succession and there was nothing the two batsmen could do about it.'

Miller's defiance ended when he played half-back to Laker. 'The off spin popped and Trueman swooped to take the chance at short leg as the ball slithered down from Miller's glove'.

The prized wicket of Harvey was all Lock's work. Harvey's 69, out of a total of 140, was a courageous accomplishment spread over four and a half hours. Bradman thought that for determination, concentration and self-discipline, it ranked as possibly the finest innings of Harvey's career.

The valiance of the little master ended when Lock, sprawling down the wicket, acrobatically took a return catch.

Australia lost their last eight wickets for 32 runs. The impeccable accuracy of Lock and Laker was reflected in their figures on the last day. Laker, firmly in charge at the Pavilion End, took 4-24 in 19 overs. He conceded only one run in his first eight overs. Lock was almost as miserly with a return of 2-16 in 15.5 overs.

Denys Rowbotham insisted: 'Both were a good deal more than just accurate. The naggingly strict length and consistent straightness of their bowling reduced to a minimum the number of balls that need not be played. They added subtle variations of flight which disguised the changing length, now drew the batsmen agonisingly forward, next forced hurriedly back and then, at crucial moments, confounded their judgement and made the batsmen move fatally the wrong way.'

It was a shared achievement between Laker, the Yorkshire exile on his homecoming, and Lock, the fiery southerner who was able to bask in the true welcome and acknowledgement of his talents so far away from his home. A remarkable pair had led England to their first victory – by an innings and 42 runs – over Australia at Headingley.

The question of the ideal cricketing wicket such as those that so disturbed the impotent tourists in 1956, was developed by Jim Swanton in the *Daily Telegraph*. Swanton said that only twice in England and never abroad could he recall Test matches in which the surface had disintegrated in such a manner. One had been the Lord's Test of 1935 – the 'leather-jacket' year – when the square was ravaged by a pestilential insect. A South African leg-spinner by the fabulous name of Xenophon Balaskas spun England to defeat. The other was the rough-cast track of a wicket at Old Trafford in 1950 upon which the West Indies were summarily dispatched. 'Both of these wickets,' said Swanton, 'were worse than those at Headingley and Old Trafford.'

Micky Stewart remembered the character of a cricket square prevailing in the 1950s. 'The pitches were nothing like they are today. It wasn't only that they were uncovered, they were also prepared differently. They wore quicker even if it didn't rain. The wickets were never as solid as they are now. Spinners could invariably get the ball to grip.'

Turning wickets were common in the 1950s as evidenced by the legion of spinners who took more than a hundred wickets in 1956. Complicit in the achievements of the off-spinners was the menace of the leg-trap which then allowed the positioning of three men, excluding the wicketkeeper, behind the wicket. Neville Cardus, in his *Wisden* tribute to Jim Laker, commented that any great performer needs to be born at the right time. 'He was clever to begin playing cricket and bowling off spin after the alteration to the lbw rule dangerously penalised batsmen who had brought to a fine art the use of pads to brilliant off-breaks pitching on the stumps and coming back like a knife.' Laker, he said, had been quick to adapt his arts to the deplorably unresourceful footwork of most batsmen of the present period. 'Moreover he has, with the opportune judgement of those born to exceptional prowess, taken advantage of the development of the leg-trap.'

Cardus added that Laker's actual finger spin had seldom been surpassed on a 'sticky' or dusty wicket. 'For sheer technical potentiality, often sheer actual spitefulness, Laker's off spin must be regarded as entirely out of the ordinary and very much his own.' To Cardus's analysis can be added the verdict of a great Australian rival, Richie Benaud. 'I thought Laker to be the best off spin bowler I ever saw in all conditions.' Benaud says that he would not deviate from this view regardless of the changes in batting and bowling techniques and pitches in the modern game.

Bert Flack, then the newly installed groundsman at Old Trafford, provided his own testimony in relating the intriguing prelude to Laker's match. During practice on the day before the Test he was completing his preparations. Gubby Allen, the chairman of the England selectors, accompanied by Tommy Burrows, the Lancashire cricket chairman, walked out to inspect his work.

'They looked at each other and spoke together without turning to me,' remembered Flack. Allen then approached the groundsman and asked him if the wicket he had just examined was to be used in the Test. Flack expressed surprise when Allen announced his displeasure. 'I'm not satisfied,' he said. There was a further conversation between Allen and Burrows. 'The chairman wants more grass off,' was the message communicated to the astonished Flack. 'Take a little more off, Bert, and that'll please him,' said Burrows. Flack was highly indignant. 'That's stupid. The match won't last three days. The surface is not all that well-knit.'

Flack pondered on his dilemma for some minutes. 'Finally, I got my cutter out and went up and down the wicket a couple of times. Then, I thought: "Well, why not, if the chairman wants a three-day match, he shall have it."' The blades were adjusted and he began his cutting again. 'And that did take the grass all off, believe you me.'

There was the fanfare of an opening stand of 174 between Richardson and Cowdrey at Manchester. It was England's best start against Australia since 1938 when Hutton and Barnett began with 219 at Trent Bridge. The brisk runs paved the way for a resplendent century by Sheppard. Before the end of the first day there were tell-tale signs of a crumbling wicket. Accusations were made that the pitch had been specially prepared for England's spin bowlers.

The maligned wicket was quite accommodating for England's batsmen on the second morning. The speed of the scoring – 152 runs in two hours and ten minutes – was an expression of urgency but did not signal the terrors ahead. England, with some ease, totalled 459. Jim Laker always reminded the critics of this score in the lingering post mortems on the match.

Before Australia's innings their captain, Ian Johnson, had looked on with distrust at the dusty wicket. He requested just a light rolling. Bert Flack made a swift exit to other duties after watching the first ball of the innings. He knew with certainty what would happen from that moment. 'I saw a puff of dust rise on a perfectly good length. Brian Statham was bowling at the Stretford End. The ball lifted over the head of Godfrey Evans behind the wicket and went for four, nearly six, byes.'

Australia, at one stage 48/0, were bowled out for 84. It was their lowest total in England since their 65 at the Oval in 1912. Their previous lowest total was 58 after a ferocious storm at Brisbane in the 1936/37 series. The debacle at Old Trafford began with Lock's dismissal of Burke, caught by Cowdrey off a half-hearted pull. It was to prove his only wicket of the match. Overshadowing all else was Laker in his meanest mood. He captured 9-37 overall; in 22 balls he claimed seven wickets for just eight runs.

Laker was convinced that the ball with which he dismissed Neil Harvey in Australia's first innings was the crucial breakthrough. It ensured that England would go on to retain the Ashes. 'Neil was the finest left-hander I ever bowled against and in our many challenging duels in the past the honours had gone very much his way. But, as luck would have it this time, I managed to bowl him a beauty first ball. From around the wicket I held it back sufficiently for the ball to drift in and pitch around the leg and middle stumps. It turned just enough to clip his off-stump.'

Of all his wickets at Old Trafford, this was the one he treasured most. Bill O'Reilly, in his account of a 'spectacular comedy', agreed with Laker on the ball which overthrew Harvey. 'It beat the little left-hander so conclusively that the dismissal prepared everyone for the dismal execution that followed.'

Jim Swanton said that Laker's first-innings performance was phenomenal enough, but its merit was clouded by the deficiencies of the Australian batting, as also by the palaver over the state of the wicket. 'There was no room whatever for argument regarding his bowling in the second innings. He bowled 36 overs, practically non-stop, except for the taking of the new ball, all the time attacking the stumps and compelling the batsmen to play. He never wilted or fell short in terms of length or direction.'

Laker wove a spinning plot as cunning as any devised by Agatha Christie. England won the match by an innings and 170 runs to retain the Ashes. Laker's figures will surely never be eclipsed. He took 10-53 in a match total of 19 wickets for 90 runs in 68 overs. Les Ames recalled: 'The Australians were not good players of off-spin. They did rather give up the ghost. Jim, with his marvellous control, turned the ball at right angles.'

Laker became the first bowler to take 19 wickets in any first-class match, surpassing Sydney Barnes's 17-159 on the Johannesburg mat in 1913. In seven matches against Australia in 1956 Laker took 63 wickets, including 46 at a cost of 9.60 runs each in the Tests. Only Barnes, with 49 wickets in four Tests against South Africa in 1913/14, has exceeded this figure.

Robin Marlar, the former Sussex captain, in his tribute written thirty years later in *Wisden*, said that there was still an air of wondrous disbelief that Laker could have taken 19 wickets. 'Lock, the most avaricious of bowlers was at the other end. Nor should it pass notice that Statham and Bailey, both unquestioned occupants in the hall of fame, sent down 46 overs between them without a strike. Even if you accept that the 1956 Australians were not one of the best sides from that country, there were still great cricketers in the team: Harvey, Miller, Lindwall and Benaud. In truth, even though it happened, we can describe Laker's feat only as incredible.'

Another Sussex player, Alan Oakman, was a late replacement for Tom Graveney at Manchester. His credentials as a short-leg fieldsman were proudly acknowledged in Sussex; he enjoyed a key partnership with Marlar, another off-spinner. Oakman recalled his alliance with Laker: 'Having the greatest confidence in Jim's accuracy, I stood nearer than usual. I can remember Keith Miller coming in, taking guard and looking round the field, particularly out to deep square leg and mid-wicket.'

Miller told him: 'That's a dangerous position, Oakie. If I middle one, they will have to carry you off.'

Three balls later he pushed forward to Laker and Oakman stooped to take the first of his catches low down around his ankles. Later that year, Oakman attended a dinner with the record-breaker. He was introduced as the man who had helped Laker by holding five catches against Australia. There was a wry smile on Laker's face. 'Alan,' he said, 'you're not still living on that?' Oakman played in only two matches for England but he has still not forgotten the fielding honours allotted to him on his last appearance. At the fiftieth anniversary dinner held to commemorate Laker's feat at Old Trafford in 2006 he was regaling all and sundry with the news: 'I'm the man who made Jim Laker famous.'

There was an amusing postscript to Laker's achievement. After the match Sir Donald Bradman and cricket correspondent Alex Bannister saw Sydney Barnes in the car park at Old Trafford. 'Well, what do you think of that?' he was asked. Barnes, the legendary bowling maestro, gruffly replied: 'No bugger ever got all ten when I was at t'other end.'

Barnes's response did, in fact, accentuate the central mystery of the match: the inability of Lock to prosper in the conditions. John Arlott wrote that never was the difference between Lock – in the days of his 'old' action – and Laker more clearly demonstrated as on that occasion. 'Lock took his wickets by the size and speed of his break in which no one in the world was his superior. But, when the ball would come through only slowly, he lacked the power – and the patience – to defeat top-class batsmen who concentrated on defence.'

Any assessment of one of the most remarkable of sporting chronicles must also address this riddle. Almost as astonishing as Laker's triumph is the fact that Tony Lock, one of the world's great spinners, sent down 69 overs and took only one wicket. 'If my performance was unbelievable, then so was his,' wrote Laker. 'If the game had been replayed a million times it would surely never have happened again. Early on he bowled quite beautifully without any luck at all and beat the bat and stumps time after time.'

Richie Benaud, as one opponent in the match, agrees with Laker. 'There is no doubt that Lock bowled magnificently from a technical point of view in Australia's second innings. We couldn't lay a bat on him because he was pitching outside the right-hander's leg stump and the ball occasionally spun straight to slip.' Benaud says that there was clearly exasperation at the lack of success in the wickets column but maintains that Lock certainly did not bowl badly. 'It was probably just that the right-handers were able to allow the ball to spin past the bat whereas with Laker they constantly had to be playing every ball.'

The paucity of Lock's analyses just did not make sense on a slow pitch tailored for him. It came down, in the view of many observers, to a mental attitude. Peter Richardson, one of the watching England fieldsmen, remembered a 'great bowler and a wonderful trier' in a fever of excitement. 'I think the more wickets Jim got the more upset Lockie became. If he had pitched the ball up and bowled at a sensible pace, he must have got ten out of twenty.'

Bert Flack recalled that Lock, from the Warwick Road End, was turning the ball so much that it was veering into the hands of first or second slip rather than the wicketkeeper. Geoffrey Howard, then the Lancashire secretary, said Lock did not use his brains and forgot his business. As the match wore on and Laker's wickets multiplied, Lock grew increasingly cross with himself. Over by over, he gestured in disbelief, placing one agonised arm across his chest and then placing the other on top of it.

For Jim Swanton the comparison between the figures was in one sense unarguable evidence of Laker's great performance. 'If the derided wicket had been such a natural graveyard for batsmen, it is inconceivable that Lock, even below his peak, would not have taken more than one wicket.' Doug Insole agreed: 'You would have backed any reasonable bowler – and Lock was far more than just that – to have greater reward.'

Tony Lock reportedly left Old Trafford in high dudgeon and the rift between him and Laker simmered for a long time. Doug Insole remembered the admissions of regret by both bowlers: 'They both subsequently said when they became more friendly how wrong they had been in their attitudes to each other. Jim said that he should have been more sympathetic to Lockie who had toiled without reward. They didn't speak to each other for quite a while. Two people more in sympathy with each other would have made the Manchester Test a more enjoyable experience.'

Laker himself later confessed that he ought to have been more understanding: 'On reflection over many years – and remembering that Tony has had to live with his "1-106" – I think I should probably have shown a bit more sympathy towards him than I did at the time. I have often tried to imagine how I would have felt if the boot had been on the other foot – as it could so easily have been.'

SEVEN

Magician in the Field

'I have seen him hold quite sinful catches, catches which were not there until his rapid hungry eyesight created them.'
– Neville Cardus

Tony Lock was as happy as a sandboy in the field. He gloried in the limelight as the entertainer who brought a theatrical touch to his catching *legerdemain*. Trevor Bailey remembered this endearing feature of Lock's cricket. 'He was seldom content to bring off a breathtaking catch but added a couple of somersaults for good measure.'

Lock was supreme in the now unregarded position at backward short leg and disturbingly agile in taking return catches as a bowler. He is third, with a career total of 830 catches, behind Frank Woolley and W.G. Grace in the all-time lists. Beneath him is a quintet of esteemed close fieldsmen – Wally Hammond and Brian Close, each with over 800 catches, and John Langridge, Wilfred Rhodes and Arthur Milton, all of whom totalled over 700. As a testimony to his all-round fielding skills, Lock also holds the world record of 202 caught and bowled dismissals amounting to 7.10 per cent of his wickets.

Raymond Illingworth, as one Yorkshire rival, considers Lock to be the best fielder off his own bowling he has ever seen. 'He had a brisk approach to the wicket and yet he could change direction and take magnificent return catches.' Illingworth remembers the consummate showman. He recalls one match at Bramall Lane when Lock, having completed a catch, went into his rolling routine. The umpire watched the antics and remarked: 'If you roll any more you'll roll yourself out of the ground.'

Lock was unmistakably a dominant figure at a time when spin was a prime attacking weapon. Every county could call upon specialist close fieldsmen. David Allen, in Gloucestershire, recalls his good fortune in having the services of Arthur Milton as a predatory ally for his off-spin.

At England level he would later discover another safe pair of hands in Lock. Milton, along with other practitioners, enthused about the values of fielding skills. 'I always felt that this was the best area of my game,' he said. 'I probably won as many matches by my catching as I did by my batting.'

Peter Walker, in Glamorgan, remembers his enlistment as the third of the short legs posted to the medium-paced off-spinners of Don Shepherd. Walker, in these formative days, stood four yards from the bat at short square leg between two of the great catchers, Allan Watkins and Wilf Wooller. 'I absorbed from these two major exponents of the art the various techniques required to hang on to the many fast-travelling edges that flew from the bowling of Shepherd and his spin partner, Jim McConnon.'

Keeping faith with the precise purveyors of spin was a forbidding task for the trusting accomplices close to the wicket. Their prowess on the turning wickets of the 1950s was grooved in harness with bowling accuracy. The spoils which accrued to these alert hands produce the verdict on the collaboration from a revered bowler, Alec Bedser. 'You're bound to have good catchers,' observes Sir Alec, 'if you've got bowlers providing the catches.' It is his way of saying that fielding standards automatically rise because a chance is expected off every ball.

Sir Alec, in his book, *Twin Ambitions*, expanded on this theme. 'The sense of anticipation is so sharpened that concentration becomes second nature. Conversely, a team without an attack to create many chances tends to relax and go through the motions of concentration. I have often thought this to be the difference between Surrey's approach and that of other teams.'

Roy Tattersall, the Lancashire and England off-spinner, rose to fame in his association with another intrepid trio of close fieldsmen – Jack Ikin, Ken Grieves and Geoff Edrich. The crucial need for accuracy was one of the early lessons communicated to him by his county coach, Harry Makepiece. '"Old Shake" told us: "Never forget that you have the lives of your fieldsmen in your hands."'

Doug Insole emphasises how necessary it was to exercise pinpoint control as a precaution against injury. 'You must remember that fieldsmen had no protection in those days – most of them didn't even wear a box.

They were very reliant on the accuracy of their bowlers. It was a fine margin of judgement – the difference between "going flat" or standing up was very real in terms of personal safety.'

The skills of another brilliant fielding side, Yorkshire in their championship reign in the 1960s, was dominated by the brazen courage of Brian Close. He crouched intimidatingly at forward short leg, often bruised but unbowed beneath the batsman's gaze. Philip Sharpe, who shared the batting plaudits with Tony Lock against the West Indies in 1963, produced other standards of excellence as a slip fieldsman. Don Wilson, one Yorkshire colleague, remembered how Sharpe used to take the ball with his 'small, very small hands' a long way behind his body which argues superb anticipation and reactions in delaying the catch until it was a certainty. 'He instinctively knew which way the ball would go as it left the bat. He stood a bit wider to me, covering first and second slip, and his agility gave us a spare man in the field.'

The miracles exerted by razor-sharp reflexes gave Surrey, in their championship heyday, legendary status in the field. Fearlessness was the key accompanied by an almost suicidal disregard for safety. Micky Stewart, in his position in 'bomb alley', often said of his captain, Stuart Surridge: 'Stewie will get us all killed one day.' Then he would reflect that Surridge was just as courageous in the helmetless cordon. He set the example and never asked others to do what he could not do himself.

It was Surridge's first belief that a batsman could be caught equally well when playing a defensive shot, as on the attack. Surridge was captain when Stewart first played for Surrey against Gloucestershire at the Oval in 1954. Formerly a cover point, Stewart had fielded once or twice in the second XI at short leg; he fielded in this position against Gloucestershire. Subsequently, he moved into the forward short leg position and was close enough to pick a batsman's pocket. If a batsman stretched his left leg to the full, Stewart was often no more than 2ft from his toe. 'If Lockie is bouncing them,' he said, 'I ought to be able to cop them off the splice.'

Stewart was later to claim the Surrey record of 604 catches; his tally of 77 in 1957, including seven in one match at Northampton, is the second highest by a non-wicketkeeper, only one short of the record established by Wally Hammond in 1928. Stewart remembers the droll reaction of Tony Lock towards his expertise. 'If I caught one or two useful ones off Lockie's bowling, he'd come to me and say: "Micky, you're the best in the world – in front of square".' Lock was magnanimous in the tribute but not prepared to concede his eminence in his favoured position at backward short leg.

Peter Walker once tellingly commented that fielding was the last remaining bastion of self-expression left to the professional cricketer. He was regretful of the passing of personalities and the accent on defensive doctrines. Viewing the athleticism of the drilled outfield patrols today gives substance to this thought. 'Fielding,' said Walker, 'as much as any other aspect of the game has the potential to keep the paying public entertained.'

Walker cited the pleasure given by his own county, Glamorgan, in its championship year in 1948. 'They had only average strength in batting and bowling. But they had a team of all-round fielders that has rarely been surpassed in the history of cricket.'

The two basic tenets of a first-rate close fieldsman came under his scrutiny. They were a set of reasonably fast reflexes – which could be speeded up by practice and conditioning in a specialist fielding position – and, interestingly, a pair of *balanced* eyes. To cleanly catch a fast-travelling five and a half ounce cricket ball, eye balance and physical co-ordination were essential.

Walker's intriguing analysis of balanced eyes was developed in consultation with a leading optician. From this source he learned that most humans initially see each object slightly double. It only took a fraction of a section to align the two images. The speed of this passage was such that few are aware of any disparity in their vision.

Walker said that this only became apparent if somebody should unexpectedly, say, throw a box of matches which were invariably fumbled. A similar confusion occurred in the split-second that elapsed as the ball travelled to the adjacent fielder. Then the slight double vision (for catching was done primarily with the eyes) would cause the fielder to put his hands either a little too low or too high, resulting in it just touching the fingers or being missed altogether.

As the possessor of perfectly balanced eyes, Walker believed that others, such as Lock and Milton, with the benefit of tests, would have discovered theirs were the same. 'For us,' he added, 'the ball image leaves in "one piece", thus eliminating the split-second of double vision. This gives us not only extra time to follow the ball, but immediately direct our hands to the same place as that travelled by the ball.'

Phenomenal is the word which readily escapes the lips in assessing Tony Lock, the magician in the field. The description gains renewed force when it is remembered that he had difficulty in diving to his left because of a cartilage problem affecting his right knee. Peter Walker remembers that Lock had a peculiar mannerism of taking two strides towards the batsman as the bowler entered his delivery stride. It brought him, with eager steps, closer to his prey than the unsuspecting opponent realised.

The spectacular Lock departed from the maxim of Arthur Milton in his close-fielding vigil. Milton, in one conversation, urged a low stance where you could pick the ball off the ground because it was easier to go up than back down. 'The great thing,' he said. 'is not to move in any direction until you sight the ball. This is the prime art. The rest you leave to your natural instincts.'

Trevor Bailey recalled that, by contrast, the one intriguing feature of Lock's work was that he did not stand motionless and crouching. 'He edges forward as the ball is being delivered and this combined with his quick reflexes and ability to anticipate have enabled him to make catches that many players would not even consider half chances.'

The flamboyant manner of this master of his trade never wavered. One typical gesture, after he had taken a low catch, was to toss the ball high in the air and not even deign to catch it again on its return trip earthwards. The extravagance very nearly denied Lock a catch in one match against Glamorgan at Ebbw Vale, one of the smallest of county grounds. Lock, ecstatic as usual, again hurled the ball into the skies, having held on a little longer than usual in taking the catch. The umpires at first doubted its validity and conferred on whether a six should be awarded and not a catch. Eventually, the decision went Lock's way after he had vigorously claimed that he had always had the ball under control.

Over the years Fred Trueman never deviated in his view that Lock was the finest of all catchers of a cricket ball. Trueman recalled one example involving his Yorkshire colleague, Len Hutton. 'On a rain-affected wicket at the Oval Len had scored 78 in one of his best innings. Len then hit an overpitched ball low on the on-side. It looked to have four written all over it, as it travelled just inches off the ground. But the next thing I remember was Tony lying full length on his back with his legs crossed and holding the ball. It was incredible that anyone could have got over that far, let alone bring off such a remarkable catch.'

The praise is echoed by another Yorkshire rival, Brian Close, who vied with Lock in his bravery in the region of fire on the leg-side. As one writer said of Lock, Close would have no more worn a helmet than he would have sported a tutu. It is salutary to receive his recognition of his Surrey rival as one of the great fieldsmen of his or any other era. Close remembers that Lock was responsible for two of the finest instances of fielding he ever witnessed. Both occurred at the Oval and in the first example Close himself was the marvelling victim of an audacious run out.

Close was partnered at this stage in the match by his captain, Ronnie Burnet, a batsman of little repute, and Yorkshire were chasing quick runs. He played a ball hard from Lock out towards Peter May fielding at deepish mid-on and called for a run. 'Lockie hurled himself to his left and while still in mid-air grabbed the ball from the ground and chucked it to hit my bloody wickets.' Close had moved two or three yards down the wicket in pursuit of the run. 'As soon as I saw Lockie with the ball in his hand, I turned round and dived.'

A magazine illustration of the time depicted Close in a horizontal position trying vainly to regain his ground. Behind him is Roy Swetman, the Surrey wicketkeeper, arms held aloft in a gleeful appeal. Fred Trueman, in his memory of the dismissal, recalled Close plunging full length in a despairing dive. As Brian, covered in dirt, was picking himself up, he saw the smiling face of Roy Swetman looking down at him. 'Even that one pitches leg and hits middle and off,' remarked Swetman.

The other fielding episode involved Frank Lowson, the Yorkshire opening batsman. Close recalled that Lock overpitched on the leg stump. 'Frank went for the drive and hit the ball out on the on-side, a little way from the cut part of the pitch. The ball travelled no more than two or three inches off the ground. Lockie threw himself from one side of the wicket to the other and caught it, right-handed as well.'

The flawless timing and instincts as a fieldsman commended Lock on both the county and international stages. Doug Insole remembered the brilliance as a 'snapper-up' of catches. Lock's favoured backward short leg position is now an anachronism because batsmen now all play behind their pads. 'The tactic today,' says Insole, 'is to position a forward short leg or a silly mid-on for the bat-pad catcher rather than the one round the corner.'

Insole mingles his recollections of a great competitor with two stories, one on an exultant note and the other when Surrey – and Lock – for once faltered in the field. The first instance was a catch off Frank Tyson at the Oval which still lingers vividly in his memory. Colin McDonald, the Australian opening batsman, was the victim. 'It was a genuine leg glance,' says Insole, 'and it sped off the bat like a rocket. Colin, expecting a certain boundary, looked round with an expression of amazement.'

The Times reported: 'The speed of the ball alone frustrated the eyesight, the dexterity of Lock was almost past belief.'

Lock was the rueful bowler, discharging the choicest words in his vocabulary, when Insole once took eight runs off one ball in a match against Surrey. 'I hit one wide of mid-on past Eric Bedser who wasn't the fleetest in the field,' recalled Insole. 'We'd run three and then chanced a fourth. Eric's throw finished four or five yards from the wicket. Lockie pounced on the ball and, with a mighty oath, missed the stumps. It went for four overthrows.'

Headingley was the arena where Lock thrice displayed his astonishing sleight of hand in personal duels with one of the great all-rounders, Gary Sobers. England's innings victory in 1957 also marked a milestone for Lock's Surrey colleague, Peter Loader. Loader took nine wickets in the match and his first innings analysis of 6-36 included the hat-trick. It was the first by an English bowler in a Test since J.T. Hearne achieved the feat against Australia, also at Leeds, in 1899.

Lock's first successful joust with Sobers at Headingley came at a time when Peter May, the England captain, was contemplating his first bowling change. He stayed his hand long enough for Loader to benefit from an amazing catch at leg slip. Sobers had glanced the ball sharply but Lock, diving to his right, cradled the ball in his hand with uncanny ease.

The West Indies, following on, displayed heady batsmanship, with Sobers at the top of the order intent on putting England to the sword. He was in imperious mood in scoring 20 runs from the first four overs bowled by Trueman and Loader. He hit four boundaries, including a vivid hook off Trueman and two sumptuous drives and a late cut off Loader.

The dramatic breakdown in the second innings had, as its catalyst, another wonderful effort by Lock. Sobers was again his victim. He hammered a ball off the back foot to the left of Lock fielding between deep point and cover. The peerless cover drive seemed certain to elude Lock and go for four. 'Sobers made off down the pitch, never suspecting that Lock would cut off the ball,' reported *The Times*. 'When he did, with the swiftness of a panther, Sobers was hopelessly stranded to resist the run out.' Lock's throw landed unerringly on the top of the stumps. It was the beginning of the end for the men from the Caribbean; from a position of relative comfort at 40 for none they collapsed to 132 all out.

Sobers had confirmed his superiority as the world's leading all-rounder when the West Indies toured England in 1963. 'Sobers was the strong man of the party' commented *Wisden*. 'He left his imprint on every field, making runs quickly when necessary, taking wickets at a vital time, and swallowing up 29 catches, mostly at slip.'

The West Indies were ultimately 3-1 victors but the series was level prior to the encounter at Leeds. Sunshine and the favour of the toss helped them to return to winning ways in Yorkshire. Lock, in his penultimate Test in England, did, as one observer put it, conceive the perfect answer to his imminent exile in Australia. *The Times* referred to the 'ironic cheers' when Lock was finally summoned up to bowl. The innings was in its 83rd over and the West Indies were 209/3. With his seventh ball Lock ended the stand between Sobers and Kanhai. It was an inswinger from which Kanhai played on as he tried to force it away on the leg-side. He was dismissed eight runs short of his century and the fourth-wicket partnership was worth 143 runs.

Lock took two other wickets in the innings in his return of 3-54 in 28 overs. He added for good measure a top score of 53 in a ninth-wicket stand of 79 with Fred Titmus. The recovery was sorely needed after England had lost half their wickets for 34 runs and subsequently stumbled to 93-8. It was, however, superseded by the stirring sight of a return catch in this match to again dethrone Sobers. The West Indian had just reached his century, his fourteenth in Test cricket and fourth against England, when Lock astounded him.

Sobers was basking in the acclaim of the crowd after the hit down to third man brought him to his hundred. A septic finger had reduced the power of his strokeplay and it meant that supporters were denied more than the occasional glimpse of his dynamic batting. His departure was, though, unexpected and rendered all the more unbelievable by the manner of his leaving. 'Sobers again made pace to Lock and struck a straight drive as well as any in the day,' commented *The Times*. 'Lock, throwing himself to his left, held the ball one-handed as he fell. For some seconds Sobers was transfixed, as though disbelieving what he saw. In Lock's career of astonishing catches few can have been better than this.'

A special catch by Tony Lock had to border on the miraculous to lift it on a plane above others for Surrey and England. Micky Stewart, who stood alongside the fielding wizard over many long summers at the Oval, says: 'He was the best in the business, the best I've seen anywhere. Lockie was magnificent behind square.' Lock's exploits in the field thrilled in a style more usually attributed to a brilliant innings or an explosive piece of bowling. 'He made catches which were applauded by the crowd beyond the boundary,' remembers Stewart.

EIGHT

The Pride of the Countryman

'Lockie was a country boy from Limpsfield thrown into the big time. He had a marvellous career and tried to act the part off the field. He always wanted to be seen in the right company and circumstances to show people what he could do.'
– Raman Subba Row, the former Surrey, Northamptonshire and England cricketer

The mask was lowered to reveal a generous man at a deserted Oval on a hot summer's afternoon in 1963. Pat Pocock, newly recruited by Surrey, had stayed on after the practices in the morning. He picked up three boxes of balls and went over to the nets in front of the Vauxhall Stand. For about twenty minutes he bowled eighteen balls into the net and then had the laborious task of retrieving them before starting all over again.

The diligence of the apprentice off-spinner had not gone unnoticed. Walking down the pavilion steps on the other side of the ground was a familiar burly figure. Tony Lock was then in his last season with Surrey and the stories about him, many of them forbidding, were legendary. Pocock had heard reports of a moody, occasionally fiery man, an aggressive loner who enjoyed his own company and resented intruders.

Pocock recalled: 'Lockie walked over to me and said: "what are you doing?"' The old campaigner listened to the explanation that the newcomer was trying to make adjustments to his delivery stride. 'Let's see what you can do,' was his response. For the next hour Lock took the boy through his action, suggesting, hinting and demonstrating how he could achieve the best outcome from his efforts.

Pocock marvelled at his senior's assistance as he digested the lessons of the unexpected tutorial. He thought: 'Here am I a raw kid of sixteen and he's the mighty Tony Lock.' On the empty ground the veteran and the pupil found a common cause in an inspiring masterclass. 'The whole staff had gone home but the great man stayed because he had found a boy who wanted to learn,' remembered Pocock. 'I was so impressed with this gesture of support and never took heed of dubious tales about Lockie after that session.'

Lock's kindness and rapport with youth was again demonstrated in coaching sessions in Pembrokeshire in the late 1980s. These were undertaken at the request of Mrs Julia White, then president of the Pembrokeshire and Dyfed Schools' Cricket Association. Julia and her husband, Ted, whose company sponsored the practices, were long-standing friends of the celebrity visitor. Julia had first met Tony when she was a schoolgirl member at the Oval. Over the years the strength of her allegiance to the county was such that she gained the title of Surrey's 'honorary twelfth man'. There was in this singular supporter-player relationship recognition on her side of the care of a dutiful man. She remembered how Tony ensured that she was safely escorted as a young girl to transport home from away matches within reach of London. 'My parents had implicit trust in him as a guardian, and so did I.'

As a member of the Wallington Ladies Cricket Club in 1950s, Julia and a small group of teammates were also the beneficiaries of coaching, given free of charge, by Tony. This was at a time when women's cricket did not have the major profile it has today. It would be true to say that their coach did not entirely approve of girls entering the cricket domain. 'If you are going to learn to play, you must do it properly,' was his watchword. 'We were expected to work hard and pay attention,' remembered Julia. Fielding practice, especially, could be a torrid experience. 'We would be wringing our hands as Tony hit the ball hard at us. We certainly learned how to catch.'

Julia never wavered in her loyalty. She recalled that Lock might appear prickly to those who did not know him. Tony was pursued by accusations that he was an outrageous 'big head' but, said Julia, he was devoid of arrogance. 'Socially, Tony was most accommodating and kind in contrast to the explosive man on the field.'

Lock's coaching sessions in Pembrokeshire involved children and young people ranging in age from nine to nineteen. 'I never saw him out of temper,' recalled Julia. 'He was endlessly patient and helpful with his pupils.' In addition to pre-arranged practices, Tony called in the more promising candidates of both sexes for extra coaching. He then umpired in a match on a rainy day so that the children, some of whom had travelled ninety miles to attend, would not be disappointed.

As the hostess at her home at Port Lion, Julia was also Lock's driver, note-taker in the nets and secretary for the detailed written reports on the boys and girls. It gave her the opportunity to observe his coaching methods. 'Tony was very much the carrot man in his dealings. He would stand in the middle of a circle of little boys. First he would ask: "What time is it?" They would all look at their watches and then be asked to remove them before practice.'

The emphasis on fielding demanded alertness from the children and there was a strict instruction to them to be on the move as the bowler came in to bowl. The punishment for the idlers was to run a full circuit of the field. 'They very quickly got the message,' said Julia.

Julia recalled the many letters of thanks from parents who were amazed by the interest Tony took in their children, and were extremely grateful for it. One local teacher wrote: 'Those of us present at the coaching sessions were very impressed by the delightful rapport Tony had with the pupils, and recognised the sure hand of a very fine tutor. The pupils responded so well that if they had been asked to walk on water they would have done so without hesitation.'

Tony Lock fully measured up to his own billing as an 'international cricket consultant' in these years. He was a true ambassador for cricket as a coach in Pembrokeshire and at Mill Hill School in London. He mingled happily with young and old companions, notably in the latter group with Julia White's elderly mother. Tony had lost his own mother when he was only eleven, a bereavement that could explain another special relationship in west Wales. 'He was devoted to her,' recalled Julia, 'and his visits, frequent postcards and telephone calls meant a great deal to my mother. She regarded him almost as a son.' Tony's funeral tribute summed up his own feelings. 'In loving memory of my second Mum' was inscribed on a note attached to his floral wreath.

The devotions rendered on these occasions made it all the more implausible that he failed to show his true self at other times. His son, Richard, remembers a 'proud man who would always speak his mind. This coupled with a strong will didn't help him during his cricket career.' Richard says that his father was wary of people who sought his friendship because he was Tony Lock. 'Some of his best friends were those who knew nothing about cricket but liked him as a person.'

The views of many contemporaries reflect the sadness of a man who failed to come to terms with his status as an international cricketer. Micky Stewart recalled: 'Lockie was basically a country boy from Limpsfield, a very kind and considerate person, particularly to junior professionals on the Surrey staff. He probably never learned how to handle the "big time" he achieved in cricket. At times he projected himself very differently from his natural self. He could be undiplomatic and this cut across the grain with some people.'

The refinements affected by Lock appeared designed to hide his embarrassment, or to present an idealised vision of himself. He rejoiced in the soubriquet of 'Beau', apparently under the impression that he was following in the footsteps of the Regency gallant, Beau Brummel, as an iconic fashion figure. It was, in fact, a less elegant form of address; the abbreviated and actual wording – 'Bo' – linked 'Beau' and his surname.

One Australian contemporary and Perth cricket colleague, Ian Brayshaw, described his friend as a 'social chameleon'. 'That was the sad thing about 'Bo'. He would put on airs and graces, particularly when he was in the company of committee men. He tried to elevate himself to a higher status. I was quite saddened by this because the real 'Bo' was a fabulous character with a lovely personality. I could never work out why he wasn't satisfied to be that person and try to be somebody he wasn't.'

Raman Subba Row and Doug Insole are others perplexed by the dual personality. Subba Row, as a former Surrey colleague, refers to the glories of a marvellous career. 'Lockie tried to act the part off the field. He always wanted to be seen in the right company and circumstances to show people what he could do.' Insole also believed that Lock was putting on an act most of the time. 'He was much less sure of himself than he might justifiably have been.'

Insole was the MCC vice-captain on the tour of South Africa in 1956/57. He remembered Lock in his social routine. 'Tony could be quite amusing at cocktail parties. He talked a very good line, full of *bon mots*.' For the South African tour Lock, contrary to everyone else, decided to include a white dinner jacket in his wardrobe. At one dinner the precious jacket was besmirched in a different colour when a fellow guest threw a glass of tomato juice over him. 'I was on the opposite side of the table and on the point of grabbing Tony to prevent a violent reaction,' recalled Insole. 'But Tony kept his cool very well. It was a measure of his attitude on that tour when he had to play second fiddle to Johnny Wardle as a bowler.'

Richard Lock remembers his father as having a dry sense of humour, quirky in the manner of the radio *Goons*, one of his favourite comedy programmes. This was best illustrated in the story of a meeting – the first for forty years – with a former Surrey colleague at his home in the hills above Perth in Western Australia. John Keeping, a fine all-rounder, had been on the Surrey staff for three years. He lived at Streatham in south London. Lock used to pick him up by car for travel to the Oval for pre-season practice and then drop him off on the return journey. Keeping, as a young boy, was very grateful for the lifts.

In the early 1990s he went out to Australia and discovered Lock's address from Ron Tindall, another Surrey exile. Tony was on his knees, working in the garden, when Keeping arrived at his home. He didn't look up as Keeping walked up the pathway. Eventually, as if suddenly aware of his visitor, he turned round and remarked: 'Where's my expenses!'

Micky Stewart relishes another story of the time when he and his wife, Sheila, were invited out to dinner by Lock at the Grand Hotel, Leicester. It occurred following his colleague's move to Grace Road in the 1960s. The interlude, amusing in retrospect, reflected Lock's unease as a host. Lock was always anxious to impress; the problem was that such attempts could spill over into farce.

The evening had started quite well. Tony had very properly asked permission of his guests to be allowed to smoke during the first course. In his nervousness he scattered an entire box of matches in his soup. He did manage to regain his composure but then came the tricky bit. An earnest examination of the wine list followed the mishap. Most people, if unversed in the subtleties of selection, would have sought advice, or chanced a choice. Tony decided to defer his decision. His inspection lasted several minutes to the confusion of the attentive wine waiter. Three times he approached the table only to be told that the order was still being considered. Midway through the fourth course the waiter tried again. 'Come on, Lockie,' urged Stewart, 'you've got to order something soon.' Tony was at last galvanised into action. He gave the list a final cursory glance. 'All right,' he said. The Stewarts politely awaited his selection. Tony gulped out the single word of his order – 'Red'.

Eccentricities, less alarming, were manifested in Lock's association with Mike Turner, the Leicestershire secretary. Lock turned the pages of a new chapter in his career when Turner recruited him as captain. 'Tony had one idiosyncrasy; he loved mowing lawns,' recalled Turner. 'He would come round to my house, often at around eight o'clock on a summer evening, and ask if he could mow my quite large lawn. We would then have a bite to eat and a glass of wine.'

The mowing task was one that Turner was happy to delegate; but he must have regarded the request as highly unusual, coming as it did from his illustrious recruit. It was obviously a gesture of goodwill from a man in his element in new surroundings. His friendship with the Leicestershire secretary was warm and secure, with origins in their rivalry as players. They often laughed about the time when Lock would look up at Turner, awaiting his turn to bat in the pavilion at the Oval. The motion of crossed hands from out in the middle would remind him of the imminent cricketing crucifixion.

Giving a helping hand to Turner's brother-in-law was another way Lock whiled away the hours after play at Leicester. The brother was a neighbour of Lock's in his temporary accommodation at Evington. The work in progress on one occasion was the re-decoration of his lounge. The wallpapering was completed with the seal of a signature. Every roll of paper that was put on the wall was signed 'G.A.R. Lock' on the reverse side before application.

Family and friends remember the startling night-time behaviour of Lock, the sudden bursts of shouting, perhaps an indication of the agitated cricketer still appealing for some decision that had gone against him. Fred Trueman recalled his experience of 'rooming' with Lock on the tour of the West Indies in 1953/54. Trueman was so riveted by the spectacle that he feared not to speak. 'It was during the first Test that I discovered Tony's sleeping habits. I had dropped off, tired after a full day in the sun, I was jolted awake and frightened to death by a piercing appeal. "How's that?" is not something you expect to hear in the middle of the night. There was Tony standing up in the middle of the bed, both arms held high with the sheet in front of him. Tony held the pose for what seemed ages and then dropped back, turned over and carried on sleeping.'

Lock vigorously denied the occurrence when Trueman broached it the following morning. Jim Laker, another tourist, smiled broadly when the Yorkshireman told him about the happening over breakfast. Laker said: 'I knew it wouldn't be long before you found out.' It was common knowledge in the Surrey camp that Lock would sometimes talk or walk in his sleep. Trueman added: 'There is no doubt that Tony was a very excitable cricketer, and it did not end there on our tour together. On another occasion he stood up in bed clapping both hands. He was congratulating somebody on a great catch.'

David Allen, his Gloucestershire rival and spinning partner with England, contrasts Lock's ferocity as a player with the care and kindness he displayed off the field. The swings in mood could ruffle this harmony. Thunderclouds descended on the Lock household when the master was in ill humour. 'Dad was quick to boil over,' recalls Richard Lock. 'But once you had had the argument it was all over.' The tantrums lost force as the 'deaf ears' of Tony's wife, Audrey, the calming influence in the family, countered them. She waited quietly for the moment of anger to pass.

Audrey and Tony were childhood sweethearts in the Surrey settlements beneath the North Downs. She lived in the neighbouring village of Hurst Green. Her father, Alfred Sage, was a good footballer and cricketer with Limpsfield and Oxted. The house in Harbour Cottages, where Audrey was born, was the Locks' first married home after their wedding at Limpsfield Church in 1952.

Graeme, their first son, was born there in August 1953. His brother, Richard, was the next arrival seventeen months later. Australia had beckoned and become their home before sister Jackie, adopted at birth, became a member of the family.

Graeme Lock remembers his mother as a 'kind and selfless woman'. 'Without her enduring long winters by herself, raising two boys and running a business, my father's cricket career would not have been possible.' Graeme's tribute is endorsed by Richard who recalls the transitional period in the 1960s when their father combined cricket in two hemispheres – at Leicester and in Western Australia. 'We only saw Dad for six months in a year. The responsibility for bringing us up was left to Mum.'

Audrey Lock industriously juggled this challenge with a variety of business undertakings, including office work and kindergarten duties. In the early years of her marriage in England there was the management of a general store and sub post-office at Hamsey Green. The family lived in a flat above the shop. Richard, with a less than nostalgic look back at a wintry clime, remembered the bleak days when he and Graeme were put to the task of shovelling snow in the tiny backyard. The two boys attended a private school at Elmhurst in Surrey during their brief time in England. When the Locks took up residence in Australia, Audrey first bolstered the family income by running, along with a friend, a fish and chip shop. She then took over as manager of a staff restaurant serving various companies in the private business sector in downtown Perth.

Audrey was one of her husband's most loyal cricket supporters. 'She was so pleased when Tony had had a good day at the cricket,' says her cousin, Nova Hearne. The trio of Audrey, Nova and their friend, Julia White, regularly attended matches at the Oval. Watching Tony sprawling to take his fantastic catches constantly reminded Audrey of another household chore. She knew the size of the task required in removing stains on the flannels, heavyweight materials in those days. Julia recalled: 'We would be watching and applauding Tony. Audrey would put her head in her hands as Tony pulled off another spectacular catch. Amid the applause, she would say: "Yes, but you don't have to wash his flannels."'

Tony Lock, contrary in so many ways, found greater ease away from the ceremonies of cricket occasions. Sporting his public persona was a trial that produced a protective wall of reserve. At home, or in the company of friends, there was no need to play the role of the celebrity cricketer. In the late 1980s Tony was employed as cricket coach at Mill Hill School in north London. His weekends were spent at the Braested village home of Nova Hearne. 'Tony used to come down to Surrey by train after giving us a ring. My husband met the train at Sevenoaks, often vainly. Tony had fallen asleep and carried on past his stop. Then we would get another 'phone call from Hastings. "Meet me on the way back," he would say.'

The congenial interludes at the Braested retreat were the perfect recipe for peace and relaxation. Tony then immersed himself in a different kind of action, the stirring film adventures of John Wayne. He shared in the passion for Western cowboy sagas with two fellow cricketers, Trevor Bailey and Raymond Illingworth. It lifted them from the humdrum into an escapist fantasy world. 'Tony would sit for hours watching the movies,' says Nova. 'Sometimes, for a change, he would get up and go down to our local – the King's Arms – for an evening game of darts and a pint of beer.'

A midnight snack of bread and cheese was one of Tony's great joys. There is the cherishable memory of him falling asleep as the gunshots echoed on the screen, and the sudden emission of loud snores as he slumped contentedly in his armchair.

NINE

Revelation on Film

'It must have been a major undertaking for an established bowler to alter the habits of many years, especially habits which brought him such success.'
– Ian Peebles

The rebirth of Tony Lock as a cricketer occurred in a time of adversity. The self-examination would lead him to the most rewarding phase of his career. On the eve of his thirtieth birthday in 1959 he was forced to urgently assess his bowling and then, having remodelled his action, find himself snubbed by England three years later.

Lock and his spin partner, Jim Laker, made their only tour of Australia in the winter of 1958/59. It was rendered possible by the dismissal of Lock's Yorkshire rival, Johnny Wardle, by his county and the subsequent bar on his services by the MCC. Even Peter May, Lock's county and England captain, regretted the absence of Wardle, who had rebelled against the Yorkshire establishment and paid the penalty. May said that it was Wardle's misfortune to play in the same era as Lock. 'Had it not been for Tony, Johnny would have played in practically every match. He was a very high-class bowler and had the great gift of being able to bowl his chinamen and googlies without seeming to practice them. It was a quite extraordinary accomplishment.'

Wardle was a wily campaigner who revelled in his foxing wrist spin and generally earned favour as an orthodox left-arm spinner over Lock overseas. The reasons behind the preference for the Yorkshireman were highlighted in Australia. Lock persisted in his quicker mode, so successful in England, to provide confirmation that his style of bowling was ill-suited to the hard rock-like pitches down under. The medium-paced spinner, as Lock then was, was rarely effective in such conditions; this was clearly proved by his overall Test figures of five wickets for 376 runs gained at a dispiriting average of 75.20.

Ted Dexter, one of the newcomers in the MCC party, said that Lock was betrayed in his efforts to gain purchase for his spin by bowling too fast. 'The Australians treated him like a straight bowler and, with his angle of approach, would just whip him through mid-wicket. Then he tried to pitch the ball a little wider and was hit on both sides of the wicket.' One of the ironies for Lock, surely not lost on him, was his later mastery – and the rediscovery of orthodoxy allied to powers of spin – in a country where he had floundered with England in the service of Australian employers.

It was a sadly disillusioned bowler who arrived in New Zealand following the series in Australia. Lock then had to take stock of his career when he saw some film of his bowling one weekend. Harry Cave, the New Zealand bowler, had filmed highlights of his country's tour of England the previous summer. They included the exploits of Lock who had enjoyed sweeping success in a rain-affected season. He achieved a series tally of 34 wickets at 7.47 runs each.

Lock and Laker shared 51 wickets, each of them illustrating their menace against hapless opponents in propitious circumstances. The fifth wicket – a typically adroit caught and bowled – of Lock's seven at Old Trafford was his one-hundredth in 24 Tests since his debut in 1952. In ten innings since the Oval Test against the West Indies in 1957 he had taken 42 wickets at just over six runs apiece.

The stark disclosure of the film evening in 1959 mocked his dominance against the Kiwis. It presented irrefutable evidence that he was beset with a host of new problems. The film, which he witnessed with increasing dismay, gave positive proof that there was a kink at the point of delivery and this had to be rectified.

Ted Dexter was one of the group invited to dinner at the Wellington home of John Reid, the New Zealand captain. After dinner the lights were dimmed for the showing of the film. It was taken from the players' balcony at Lord's. Lock was pictured running in to bowl but in slow motion. The images were sharp and clear, and from the very first ball there was a pronounced bending and straightening of the arm. Several in the room gasped out loud and the mirth was barely concealed.

Dexter described the reaction of the onlookers: 'There was much hilarity from the England players but, when the lights went up, there was the absolutely ashen-faced Tony Lock. He was stunned and very quiet, and was not prepared to speak to anybody. He was obviously deeply shocked and affected by what he had seen.'

The delivery was now revealed to be not just suspect but a blatant throw. But Lock could hardly have feigned his horror had he been previously aware of a glaring aberration. Perhaps, as Dexter suggested, he had not seen his action before in such slow motion, or from the angle on film.

A contrite Lock came to the ground the next morning and bowled very slowly with no sign of a quicker ball, as he desperately tried to keep his arm straight. Lock claimed that he had no idea about the way in which he was bowling and was not prepared to continue in a similar fashion.

According to Peter Richardson, another tourist, Lock was so distressed that he told Peter May, his captain: 'Skipper, I can't bowl today.' It required a good deal of cajoling from May and other players to persuade him to bowl anything like presentably in that game.

In his despair, Lock had, unknowingly, reached a turning point in his career. Jim Laker recalled: 'The events of the next few years saw a remarkable change in his cricket life which he could never have visualised. In an incredibly few short months he once again reconstructed his action so well that he was ready to embark on a new career and carry on for another ten years without a single objection to his bowling action.'

An intensive period of reappraisal preceded a fresh beginning. At an advanced age, Tony Lock was faced with a challenge, amounting to a command, to eliminate an action which had made him a Test bowler. He had to replace it with a different delivery to satisfy an extra vigilant jury. Ian Peebles, an England spin bowler of another era, considered Lock's dilemma: 'It must have been a major undertaking for an established bowler to alter the habits of years, especially habits which had brought him such success.'

Sir Alec Bedser and Arthur McIntyre, two former Surrey colleagues, are at variance on the process of rehabilitation. Sir Alec maintains that Lock did not have to remodel his action; he simply reverted to the orthodoxy of his youth – 'the way he was born to bowl.' Judging by the comments of others, it is not quite as clear-cut as that. McIntyre presents a more formidable task confronting Lock. He remembers the work Lock put in at the Oval nets. 'He used all sorts of styles until he hit on the right one. I don't think I've seen a greater trier than Lockie. Sometimes the blood would be pouring from his fingers as he slogged away to get it right.'

Lock, though, was on probation as a bowler over many tense months. His efforts did lead to unreserved praise. Ted Dexter, his captain on the 1961/62 tour of India and Pakistan, said: 'Lockie bowled superbly for me on that tour. There were all the flight and variations you could wish for.' Dexter remembered the tireless efforts and enthusiasm of a wonderful competitor. 'He would willingly bowl all day, but more than that, in those hot, dry conditions, he left me with two abiding memories. He would always come off the field absolutely covered in dust from head to foot because he had hurled himself around after the ball all day.' Lock was rarely challenged in the fielding stakes. The custom then was decorate the chosen player with a garland of rupees. Lock was invariably bedecked with his garland at the end of the day.

There were, inevitably, those batsmen intent on revenge as Lock persevered in remodelling his action. David Allen, the Gloucestershire and England off-spinner, remembers one of them: his county colleague, George Emmett. 'Tony came down to Bristol with the Surrey seconds at the beginning of the 1960s. George was our coach and skippered the second eleven.' Emmett was in a belligerent mood against his old Surrey rival. He had long memories of their duels and said: 'I'm going to make up on this bloke after being thrown out so often.' Allen adds: 'Lockie was working on his new action and George cut and lapped him all over the ground.' The embattled Lock took the assault in his stride. It was a new beginning for a bowler, who was one of the few able to change and perform in a legal manner.

Allen, Lock's spinning partner in India and Pakistan, enthuses about their alliance. 'Lockie was a super bloke to bowl with. There are many bowlers who work in their own interests. They will ask you to keep a certain batsman down at the other end – and not allow them to take a single off the sixth ball. That was never the case with Lockie. We always bowled in tandem.'

Allen remembers Lock's generosity as a bowling partner. In India there were a number of small competitions with prizes of a vase or other trinkets going to the bowler taking five wickets. On one occasion he and Lock had each taken four wickets and were trying to get the last man out. 'Tony, the fair-minded man, proceeded to bowl an over of donkey drops, so he wouldn't get the additional wicket and I could.' Ted Dexter, their captain, intervened on this arrangement. He said: 'Settle this argument, you two. I want Lockie to bowl properly.'

The tour of India and Pakistan in 1961/62 coincided with a boom in the popularity of the game on the subcontinent. The origins of their global prominence today were seen in the attendances. Close on 2 million people watched the MCC team, with approximately 1.2 million at the eight Tests. Ted Dexter and his team took part in one of the most strenuous of tours, lasting over four months, by any side. They played twenty-four matches in India, Pakistan and Ceylon, including three Tests in Pakistan and five in India. India won the fourth and fifth Tests, the first three having been drawn, to defeat England for the first time in their history. England gained partial compensation by winning the rubber in Pakistan 1-0.

Tony Lock and David Allen bore the brunt of the bowling in the Tests. The tour figures once again indicated Lock's enduring qualities. He had bowled 1,266 overs for 127 wickets in the previous summer in England and the total was advanced by another 472 overs in the 1961/62 series. His partnership with Allen was fulfilling in its mastery. In India they shared 608 overs and 43 wickets. Their return in Pakistan in the two Tests in which they played together was 291 overs and 18 wickets.

In the second Test against Pakistan at Dacca, Lock took his 150th Test wicket during the drawn match in which he bowled 115 overs, including 73 in the first innings. Allen also bowled 62 overs in the same match. He recalls their industry on a gruelling tour. 'We took all those wickets together. It was my great pleasure and privilege to bowl with him.'

One correspondent in the *West Australian* would later comment that the origins of Lock's future success in Australia lay in the bitterness of demotion. He wrote that Lock was in a jilted mood after a surprise development in 1962. The Surrey bowler was the only England player in the Test against Pakistan at Trent Bridge not to be chosen to tour Australia the following winter. Like a lovelorn swain he was caught on the rebound and enticed to Western Australia. .

David Allen considered that the omission of Lock from the Australian tour was one of the biggest mistakes in selection he had ever witnessed in his international career. 'Someone had a brainstorm in taking three offspinners.' They comprised Titmus, Illingworth and himself. The selectorial policy was presumably dictated by the vulnerability of the Australians against this form of attack. The theory was misguided on the grounds of bowling variety, and the absence of Lock also deprived England of a key close fieldsman. In a series of missed chances, they would rue leaving him behind. *Wisden* adopted a similar stance to Allen in its observations on Lock with Surrey in 1962. 'Lock was his true self, a grand team man, and the majority of the Surrey supporters were astounded when the selectors did not choose him for Australia.'

John Arlott voiced the concern of many admirers as Lock grimly withstood the handicap of a troublesome knee in re-establishing himself in the early 1960s. Arlott, like others, thought Lock's courage was misplaced and that perhaps it was now time for him to retire. 'Sometimes it was agonising to watch him drive himself on that wretched leg. Lockie – because he was Lockie – fought on.'

Arlott recalled the first signs of a breakthrough. 'In 1961, against Yorkshire at the Oval, Lock bowled like one of the classic slow left-arm bowlers: through a higher arc than in his "slinger" days but with a truly straight arm, artful variations of flight and pace and, once more, genuine spin.'

The admiration was mingled with relief at the transformation. But long-held suspicions were hard to dispel and Lock was only intermittently able to convince the selectors of his worth. The failure to win favour despite the sweat and toil in remodelling his action did, it seems, have political overtones. Lock was a victim of his past misdemeanours. There was undoubtedly concern not to rock the boat during high-level discussions on illegal bowling at the turn of the 1960s.

In the 1958/59 series the Australian 'chuckers', Ian Meckiff and Gordon Rorke were among the savage aggressors who capsized England. Even former Test cricketer, Jack Fingleton, one Australian spokesman, thought that they would have been more at home 'knocking down coconuts on Hampstead Heath'. Meckiff had been considered too wild and uncontrolled to pose a major threat. In the second Test at Melbourne he suddenly found direction to confirm his hostility, taking 6/38 in the rout of England for 87.

The disorder of illegal bowling tactics was perceived in Australia by Meckiff's captain, Richie Benaud. He attended, along with other state representatives, a dinner hosted by Sir Donald Bradman at his home in

Adelaide in January 1963. They were shown a selection of intriguing films, which Bradman had assembled over the years, spotlighting various bowlers who either had suspect actions or actions slightly out of the ordinary. Benaud was deeply affected by the parade of indiscretions. At the end of the evening he said that in future he would not continue to bowl anyone called for throwing by an umpire. Furthermore, he stated that he would not bowl anyone whom he considered to have a suspect action.

Gordon Rorke, one of the notorious bowlers against England in 1958/59, was the first to test Benaud's resolve in a match between New South Wales and South Australia. Rorke was underbowled for reasons not primarily connected with legitimacy. Benaud was firmly told that his duty was to captain the side; they, the selectors, would determine whether their nominated bowlers erred in fairness. Benaud was not to be bullied out of his convictions. He told the selectors that he would continue his crusade against illegal bowlers. To drive home his point, he would not only sideline them but open the batting with them as well.

The sequel involving Ian Meckiff came at Brisbane in December 1963. Meckiff, reinstated in the Australian team against South Africa, was no-balled four times in his opening over. Benaud, in the light of his high-profile campaign, had no alternative but to remove him from the attack. 'It was very sad because it had a detrimental effect on one of the nicest men ever to step on to a cricket field. Ian never played first-class cricket again. It left a hollow feeling with everyone who had taken part in the game.'

Lock's last years in England were still shadowed by the throwing investigations. In 1959, when India were the visitors, he did not play in a home Test for first time in eight years. He was also omitted from the series against South Africa the following year. Subsequently, he played in nine home Tests against Australia, Pakistan and the West Indies. His figures give credence to diminished ability during his rehabilitation as a bowler. After 1958 he passed 100 wickets four times, achieving a total of 573 wickets at averages ranging from 21.42 to 28.48. His workload of over 5,400 overs in five seasons showed his stamina to be in good order. He was, at the very least, still effective as a key bowler even if he lacked his former dominance in the reversion to the slower style.

Among those wishing Lock a bumper benefit in 1960 was E.M. Wellings of the *London Evening News*. Writing in the match brochure on sale at Oxted, Wellings paid tribute to Lock's spirit and attitude. 'He gives everything he has of skill and eager energy to his team and has outstandingly succeeded in entertaining the public.'

Wellings said that Lock was most admired for the remedial work on his bowling. 'Others, whose actions incorporated the motions of a throw, had seen themselves on film but were prepared to continue in their errant ways so long as they could pull the wool over umpires' eyes. Lock, on the other hand, without being prompted, took immediate action and missed Surrey's early matches in 1959 while working in the nets to smooth out the kinks in his delivery.'

The *London Evening News* cricket correspondent cited the reward for Lock as a result of an improvised and temporary new action. 'He returned to take III wickets during a season unfavourable for spin bowlers, least of all for one experimenting with his methods, and so raise his career aggregate to 1,646 wickets. Since then he has devised yet another new method which helped him to take nine wickets in the county's opening match of 1960.'

The 'magnificently aggressive bowler and admirable character' of Wellings' tribute was stunned by the response to the appeal of his benefit year. Not the least of his setbacks was the final benefit figure of £4,700, quoted by Jim Laker, and another even lower estimate of £3,500, which at best was less than half the proceeds received by Alec Bedser and Laker himself. It was the lowest benefit of a Surrey player through the entire 1950s. Laker recalled: 'No Surrey player in my time deserved a benefit more than Tony yet when it came in 1960, it proved to be something of a disaster. His tremendous efforts for the county should have been rewarded with the sort of return that had come the way of Alec and myself.'

Doug Insole remembered that Lock was bitterly disappointed at the result of his benefit. 'Tony was quite jealous of Laker's reputation. He wanted a house like the one Jim owned and he couldn't really afford the detached house he did buy in an affluent Croydon suburb.' David Sydenham, a younger Surrey colleague at the time, considers that Lock was not prepared to undertake the necessary groundwork and public relations duties to ensure a successful benefit. Given his character, Lock probably found this demeaning but it is a cross even star beneficiaries have to bear to pull open the purse strings. 'Tony's reward was poor for such a great cricketer,' says Sydenham. 'He believed that because he was Tony Lock the money would flow in but it just did not happen.'

John Inverarity, the former Western Australia captain and Test player, was among those welcoming the angry and disappointed Lock to Perth in 1962. 'Tony was considered a certainty for the 1962/63 tour of Australia. The England selectors chose three off-spinners and not one orthodox slow left-arm bowler. It was a very surprising omission. Western Australia at that stage was struggling as a cricketing state. Tony jumped at the opportunity afforded him and replaced Rohan Kanhai in our ranks.'

The doors opened to a new and unexpected opportunity. One commentator said that Lock took to Australia like a kangaroo to the plains. He thought that the newcomer possessed a character more typical of Australia than of England. 'He has the old, prickly competitive attitudes that communicate themselves so quickly to the uninhibited barrackers on the outer at our major grounds.'

Lock, in one account, was said to have heard from a Nottingham newspaper of his omission from the Australian tour party in 1962. He felt the rejection so strongly that he considered abandoning county cricket and possibly playing in league cricket. 'In the last few years I have had to overcome setbacks. I had completely remodelled my action when I played against Pakistan at Trent Bridge. I was sure that a left-handed spin bowler would be picked for Australia. Then I heard that I was out. I couldn't believe it.'

The initiative in the plan to lure Lock to Australia had been taken by Perth bookmaker, Jack Walsh. There were consultations with the West Australian Association committee and secretary, Les Trueman. All were agreed that state cricket was at a critical juncture and that the need was to enlist a player with the drawing power of a big name. Lock was asked years later how he had responded to the offer. 'It was like a bloke in a passing dinghy asking a drowning swimmer if he was interested in a lift back to the shore.'

Richard Lock, Tony's youngest son, recalls that his father initially had only a six-month contract in Perth. 'From our point of view, as a family, that was fortunate because it enabled us to have a look at the country we were going to live in. It was a marvellous opportunity for Dad as a cricketer but also quite a gamble.' Richard remembers that, even as children, he and his brother, Graeme, were impressed by the phenomenal lifestyle in Australia. They were immediately struck by the comparison of the wide, open spaces of the sunny state with England.

The West Australian offer meant that Lock senior could fly to Perth ahead of the shipboard MCC party by a few days. He was there to meet them when the *Orcades* steamed into Fremantle harbour.

Consternation probably ruled among his former England colleagues when Lock took 4-68 for Western Australia against the MCC at Perth. He followed this with 3-73 for a Combined XI in the victory by ten wickets over the tourists. Honour, if only in a small degree, was salvaged for the exile. 'I never thought,' said Lock, 'that the day would come when I would take any comfort whatsoever from an English defeat. I have to admit, though, to this feeling as I walked off the WACA after that match.'

Lock returned to England to play his last season for Surrey in 1963 and to tidy up his affairs and make the necessary arrangements for his wife and two young sons to join him in Perth. It was the end of an illustrious era at the Oval. In 385 games for Surrey he had taken 1,713 wickets, the highest aggregate for the county in the last century.

A powerful factor in the thinking of Tony and Audrey Lock – as it is with all migrant families – was what the future in a fast-growing city in a new country could offer their children. Graeme and Richard, at respectively ten and eight, were an ideal age for migration, young enough to shrug off the old loyalties that can affect a migrant for life and prevent total fulfilment.

Graeme Lock today acknowledges his debt to his parents in what he believes must have been a difficult decision to migrate to Australia. The opportunities presented to him over the years would have been less forthcoming in England. A daunting flight involving seven stopovers but without alighting took the Locks to Perth to take up permanent residence in March 1964. Their first home was in the suburb of Embleton in a new three-bedroom house on a quarter-acre site. Graeme remembers the lavish welcome on arrival and says that they were overwhelmed by the hospitality extended towards them. Above all, there was the bright sunshine, yellow sands and a quiet relaxing environment. Perth is today transformed as a vibrant city and beginning to rival Sydney and Melbourne in prosperity. But it still charms the visitor, with its sails on the river, bustling and attractive shopping malls and arcades, and the majestic King's Park high above the city. As Graeme says, there are few places in the world where housing within one mile of the beach and with ocean views is reasonably affordable.

Admiration jostled with regret in the report of *The Times* correspondent after Lock's departure. 'Lock had character as well as greatness, two commodities which English cricket will be loath to export. He will be missed for many things: his breathtaking catches round the corner, his belligerent bowling, and his inexhaustible spirit and not least the delight he took when he managed to make batting look easier after superior batsmen had floundered.'

Jim Laker considered that, in the ensuing years, Lock was at his greatest as an exponent of the art of left-arm spin bowling. 'If any Surrey player of the 1950s had visited the WACA ground at Perth during these years they would hardly have credited that such a transformation had taken place.'

Laker explained: 'In contrast to the immature medium-pace spinner striving the whole time to pitch on leg stump and hit the off, they would have seen the smooth flowing action of a genuine left-arm spinner, making intelligent use of the breeze, and capitalising on his thoughtful study of batsmen's weaknesses.'

Equally remarkable was his leadership, the key turning point in his fortunes. The responsibility brought the best out of him and made him the complete cricketer. The boyish enthusiasm, which was always a vital part of his character, provoked a self-belief in his charges. Lock rediscovered his appetite for county cricket in his galvanic captaincy at Leicester, where he drove the Cinderella county to their highest ever rung on the championship ladder.

More amazing still in an epic story was that he could perform the oracle in two hemispheres, 12.000 miles apart. His feats at Grace Road were but a curtain-raiser to other memorable summers in Australia. The fervour would carry his disciples on both sides of the world from lowly estate to unimagined heights.

TEN

The Astounding Veteran

'Lockie led by example and never allowed a game to drift. He always tried to make things happen. We watched him tumbling and diving around. You could not help but be infected by his enthusiasm.'
– Jack Birkenshaw

Everyone associated with Tony Lock in his twin enterprises remembers the excitement he engendered as a captain. He was a man who disdained the notion of surrender. The invigorating leadership won instant commendation at Leicester. One observer recalled the portentous arrival of the veteran. 'Lock's effect on the county was electrifying, the players were captivated by his infectious enthusiasm and came to believe, for the first time in Leicestershire's history, that they were capable of beating any other county.'

Leicestershire were indebted to the persuasive powers of Mike Turner, their campaigning secretary, in enticing Lock to Grace Road. The signing of Lock was an audacious coup and one that would lay the foundations for a proud new era. Turner was astute enough to realise the need for recruitment outside the county if the club was to compete in the championship. Leicestershire, like their Midland neighbours, Northamptonshire, were the poor relations in player assets. In other days, the lauded George Geary and Ewart Astill, both England stalwarts between the two world wars, were dominant all-round forces at Leicester. Yet the exploits of this redoubtable long-serving duo could not alone breach the strongholds of the premier counties in north and south.

Leicestershire remained mired in the lower reaches of the championship and it was not until 1953, when they finished third under the captaincy of Charles Palmer, that the county mounted a creditable challenge. Grace Road, their first home on the foundation of the club in 1879, was purchased in 1966. It was popularly thought to be named after W.G. Grace but the address, in fact, commemorated a local property dignitory. Economic reasons had forced Leicestershire to relinquish the site at the turn of the last century and they spent the intervening period at nearby Aylestone Road. The purchase of Grace Road and the transformation of the ground, previously used as a school playing field, was an important stepping-stone in the progress of the club. The building of a fine new pavilion suite and a radical overhaul of the spectators' accommodation provided a headquarters to earn praise as one of the most attractive urban grounds in the country.

The enhanced facilities were now a magnet to attract top-class players to Leicester. By the early 1960s the nucleus of the playing staff had retired. The loss of Charles Palmer, Jack Walsh, Vic Jackson, Jack Firth – followed by the sad death of Maurice Tompkin after an operation at the age of thirty-seven – severely depleted the county ranks. Mike Turner commented at the time: 'Since then our whole recruiting drive has been to create a balance between young and old talents.' Eight of the first eleven in 1966 had joined the county in the previous five years.

Sweeping away the cobwebs of the old regime was the main objective at Leicester. Tony Lock was the banker in Turner's desired collection of new recruits. He had severed his links with Surrey and was the prime candidate to help bolster the strengths of a faltering county. The offer from Leicester in 1965 was another spur to Lock in re-establishing his career. He was irresistibly drawn to the prospect of combining his duties in Western Australia with county cricket in the English summer months.

Mike Turner recalls the rewarding pattern of his recruitment drive at that time. 'The team had started to improve and then Lockie came along to galvanise the side.' Turner emphasises his good fortune as the club secretary. 'Charles Palmer – a great cricket man – was chairman. I was extraordinarily lucky because when I became secretary in 1960 I had William Bentley, a very successful industrialist, as president. Those two gentlemen held the offices for twenty-five years at Leicester. I had a fantastic working relationship with both of them.'

In 1965 Tony Lock signed a three-year contract with Leicestershire but, according to Turner, he had omitted to disclose that he had a prior agreement with Ramsbottom in the Lancashire League. Consequently, in the first season, he was restricted to eight mid-week county games. It did give Lock the opportunity to assess his new colleagues and also take 35 wickets in a curtailed season. His Leicestershire debut was against Lancashire in May which yielded three wickets and 40 runs – 'a colourful innings' reported one observer – and including six lusty boundaries. 'True to his reputation. Lock provided an inspiration with his tireless energy and brilliance in the field,' commented *Wisden*.

Turner's version of Lock's divided loyalties in this season is at variance with the account offered by Geoffrey Bladen at Ramsbottom. He says that his club did agree to release Lock from his coaching duties in order to assist the county on weekdays in a maximum of eight matches. Bladen recalls that as a compensation to his club it was verbally agreed that Leicestershire would send a representative side to play at Ramsbottom. By some oversight this did not happen, which was a little unfortunate since the Lancashire club had paid all Lock's travel expenses from Australia and his full contract fee.

At Rambottom Lock followed the West Indian Seymour Nurse and Australian Ian Chappell as professional. In the few short months of his engagement he renewed his contests with his old Yorkshire rival, Johnny Wardle, his counterpart at Rishton. The competition between the two foes was sharpened rather than diminished in the one-to-one battles between professionals. Lock and Wardle were expected to give forthright leads to amateur colleagues and they did not waver in their direction. Their respective figures for the season demonstrated the keenness of the rivalry. Rishton, as league runners-up, could point to the bonus of Wardle's 114 wickets at just over nine runs apiece. Lock's 92 wickets for Ramsbottom were garnered at an identical cost and supplemented with 520 runs with the bat.

Bladen was acting captain in one game at Ramsbottom. It provided an instance of Lock's ultra-competitive nature. 'We were coasting towards victory with the opposition nine wickets down and some distance from our score.' There was one other issue to be resolved: the recipient of the collection for the best bowling performance. Lock, as the professional, was one short of the six wickets to qualify whereas his amateur partner, Bill Savage (the younger brother of Lock's later Leicestershire colleague, John Savage) had four of the coveted five-wicket haul. Bladen recalls: 'Tony was, of course, keen to take his reward and he needed some persuading to run out the last batsman.'

Tony Lock was fully committed to Leicestershire in 1966 when he succeeded Maurice Hallam as captain. He piloted the county to eighth in the championship and claimed eight victories along the way. He bowled nearly 1,000 overs, took 109 wickets at less than twenty runs apiece, and scored over 600 runs. It was his highly stimulating leadership that caught the attention of *Wisden*. 'Lock's urgent approach to his new duties delighted spectators and brought a lively response from the players, evidence of which was often seen in the field,' commented the almanack. Leicestershire were rated among the best fielding sides in the country.

Mike Turner remembered how Lock, then in his late-thirties, maintained his extraordinary prowess in the field. 'Often, during the first two or three overs of a game, Tony would make an electrifying stop in the field and that set the tone for the day. He exuded confidence himself and this was transmitted to the rest of the team.'

The astounding veteran continued to surmount the handicap of discomforting knees. Turner says that Lock was impervious to injury, and believes that in many ways he exemplified the attitudes of the old county professional who was prepared to play with all manner of injuries. 'Tony would arrive at the ground an hour before anyone else to go through the ritual of bandaging his knees.' The intensity of Lock's character was revealed in another memory. 'Lockie used to get himself so worked up during matches, especially at critical moments, that he could be physically sick on the field.'

The enormous self-belief, an attribute shared with Raymond Illingworth, Lock's successor at Grace Road, was at the heart of a born winner. Turner remembered one match at Queen's Park, when Chesterfield played on a beautiful batting wicket. 'It was a very flat pitch and I ventured a question to Tony: "Who's going to get them out? You won't get much turn here."' Lock immediately countered Turner's pessimism. As usual, he was undaunted by the conditions. 'I'll bowl 'em out," he replied. It was no idle boast. Instead of the expected toil, he ran through his teasing variations to take 6-20.

On this and other occasions Lock revelled as the master in his new kingdom. *The Times* acknowledged the renaissance and presented the claim that Lock was 'still, surely, the best English spinner.' The correspondent also welcomed 'the old-fashioned aggression which had helped to inspire his colleagues. Lock's return certainly adds lustre to the game.'

Among those at Leicester sharing in Lock's bounty was Yorkshire-born all-rounder, Jack Birkenshaw. 'These were exciting times – the best years of my career – with Lockie at Grace Road because it was a new experience for us to enjoy success.' Birkenshaw had made his championship debut for Yorkshire at the age of seventeen in 1958. His off spin twice confounded Jim Parks in the match against Sussex. In all he played thirty games for Yorkshire but failed to win his county cap, and in 1961 he went to Leicestershire in search of better times.

Birkenshaw, doubtless under the influence of the new captain, prospered following lean times at Leicester. After the departure of another off-spinner, John Savage, to Lancashire he won a regular place in the team. Splendid profits would accrue to him in his bowling association with Lock. Transcending his personal fortunes was the fact that Leicestershire learned how to win under Lock's captaincy. 'Tony came to us from a tough, competitive environment at the Oval. With Surrey, he was subjected to bullying by Stuart Surridge, as a means of goading him to greater effort.'

As captain at Leicester, Lock tried to replicate the Surridge doctrine. The dictatorial tactics had a short life. They ended in failure when Peter Marner, a Lancastrian, stepped in to calm him down. Marner, who wielded great influence as a senior lieutenant, responded to the abuse in the same coin. 'Lockie became a much nicer person after Peter's intervention,' says Birkenshaw. 'Before this happened he could frighten young players. Barry Dudleston eventually became a very good batsman but for a while he was terrified of Lockie – he couldn't catch a cold.'

Birkenshaw played under both Lock and Illingworth at Leicester. He remembers their differing personalities. 'Lockie was the showman whereas Illy was quieter and more down to earth. Each of them had tremendous self-belief. Lockie led by example. He never allowed a game to drift and tried to make things happen. It was all "edge of the seat" stuff and spectators as well as players responded to him. We watched the veteran tumbling and diving around. You could not help but be infected by his enthusiasm.'

There was also, from Birkenshaw's perspective, the capital of bowling in tandem with Lock. 'He was a brilliant bowler, clever at orchestrating appeals and putting pressure on umpires as well as opponents. I profited because he was so good at applying pressure and took wickets at the other end. He had then reverted to the orthodox style of his young days.

He stood tall with a high arm at the bowling crease, side-on in delivery stride. But occasionally, when he encountered an especially obstinate batsman, he would let rip his faster one.'

The trademark fielding did not waver as the years advanced. Birkenshaw remembers: 'He was a good fielder anywhere but especially in the familiar short leg position. All his catches, not just the spectacular ones, involved the obligatory somersault in celebration. It was showy but he always wanted to be noticed.

'He once ran me out in a match for Yorkshire against Surrey at the Oval. I drove a ball from Eric Bedser past silly mid-on, ran one and mistakenly went for a second. He pounced on the ball to run me out. The speed of his arm was incredible.'

Other incumbents at Grace Road included the long-serving Maurice Hallam, who had preceded Lock as Leicestershire captain. He was a popular man but regarded as too much of a gentleman to rule in an often fractious dressing room. One apocryphal story involving Hallam and Tony Lock illustrated the humour of a man who preferred not to be the victim of his captain's affectionate hugs. The embraces, uncommon then, were the equivalent of today's 'high fives' and congratulatory huddles. Tom Graveney recalled: 'Lockie was so demonstrative when he took a wicket. In one game Maurice, who normally fielded at first slip, had sought the sanctuary of third man. One of the spectators inquired: "What are you doing down here?" Maurice replied: "Because I can't bear the thought of being kissed by Lockie at 11.32 in the morning."'

The cuddles usually replaced bullying expletives but the severity resurfaced if any spectator sought to challenge Lock's authority on the field. The quiet of one summer afternoon at Grace Road was broken when one lone voice in the crowd noisily harangued the Leicestershire captain. It echoed around the ground as if borne by a loudspeaker. Play was suspended as Lock marched to the boundary to scold the spectator. Brisk words were exchanged to silence the critic. Lock, with his prestige restored, then returned to direct operations and the match resumed.

Maurice Hallam was the fixed point of Leicestershire's batting through the 1950s and 1960s. His career figures of 24,488 runs did not truly reflect the quality of his play. At his most imperious he could wreck attacks and score quickly with style and power. Four of his 32 centuries were doubles and twice he achieved the rare feat of 200 and 100 in the same match. Hallam was a local boy and first won notice as captain of the Leicester football team that won the National Schools Trophy in front of a full house of 35,000 at Filbert Street in the 1945/46 season.

At cricket, rather in the manner of Sussex's John Langridge, he was considered unlucky not have played for England. Hallam was later the Leicestershire second XI captain and coach at Uppingham School, where his pupils included Jonathan Agnew and James Whittaker, the latter a successful Leicestershire captain in the 1990s.

Tony Lock was united with fellow exiles at Grace Road in 1965. They included John Cotton from Nottinghamshire, who shared the new ball with Terry Spencer. Peter Marner joined another Lancastrian, Brian Booth, who had moved from Old Trafford the previous season. Marner was considered erratic in some quarters but *Wisden* did not subscribe to that view. 'His presence made a big difference to the Leicestershire batting. Marner was one of five players who scored more than a thousand runs and also accomplished some useful bowling, taking 52 wickets.' John Cotton, in the same account, seized his chance and 'lent fire to the attack with his speed.' Cotton finished second to Lock with 76 wickets in the county's bowling averages. They included a hat-trick in Leicestershire's victory by six wickets over Surrey at the Oval.

The exploits of Singhalese batsmen, Stanley Jayasinghe (styled by his home supporters as the 'Denis Compton of Ceylon') and Clive Inman, afforded glimpses of the flair and effervescent style of the modern batting exponents in Sri Lanka. Jayasinghe had been recruited from the Lancashire League and he, in turn, recommended his fellow countryman. Inman outstayed his compatriot in a productive reign at Leicester and passed 1,000 runs in a season eight times. He also recorded the fastest fifty in first-class cricket – 51 in eight minutes – against Nottinghamshire at Trent Bridge in 1965. Others contributing to Leicestershire's considerable all-round strengths were Roger Tolchard, the Devonian wicketkeeper-batsman, and David Constant, from Kent, who would later become the youngest first-class umpire since Frank Chester.

The boundless enthusiasm of Tony Lock was seen at its best in these times. He was quick to praise the efforts of those under him and was almost too effusive in his reactions to a successful ploy in the field, often embracing the recipient of his freely distributed congratulations. The exultant warrior led from the front and Leicestershire responded to his fervent command in the climb up the championship table in 1966. *Wisden* commented: 'Lock invariably came along with a destructive burst of highly skilled bowling which sometimes encouraged the belief that he should be recalled to Test cricket.'

Lock unfurled a sequence of match-winning performances, including his then best analysis for the county of 8-85 in the one-wicket win over Warwickshire. He returned figures of 12-71 (7-31 in the first innings) on a 'lifting, turning wicket' against Derbyshire. The victory by two wickets over Lancashire – with the captain hitting the winning boundary off Brian Statham – was exceptional for the part played by Lancastrian exiles. Marner, with 59, was top scorer in the first innings; Savage took 7-64; and finally Booth hit a century. Others, even including the mighty Surrey, laboured against the former championship minnows. They tumbled at one stage to 19/6 and were bowled out for 81 at Grace Road. Marner's opening spell gave him three wickets for two runs, and then a full analysis of 4-25. Lock, at the other end, served notice of his unwavering command in taking 3-18 in twelve overs against his former colleagues.

Lock, at thirty-eight returned to Leicester for what would prove to be momentous last season at Grace Road in 1967. He had won other laurels in the previous Australian season in becoming the first post-war bowler to take fifty wickets in the Sheffield Shield, surpassing the record of 47 wickets set up by Garry Sobers in 1963/64. Lock's farewell to his Midlands hosts was studded with heroic deeds. One was the stunning conquest, which defied all predictions, over Somerset in June. A crowd of over 5,000 watched a fluctuating drama. Leicestershire tottered like a crumbling castle against the spin of Robinson and Langford. Facing a Somerset total of 402, they lost five wickets for 84 runs. Inman rallied his team with a spectacular assault, striking 14 boundaries in scoring 76.

Leicestershire were then 148/6 and the follow-on loomed. 'But we had reckoned without a Yorkshireman's gritty approach,' reported the *Leicester Mercury*. 'For Leicestershire this was Birkenshaw's finest hour, his batting was at times studiously inhibited with normal caution but also included a dazzling array of boundary shots.' Birkenshaw's vigil did, though, seem to be in a lost cause. When the ninth-wicket fell Leicestershire were still 41 runs short of avoiding the follow-on. The last wicket stand, with Cotton hoisting two enormous sixes, harvested 52 runs to steady the fears. Birkenshaw was unbeaten on 73, poised and resolute in a Leicestershire revival against the odds.

The alarm of the previous day was dispelled by helter-skelter batting. It carried Leicestershire, winners by two wickets, alongside Hampshire at the top of the championship. Lock's spin and guile had gained 6-45 before the Somerset declaration at lunch. His successes did emphasise the task of scoring 296 to win in four hours. Four wickets fell in a rush to seemingly exclude all but saving the match. Dudleston and Norman eased the situation in a partnership lasting over three hours.

The outlook looked ever more forlorn with 150 required in the last ninety minutes. At the last, 98 runs were required in three quarters of an hour, then 68 in the extra half hour. Birkenshaw and Tolchard momentarily flagged and appeared to have given up the chase. The stand regained momentum after frantic signals from Lock from his pavilion lookout. His clenched fist demanded an all-out attack and it was not ignored. The Leicestershire pair now cut and drove with abandon to stampede the bewildered fieldsmen. Langford was hit for eighteen in one over. Sixteen runs were needed in ten minutes when Birkenshaw skied a catch into the covers and Tolchard, snared lbw, quickly followed.

The stage was now set for Lock in the final pulsating over. He hit the first ball from Rumsey for two runs but there was no addition from the next three balls. The fifth and final ball of a nerve-tingling game was square-cut by Lock for four winning runs. 'There was,' reported the *Leicester Mercury*, 'the ecstasy of Tony Lock throwing his bat to the high heavens as he made the winning hit.'

The gesture was that of an ebullient man still manifestly enthralled by the game. Lock was in his thirty-ninth year but, as a testimony to his endurance, in his last season at Leicester he bowled 1,154 overs and his 128 wickets cost him only 18.11 runs each. In one memorable week in August he took 10-61 in the match against Worcestershire and 13-118 against Northamptonshire. Jack Birkenshaw was in his element, too, as Lock's comrade in arms. At Cheltenham he shared batting and bowling honours with his captain. Between them they dismissed Gloucestershire for 106 after the opening pair of Nicholls and Milton had scored 49. They were then associated in an eighth-wicket partnership of 119 in ninety minutes. Lock's 81 not out was then his highest in first-class cricket.

Birkenshaw, for so long a fringe player in Leicestershire's ranks, took full advantage of his security as a capped player to take 111 wickets. The gain of another 100 wickets in 1968, three centuries with the bat and solid consistency in the following seasons brought a diligent cricketer England recognition when he toured India and Pakistan in 1972/73.

Mike Turner today maintains that criticism of the pitches at Grace Road during Leicestershire's title challenge in 1967 was unjustified. The wickets, he says, did take spin but were normally slow-paced and Lock, as their premier bowler, did not receive extravagant help in his successes. It was somewhat ironical that Bert Lock, the MCC's inspector of pitches, had himself, as the Surrey groundsman, been criticised for preparing pitches to aid his own bowlers at the Oval. There was, however, a distinct threat of the closure of the Grace Road ground after it was named among five other grounds where pitches had fallen below required standards. Bert Lock had made two visits to Leicester before the Lord's directive warned about the 'vital necessity for improvement in the future.'

The wheel had turned full circle from the tradition of true wickets at Leicester in the 1950s to the purported treachery of this time. One match report in *The Times* referred to a 'thinly grassed pitch which reacted appreciably to spin by the middle of the first afternoon. It had been covered at night and suffered no adverse weather but yesterday from the loose patches the ball spun frequently, turned vastly and came up in extremely steep though slow bounce.' Trevor Bailey, as one opponent from Essex, offered a humorous viewpoint on the situation. He was said to have taken a deck chair out to the middle at Grace Road and sitting in it beside a little mound of sand. 'All I need now is a bucket and spade,' he said.

Mike Turner offered emollient words in response to the allegations. 'Our efforts to produce the desired type of pitch have not been successful. But we shall persevere and all I can say is that we shall continue to work on the lines which will produce the variety of wickets requested.' The local newspaper was stoutly loyal in the furore. It poured scorn on the boredom induced by featherbed pitches. It had led to the inevitable huge totals and to cravenly drawn games. The ideal wicket was, he considered, something of a mirage. 'If it is a perfect pitch, in essence it means it is perfect for batsmen and the bowlers to bowl their hearts out. In these circumstances cricket becomes less of a contest and more a marathon test of physical endurance with the odds firmly on the batsmen.'

The upsurge of criticism did not deflect Leicestershire in their title pursuit. In August a crowd of nearly 8,000 – the biggest of the season – voiced their acclaim at Grace Road. The *Leicester Mercury* reported: 'The lion of Leicestershire cavorted excitedly in his ninth victory jig of the year, as well he might, for this was one more day of splendour in the life and times of that astonishing cricketer, Tony Lock.'

Leicestershire, in less than two days, had beaten Worcestershire by an innings. It hoisted them again to the top of the championship, eight points ahead of Yorkshire and twelve points superior to Kent. The artifice of Lock was the glowing masterpiece. On the final afternoon he claimed four first-innings wickets for four runs and a subsequent 6-20 when Worcestershire batted again. His match analysis was a stunning 10-41.

'When it was all over,' enthused the writer in the *Leicester Mercury*, 'one pondered long on this mesmeric performance and Lock's season-long brilliance. The conclusion was that if England's team flies off to the West Indies without Lock in their party, then we are more richly equipped in spin bowlers than I think we are.'

Jack Birkenshaw recalls the tense closing stages of the championship quest. Kent were the main challengers to Leicestershire in the attempt to overhaul Yorkshire. The match at Canterbury for Stuart Leary's benefit was drawn. Lock took 6-54 runs in 49.4 overs in Kent's first innings. *Wisden* reported: 'Having toiled for six hours and forty minutes to get Kent out once, Lock was in no mood to take chances in setting them a target. It was obviously an impossible task for him to win the match.' Birkenshaw says that the Kent supporters roundly abused Lock after he had bowled little medium-paced seamers outside the leg stump to deny his rivals important points. 'It didn't faze Lockie at all. He quite enjoyed this hostile reception. He had won this little battle.'

Leicestershire's hopes of the first championship in the history of the club were cruelly dashed by the weather in the match against Sussex at Hastings. 'We were in pole position with Sussex requiring around 300 to win on a pitch where the ball was turning square,' remembers Birkenshaw. The actual state of the game was that Leicestershire held a lead of 238 runs, with five wickets left. Birkenshaw had worried all the Sussex batsmen in taking seven wickets on the second day.

On the fateful last day the Leicestershire players awoke to find the town shrouded in a blanket of mist. A sea fret had descended on the Central Ground after the cloudless blue skies of the opening days of the match. There was an anxious wait for it to lift but play was eventually abandoned. Ironically, as Birkenshaw recalls, the Leicestershire party had motored only a few miles north for home when they ran into sunshine and perfect cricket conditions. It was the key turning point in the championship race. The expected victory over Sussex would have given the challengers a vital twelve points – eight for the win and four for the first-innings lead. Had they won the match, it would have clinched the title. Yorkshire, with 186 points, were only 10 points in the lead.

A caprice of south-coast weather denied Leicestershire the ultimate triumph. They had to be content with joint-runners-up place with Kent. It was their highest placing since they entered the championship in 1894. The previous best was third under the captaincy of Charles Palmer in 1953. *Wisden* duly noted the advance in status. 'The change in Leicestershire's fortunes since Lock took over the captaincy in 1966 has been extraordinary. In two seasons under his drive and brilliance in the field they have ascended from fourteenth in 1965 to eighth in 1966 and now second in the championship.'

The *Leicester Mercury* also waxed lyrical in its assessment of a magnificent achievement. 'Lock's leadership has been inspirational but he has had the fullest support and co-operation from his team. He and Birkenshaw both soared to the triumphs of more than 100 wickets apiece. For the quiet, likable Yorkshireman it has been a season of wonderment with bat and ball, hardly won and deserved reward after seasons of much frustration and many disappointments.'

There were also tributes to the pacemen, Cotton and Spencer, and the batting eminence of Norman, Hallam, Inman, Booth and Marner, each the scorers of 1,000 runs. A summer of splendid attacking cricket had failed to yield the crowning distinction of the championship pennant by the narrowest of points margins.

Mike Turner remembered an emotional September day after Leicestershire had registered their tenth victory of the season. It was achieved on a pitch, which, as one observer described it, was a 'fiery instrument in Lock's hands.' He signed off as Leicestershire captain with thirteen wickets in the match. It completed a remarkable week of dominance with the ball. A few days earlier he had taken ten wickets in the innings victory over Worcestershire.

The last ball of the season had been bowled and the spectators spilled over the field to station themselves in front of the pavilion. 'We had beaten Northamptonshire and were just ten points short of winning the championship,' says Turner. 'There was a big crowd that day. I shall always remember Tony standing on the balcony. He raised his arms to the crowd. He just looked like Jesus standing there.' The delighted captain addressed the excited throng of people: 'Next year we will win the championship,' he told them.

Tony Lock was unable to fulfil his promise but his dynamic captaincy had laid firm foundations at Grace Road. The exhilarating manner of his leadership had given rise to the talking point that he possessed the credentials to captain the MCC on the forthcoming tour of the West Indies. Brian Close had been stripped of the England captaincy after the timewasting furore against Warwickshire at Edgbaston, Many observers, especially those with a Leicestershire bias, thought Lock was the preferable to Colin Cowdrey, Close's eventual successor.

Leicestershire own fortunes, under the leadership of Raymond Illingworth, soared to even greater heights. They would go on to win their first championship in 1975 and become undisputed one-day masters. Lock's leavetaking was sudden and hugely regretted at Leicester. Family commitments detained him and another cricket mission beckoned across the world. He was soon to be hailed as a saviour in Australia. Before long, a proud Englishman would be loved and respected as one of their antipodean own.

ELEVEN

The Pom in
His Australian Pomp

'Tony Lock was a fierce, uncompromising and tough cricketer. He brought all this vigour to inspire us when we were at a junior stage.'
– John Inverarity

The halcyon days in the sunshine state in the 1960s were enlivened by the renaissance of a spurned cricketer. Tony Lock, the deposed monarch from England, was newly crowned in Western Australia. His admiring young courtiers in Perth hailed him as a saviour. Lock was the tutor who would guide many of them towards worldwide renown. There was a feeling of near disbelief at the recruitment and incomprehension among his hosts at the exclusion from the England ranks. Ian Brayshaw, as one colleague and later a close friend, remembers the thrill of the presence of a 'famous international cricketer' and how it was 'a fantastic opportunity to have him coming to us.'

Tony Lock had been deeply hurt by his rejection by the England selectors in 1962. His response was akin to that of a gamekeeper turned poacher and the aim was to exact retribution. He brought to bear in this quest the lessons of ruthlessness sharply honed in the cut and thrust of competition back home. The desire to win was undiminished and it spurred his recruits who were only too willing to reap the benefits of his leadership. It was a beguiling time for them and the master at the WACA.

There were regretful voices in England at the loss of such a wholehearted cricketer. One Devonian supporter, writing in *The Cricketer* in 1963, commented: 'I believe that had Tony Lock been an Australian he would have played in the last series out there. Sir Donald

Bradman has been reported as having described Lock's bowling as the best of its kind. Robins and his English co-selectors must be blamed for letting spectators down with their unbalanced selections.'

Another outraged correspondent penned his protest at the exclusion of Lock in the *Playfair Cricket Magazine*. 'Our man in Australia has proved beyond doubt by his magnificent performance with Western Australia that he should have gone [with the MCC]. The greatest close-to-the-wicket catcher in the world let alone a wonderful bowler. His fielding and catching would have set an example to the rest of the team.'

More discerning disciples in Australia would count their blessings at securing the services of a seasoned veteran. Lock had been playing first-class cricket since 1946. The wild exuberance that marked his early appearances for England might have faded after the strenuous years of combat in international cricket. But one Australian observer said that even in physical decline the hands were as sure as when he first miraculously held the fielding stage. 'The determination to win was as strong as ever, and the means of doing so in Australian conditions actually enhanced by the experiences which curtailed his England career.'

The turning point, continued the writer, had been the reaction of the English authorities to a suspect action, which had seemed obvious for some time to the growing television audience in the 1950s. Lock's completely remodelled action gave him mastery of flight as well as spin.

'The old Lock, sometimes bowling his orthodox left-arm spin close to medium pace, would have been less likely to winkle out the tail-end batsmen with the economy and dispatch that became his hallmark in Western Australia.'

Ted Dexter, the England captain on the 1962-63 tour of Australia, echoed the comments on the new beneficial style. He remembered how the exiled Lock took wickets against the MCC in the opening matches. 'The Perth wicket was one of the fastest and bounciest in the world. Yet Lock, who was by now an orthodox spinner, was particularly successful in that season. There was not another spinner in Australia as effective as he was.'

Conversely, Richie Benaud takes another view and maintains that, rather than hamper Lock as a bowler, the Perth wicket actually benefited him. 'It is something of an illusion that the WACA pitch square was not suitable for spinners. I always enjoyed bowling there for New South Wales.' Benaud says that the problem was to get on to bowl because the pitch was most favourable for swing bowlers. The key was the 'Fremantle Doctor', the name given to the cooling breeze that blows up after lunch and springs from the nearby Swan River. Opinions differ as to how much help it gives both types of bowlers. But, according to Benaud, the 'Doctor' blowing from fine leg at the then Members' End, was perfect for the right-arm over-the-wrist spinner and the orthodox slow left-arm bowler. Tony Mann, the West Australian leg-spinner, recalls that Lock was not unaware of the advantage. For Mann, there was a conflict of interests. 'The crucial thing for me, as a leggie, was that I had to bowl into the wind but then so did Tony.'

One of the ironies of the recruitment of Lock by Western Australia was the perennial quest by the authority to sign a batsman. The concern was for reinforcements in this department. A regular item in the minutes was: 'Engagement of leading batsman to play in WA next season.' The signing of Rohan Kanhai in 1961/62 was not considered satisfactory because of his commitments in the West Indies. Other players coming under scrutiny were Norm O'Neill from New South Wales; the Mohammads, Hanif and Mushtaq, from Pakistan; and Roy Marshall, the West Indian, then playing with Hampshire in England. Serious approaches, it is claimed, were also made to Ted Dexter and Ken Barrington. Yet, amid the feverish hunt for a batsman, the most significant import of this or any other era was a bowler.

Lock's arrival in Perth also upstaged potential spin rivals – the leg-spinners, Terry Jenner and Tony Mann, and off-spinner Ashley Mallett. All of them were quickly conscious that their opportunities would be limited because of the commanding presence of the Englishman. Mann, along with Jenner and Mallett, watched keenly from the pavilion as Lock took wickets for Western Australia against the MCC tourists at Perth in 1962. Either of the two leg-spinners, while acknowledging the mastery of the Englishman, had reason to believe that they could complement Lock with their varying spin. It was quite common for two spinners to bowl in tandem at the WACA. Some time would elapse before Mann rose to eminence but he remembers the later press comments of his captain that he had a role to play in the state attack. A particular regret was the departure of Mallett. 'It was amazing because he was a leading off-spinner and would have been a great asset to Western Australia,' says Mann.

The general view at the time was that Western Australia was not big enough for two spinners. Jenner, together with his friend, Mallett (who never played for the state) left for South Australia and speedy recognition by the Test selectors.

Mann would later embark on a long career with Western Australia and make a major contribution to the state's rise to the top of inter-state cricket. He had played cricket for Midland-Guildford, one of the strongest Grade sides in Australia, at fourteen and a year later represented the Combined High Schools XI against a Governor's XI which included Test players Richie Benaud and Neil Harvey. John Inverarity was captain of the schools' side and Rodney Marsh was the wicketkeeper. Mann took 7-45 and had Harvey stumped down the leg-side by Marsh. In 1963/64 he made his debut for Western Australia. He was unable to retain his place and did not play for the state again for another two years.

The campaign to revive the fortunes and esteem of Western Australia had begun in the reign of Barry Shepherd. Ian Brayshaw refers to the periods of major influence in the rise of the state to prosperity. The signing of Lock, who took over the captaincy in 1967/68, had coincided with a five-year action plan of fitness, a training regime drawn up by Shepherd and the state selectors. 'Shepherd drove this campaign and then Lock came along to teach us the habit of winning, not just one game, but again and again,' remembers Brayshaw.

Shepherd belonged to an elite cadre of sporting prodigies. In December 1955, as an eighteen-year-old, he became the youngest player to be selected for Western Australia in Sheffield Shield competition. His 103 not out in the second innings against Queensland at Perth was compiled in a record seventh-wicket partnership with Keith Carmody. He was the youngest West Australian to score a century on his debut.

The burly left-hander established himself as a crowd favourite with hurricane hitting. The fervour of his batting assaults was recalled with pride long after his retirement. Shepherd was the first from the state to score a double century – 212 not out against Queensland. It was part of another record stand of 223 for the third wicket with Rohan Kanhai. Shepherd hit six sixes and 20 fours and struck his last 112 runs in sixty-eight minutes.

Shepherd scored another double century (219) against Victoria at Melbourne in 1962/63 and in this season he made his Test debut against England at Sydney. He was unbeaten on 71 as he ran out of partners. There was justifiable concern, especially in his home state, at the shabby treatment of a resolute cricketer who narrowly missed selection for the tour of England in 1964. It was a major disappointment for the WACA

1 & 2   A cricket awakening in rural Surrey. Tony, above left, perky in the classroom, and Sir Henry Leveson Gower, above right, the squire of Limpsfield and, as President of Surrey County Cricket Club, a key influence in the recruitment of the boy at the Oval. (Bryan Lock)

3   The ten-year-old Tony, back row, third from the left, as a member of his school XI in 1939. Leonard Moulding, his headmaster and the first of his cricket mentors, is pictured third from the right. (Limpsfield School)

SURREY COUNTY TEAM 1950

4   On top at the Oval: The Surrey team, captained by Michael Barton in 1950, shared the title with Lancashire. Lock was in his first season with the county as a capped player. (Surrey CCC)

5   Lock in contemplative mood at the Oval at the start of his first-class career in 1946. At seventeen, he was the youngest player to represent Surrey. (Bryan Lock)

6   Stuart Surridge,
sometimes a tyrant as captain
but the epitome of enterprise
and adventure in Surrey's great
years. (Surrey CCC)

7   The victorious Surrey team who won a fourth successive Championship title in 1955.
(Surrey CCC)

8 Selected for England: Jim Laker, Alec Bedser, Peter May and Tony Lock were all chosen to play against India at Manchester in 1952. (Surrey CCC)

9 Lock with umpire Fred Price, who first no-balled him at the Oval in the match against the tourists before the Test at Old Trafford. Controversy would stalk him as a bowler throughout the decade. (Nova Hearne)

10   A revealing action picture of Lock from 1953 showing the fingers at the end of the release while the bent elbow is in the process of straightening. The perceived illegality of the action incensed Johnny Wardle, his Yorkshire rival for England honours.

11   The Australian fast bowler Ian Meckiff, below, was unpredictable in line and length, and caused much consternation in the England ranks on the 1958/59 Ashes tour.

12   Derby rivals in distress at Blackheath: Lock took sixteen wickets, including all ten in the second innings, against Kent in 1956. (Surrey CCC)

PROGRAMME 3d.

Intervals
Lunch   1.30 — 2.10
Tea   usually 4.15

Umpires
Harry Elliot
W. F. Price

Scorers
W. Hansford and
H. Strudwick

‡ Captain
† Wicketkeeper

New ball is due after 200 runs, or after 75 overs have been completed.

Membership:—
The Kent County Cricket Club welcomes new members. For full particulars apply to the Secretary, St. Lawrence Ground, Canterbury or to any K.C.C.C. official on the Ground.

This Card does not necessarily include the fall of the last wicket.

Next Home Matches
MAIDSTONE WEEK
JULY 14th, 16th, 17th
Kent v Northants
JULY 18th, 19th, 20th
Kent v Middlesex

Please put your litter in the receptacles provided for the purpose.
The K.C.C.C. Annual can be purchased on the Ground, price 2/- or from J. A. Jennings, Ltd., the publishers.

Printed on the Ground by J. A. Jennings, Ltd., Canterbury.

Completed Cards at close of each day's play.

BLACKHEATH   —   JULY 7th, 9th and 10th, 1956
KENT v SURREY

Hours of Play : 1st day 11.30 - 6.30 2nd day 11.30 - 6.30 3rd day 11.30 - 6.0 or 6.30

Surrey won toss and elected to bat   **SURREY WON**

KENT	1st Innings		2nd Innings	
1 M C Cowdrey	c Swetman b Bedser A V	49	lbw b Lock	8
2 Phebey A H	b Lock	22	b Lock	12
3 Wilson R C	c Barrington b Lock	2	b Lock	32
†4 Evans T G	b Loader	1	c and b Lock	19
5 Fagg A E	c Stewart b Lock	2	c Bedser A V b Lock	21
6 Dixon A L	c May b Lock	13	b Lock	2
7 Ufton D G	b Lock	0	not out	17
8 Ridgway F	c Surridge b Lock	6	c Stewart b Lock	7
9 Halfyard D J	c Pratt b Bedser A V	1	c Barrington b Lock	0
10 Page J C T	not out	1	b Lock	0
‡11 Wright D V P	c Loader b Bedser A V	2	b Lock	0
	l-byes	2	byes 6 l-byes 5 Nbs 1	12
	Total	101	Total	130

Runs at fall of wicket	1	2	3	4	5	6	7	8	9	10
1st Innings	55	63	64	67	91	91	91	96	98	101
2nd Innings	20	29	60	84	101	104	130	130	130	130

Bowling Analysis	O	M	R	W	Wd	Nb	O	M	R	W	Wd	Nb
Loader	16	6	38	1	....	....	8	3	7	0	....	....
Bedser A V	11	0	28	3	....	....	16	5	41	0	....	1
Lock	21	12	29	6	....	....	29.1	18	54	10	....	....
Bedser E A	3	2	4	0	....	....	18	10	16	0	....	....

SURREY	1st Innings		2nd Innings	
1 Stewart M J	c Fagg b Wright	13		
2 Clark T H	b Ridgway	191		
3 Barrington K	c Ridgway b Wright	32		
4 P B H May	not out	128		
5 Pratt R	c Phebey b Page	21		
6 Bedser E A	not out	11		
†7 Swetman R				
‡8 W S Surridge				
9 Lock G A R				
10 Bedser A V				
11 Loader P J				
	l-byes	8	byes	
	Total (for 4 wickets dec.)	404	Total	

Runs at fall of wicket	1	2	3	4	5	6	7	8	9	10
1st Innings	47	145	319	360						
2nd Innings										

Bowling Analysis	O	M	R	W	Wd	Nb	O	M	R	W	Wd	Nb
Ridgway	15	3	53	1	....	....					....	....
Halfyard	28	4	104	0	....	....					....	....
Wright	25	3	85	2	....	....					....	....
Page	25	2	107	1	....	....					....	....
Dixon	9	0	44	0	....	....					....	....
Cowdrey	1	0	3	0	....	....					....	....

13   Lock's figures against Kent recorded for posterity on the match scorecard. (Kent CCC)

14   Lock is the hero of the hour, having taken seven second innings wickets in Surrey's victory over the Australians at the Oval in 1956. (Surrey CCC)

15   Lock and Laker at Leeds where they shared eighteen wickets in stark contrast to the mysterious Test at Manchester, where the wicket count was 19–1 in Laker's favour.(PA Photos)

16   An Ulyett cartoon illustrating the venom of their partnership in a memorable summer for both England and Surrey followers.

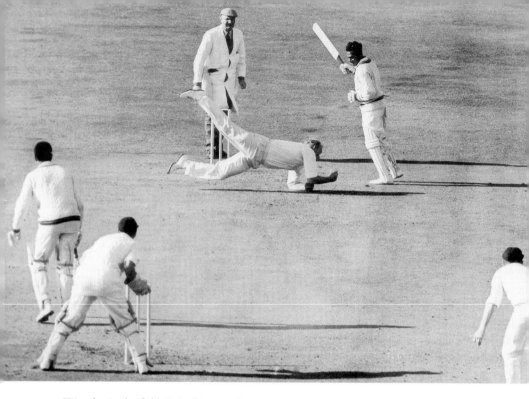

17 Wizardry in the field: Swivelling to take a return catch to confound Garry Sobers at Leeds in 1963. (Richard Lock)

18 A typical gesture of jubilation as Lock bowls South African Hedley Keith in the Oval Test in 1955. (Surrey CCC)

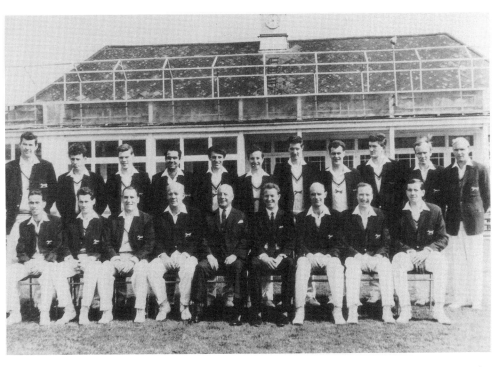

19 The Leicestershire team which was inspired by the self-belief of the veteran at Grace Road. The zest of Lock's captaincy was the prelude to a remarkable final phase in his career.

20 Jack Birkenshaw, the Yorkshire exile and Lock's key bowling ally at Leicester, whose own fortunes were transformed in the 'best years of my career'. (Leicestershire CCC)

21 Sheffield Park, the home of a pioneering Sussex Lord and cricket benefactor, in its Victorian heyday. The illuminations at the park were to welcome the touring Austalians in 1893. (Fletchling CC)

22 The Australian team group of 1884 includes Billy Murdoch who would go on to represent both England and Sussex. (Sussex CCC)

23   Pavilioned in splendour: The palatial cricket setting at Sheffield Park, above, soon to be revived as a venue, was given royal patronage to seal the last visit of the Australian tourists in 1896. The Prince of Wales (later Edward VII) is pictured leaving Lord Sheffield's private pavilion during the match. (Sussex CCC)

24   The newly refurbished Sheffield Shield, originally donated by Sheffield for inter-state competition, began an Anglo-Australian tradition which lasted for over a century. It would have special significance for Tony Lock, another English visionary, as West Australian captain. Capturing the magnificent trophy in 1968 gave him exalted status in the land where he made his home. (David Studham, Melbourne CC)

25   The WACA, the West Australian cricket headquarters at the time of the inaugural Test at Perth during the 1970/71 season. It was a ground upon which Lock reinvented himself as a bowler. Against all expectations, he performed record-breaking exploits in alien conditions for a slow left-arm bowler. (WACA)

26   Lock and the victorious West Australian team arriving back in Perth after their Sheffield Shield triumph at Melbourne. Left to right, back row: Keith Slater, Graham McKenzie, Murray Vernon, Gordon Becker, Jock Irvine, Tony Mann, Laurie Mayne. Front row: Ian Brayshaw, Tony Lock, Ross Edwards, John Inverarity, Derek Chadwick. (*West Australian*)

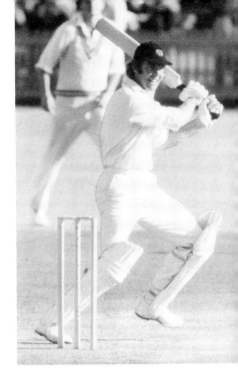

27, 28 & 29   Renowned pupils of the English master. Above left: Dennis Lillee, whose innate aggression as a novice bowler won the approval of his like-minded captain. Above right: John Inverarity, another future Australian Test player, who prospered in succession to Lock as an astute captain in his own right. Below: Lock leads the applause for Ian Brayshaw after he had taken 10-44 in an innings against Victoria at Perth in October 1967. (West Australian Cricket Association)

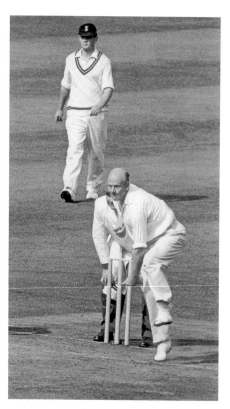

30   The remodelling of Lock's action – and reversion to the orthodoxy of youth – first began after viewing himself on film during a private showing in New Zealand in 1959. It would lead to an extended career as a purveyor of alluring flight which teased even the best of Australian batsmen, many of them Test players, into submission. (Leicestershire CCC)

31   Below: Lock was never to be under-estimated as a batsman; he was just as aggressive in this mode as he was as a bowler. His recall in his thirty-ninth year to England colours in the West Indies during 1968 provided ample evidence of his prowess. He flayed the home fast bowlers in a rescuing ninth-wicket partnership at Georgetown, Guyana, and hit 89, his highest score in first-class cricket. (Surrey CCC)

32 A family interlude: Audrey and Tony Lock at their wedding at Limpsfield Church in 1952. Lock was a devoted husband and his marriage withstood the unfounded allegations of sexual abuse which cast a huge shadow over the final years of his life. A proud man was deeply hurt by the slur on his name – and that of his family – but was able to find solace in the tragedy through their support and that of many friends and cricketing contemporaries. (Bryan Lock)

33 Happier times with Audrey and their two sons, Graeme (left) and Richard. (Richard Lock)

34 Above: Lock, now an Australian citizen, is reunited with former Surrey colleagues Peter Loader, Ron Tindall, Jim Laker and Ken Barrington at Perth. (Surrey CCC)

35 Envoi: the smiling country boy, a fighter in adversity and a kind, generous soul behind the formidable mask. Cricket always remained an integral part of his life. His courage was legendary. Nobody pursued a passion with more fervour or more wholehearted endeavour. (Roger Packham)

captain. Over thirty years later he still possessed the sumptuous leather cricket bag embossed with the name 'R. Benaud', given to him by that noted rival and friend in the confident expectation that he was a certainty for the tour.

Shepherd played in another eight Tests against the West Indies, England, South Africa and Pakistan. By the time of his premature retirement in 1966 he had scored twelve centuries and the highest number of runs – 6,834 – in both the Sheffield Shield and in all first-class matches for Western Australia. Interestingly, his averages in both state and Test cricket were almost identical at a little over 41 runs each. Shepherd later embarked on another influential career as an administrator. He vied with Sir Donald Bradman as one of the longest-serving Cricket Australia Board directors until his forced retirement due to his diabetes, an illness that led to death.

Shepherd captained Western Australia thirty times, a record that has only been overtaken by John Inverarity. Many contemporaries consider Shepherd's efforts in this capacity to be his major contribution to West Australian cricket. In the 1961/62 season the state selectors turned to the twenty-four year-old Shepherd as captain. 'It was in that role that this powerfully built, yet surprisingly nimble young leader made his most enduring impact,' commented one observer.

Tony Lock, who joined Western Australia in Shepherd's second season as captain, would soon stir his own inspirational brew. It is, however, Shepherd who wins the plaudits for the crucial introduction of young players in the early 1960s. John Inverarity, who had been surprised by his own elevation as an eighteen-year-old – at a time when he was not even in the state squad – recalls Shepherd as one of the great captains of Western Australia. 'He was, in my view, the player who began to transform the culture of our state cricket. He led from the front, he was intelligent and innovative and had a strong impact on the young fellows coming into the side.' Shepherd's aggressive approach kindled the enthusiasm of the youthful Inverarity who was besotted with cricket and had been fired with state pride from his infancy.

Other young players who came under Shepherd's and later Lock's captaincy were Ross Edwards, Jock Irvine, Derek Chadwick, Bob Massie, Rod Marsh, Dennis Lillee and Graham McKenzie. 'Barry Shepherd had the good fortune to lead a group of passionate West Australians simply waiting for the light of battle to be lit. But none of them would deny that he provided the spark in a uniquely compelling way,' wrote Anthony J. Barker in his book, *The WACA – An Australian Cricket Success Story.* 'He developed a potent mixture of intense state parochialism and innovative preparation that left Western Australia poised for a great future.'

The chain of command was enriched by Shepherd's legacy and his baton conjured new wonders when it was passed on to Tony Lock. The spell cast by the English exile on the team – and a generation of boys young enough to be his own sons – was sourced deep in hard-nosed professionalism. The veteran brought another dimension to the local scene. 'Tony was a big man, an imposing figure on the cricket field,' recalls Ian Brayshaw. Lock seemed to others to grow ever more formidable as he grew older, his weather-beaten visage produced a distinct impression of a grizzled seafarer. Quite clearly there was no danger of mutiny while he was on deck.

The menace of Lock's bowling was cloaked in a cunning to overcome the seeming handicap of an alien setting for spinners. Brayshaw attests: 'The fact that he rarely spun the ball – not many did, especially at Perth – on Australian wickets did not surprise me. Where he succeeded was as a master of flight and variations. Sometimes he bowled two yards behind the bowling crease. His control of line and length even from this position was so good that he invariably landed the ball perfectly. He would hold them back; yet another ball would be delivered with a round arm; and then, occasionally, with a bit of a "double whirl", he proceeded to bowl his quicker ball.'

Only rarely, it was said, did Lock revert to his bad old ways and one of them was against the redoubtable Norm O'Neill, who was generally considered unstoppable when firmly installed at the crease. His dismissal by Lock in one match against Western Australia occurred when he was in the seventies and seemingly assured of a century. O'Neill was doubly incensed, having just been omitted from the Australian team to tour South Africa. The unfairness of his downfall added to his gloom.

After the years of acceptance of Lock's looping Australian style of bowling, the umpires were not looking for a suspect action. When he suddenly penetrated O'Neill's backlift with a blatant throw it was greeted with general hilarity by the fielders. John Inverarity remembered the bemusement of their dumbfounded rival. 'Norm was a handsome striker of the ball and he was 78 not out and cruising towards a century. He was insistently coming down the wicket and getting after Lock. Tony came in to bowl. I was fielding at first slip and Gordon Becker was the wicketkeeper. Lockie thereupon threw the ball as hard as he could; it hit Norm on the toe and he fell flat on his face trying to avoid the ball. It smashed into his stumps. Becker claimed in the ensuing wreckage – and the clatter of bails – that he nearly swallowed a stump.'

Wisden refrained from judgement in its report: 'Lock, with his customary guile and accuracy, took nine wickets in the match.' There was no mention of the 'really accurate chuck' which had capsized O'Neill.

The obdurate O'Neill had roused Lock to an indecent action. More orthodox measures easily prevailed against the late-order batsmen. Ian Brayshaw extols Lock as the expert in routing the tail. 'He would position a long off and a long on and then bowl two or three fast darters. In those days tail-enders didn't really guard their wickets. Then he would toss one up and the batsman would have a swing and be caught in the deep.' The strongest memory of Lock the bowler is his unerring accuracy. 'I reckon that you could have blindfolded him, so he didn't know where the wicket was and he would still have dropped it on a length.'

An extract from the *WACA Annual Report*, in one of Lock's early seasons at Perth, also referred to: 'Uncanny control and accurate bowling ... [sustained for] long hours under trying heat conditions. Any match in which Tony Lock plays is stamped with the personality of a volatile player. His keenness in the field, the voicing of his appeals which test his own vocal chords (and the nerves of opposing batsmen and umpires) and the gamesmanship in his batting has delighted crowds in Australia.'

John Inverarity also reflects on the hunting instinct, a predatory attitude that Lock shared with all the great bowlers in the history of the game. 'It is a division of skills and psychological powers,' he says. 'Shane Warne gets ten out of ten in each category. Lock was not far behind with eight and half out of ten in the skills department and ten out of ten in the other.'

Inverarity recalls Lock's ability to create a presence by talking with the umpires and the way he orchestrated his appeals. 'First there was the stifled appeal, then he gave it full throttle. He crowded the tail-enders, bowling it flat for three or four deliveries and then tossing the ball a little higher to tempt the unwary opponent into a big hit and the inevitable catch on the boundary.'

Ian Brayshaw also delights in recalling how Lock outfoxed inexperienced players: 'Lockie would work the umpires and have Colin Milburn (another English import) in the bat-pad position to make them feel he was doing more than he was with the ball. He would call up Ollie for a mid-wicket conference and the young bloke at the batting end was shaking in his boots.'

John Inverarity describes Lock as a shrewd 'animal hunter'. It is an appealing big game analogy. Lock stalked his prey with the relish of a man on a jungle safari. 'Most people don't realise how astute Tony was in this quest. He created a dynamic in which many opponents got out *knowing* he was bowling. It is a subtle attribute but also very real. Lock was a fierce, uncompromising and tough competitor. He brought all this vigour to inspire us when we were at a junior stage. The most significant part of his captaincy was that he led from the front. It was the never-say-die attitude of a brave cricketing warrior that rubbed off the rest of us.'

Dorham Mann, who now works as a winegrower and consultant in Perth, was another of Lock's protégés in Western Australia. He shares this distinction with his brother, Tony, the Australian leg-spinner who did not come to fore as a Test player until 1977. The younger Mann was aged thirty-two when he was chosen to bolster an Australian attack depleted by the loss of players who had defected to Kerry Packer. In his second Test he was sent in as nightwatchman against India at Perth. Mann hit 105 and his innings enabled Australia to win by two wickets.

Dorham endorses the views expressed by his contemporaries on the reinvention of Lock as a bowler. 'Tony was now a superb orthodox flight bowler on our hard, bouncy wickets.' The veteran, with his balding pate, was sometimes known as 'Coco', a misleading soubriquet. 'Occasionally, he would become frustrated after a long bowling stint and unleash one of his jerked faster deliveries to confound the batsman.'

There is a memory, too, of Lock's tactical acumen in First Grade cricket with the Guildford-Midland club. The beam of his personal radar enabled him to anticipate an opponent's intended stroke by precisely placing a fieldsman to guard the area. More often than not the noose had been tightened to snare a catch. Lock again showed how adept he was at causing confusion in the minds of incoming batsmen. On one occasion at South Perth the victim was a future Test player, the sixteen-year-old Bruce Laird. Mann recalled that 'Steamer' Wilson, a fiery paceman, opened the bowling. Lock motioned to Dorham to take up a position at silly mid-on.

The young Laird watched the manoeuvre with his hands trembling with anxiety. 'It was like taking a bone from a blind dog,' Dorham wittily explained. Wilson's first ball was nervously edged straight to slip.

Tony Mann has referred to his brother's tribute to Lock as the finest of batting coaches. It seems at first like a contradictory statement when applied to a bowler. The answer lay in Lock's sharpened antenna in gauging the strengths and weaknesses of batting opponents. He was also not to be under-rated as a batsman himself. He did score 10,000 runs, without a single century, in his career. Dorham Mann recalled that, due to university commitments, practice on turf had been denied him. Consequently, he had little or no experience of playing swing bowling. Lock advised him to change his wide stance at the crease to reduce his vulnerability against late swing. He advocated the more orthodox English style of placing the right foot behind the bat. Dorham says that this had the effect of allowing him to play straighter, control his head movement, and judge the direction of the ball with greater certainty.

All who played with Lock in Western Australia are in thrall to a bowler who often won matches with his own remarkable performances. He was an instinctive captain rather than a strategist. Self-belief was the over-riding feature of his leadership. 'Just follow me, boys,' he would say. 'You make enough runs and I'll bowl 'em out.' Ian Brayshaw remembers an article by Jack Lee in the *West Australian*, which referred to one of Lock's decisions as a 'folly'. 'Next day Lockie responded to the criticism with a notice on A4 in his own handwriting pinned to the dressing-room door. It read: "Welcome to Lock's Folly." Anyone wanting to come in knew without doubt that he had taken objection to the article.'

It is the commanding presence which lingers in the memories of those who played with Lock in Western Australia. Lock was unyielding to the opposition and never allowed his own players to become smug and satisfied. 'You certainly knew who was captain,' recalls Inverarity. 'He could be pretty savage on any indiscretion on the field of play.'

For the young Dennis Lillee, who entered the WA team only after the 1967/68 season, the toughness was inspirational. 'Lockie didn't suffer fools gladly. If he didn't like you, it was better to keep your distance. Fortunately, he took a shine to me. Perhaps he saw something of himself in my personality. I was very lucky as a young player in Perth to come under his influence. Lockie made a major impact on me in terms of my aggression and professionalism.'

The sense of theatre, which Lock brought to his cricket, would later manifest in Lillee's menace at the bowling crease. 'Lockie taught me the need for a "hold-no-quarter" approach to playing the game. I had a lot of that in my make-up but to see my captain with the same attributes endorsing this was very important for a youngster. Lockie was happy with my attitude. It was what he wanted as, day by day, he revved up his troops.'

The camaraderie between Lock and Lillee produced an incongruous situation of an English professional fostering the aggression of his pupil to, ultimately, his own country's alarm. 'There might have been a lot of people in England cursing Lockie when I went there and played for Australia,' says Lillee. 'In actual fact, the English crowds took me to their hearts as much as any Australian could be.' The dark matinee idol of yesteryear still threatens in a magnificent action sculpture – a recent addition to the pantheon of Australian cricket heroes that ring the perimeter of the Melbourne Cricket Ground.

Tony Lock was revered as an 'extraordinary imaginative and creative bowler' and earned his own place in the gallery of cricketing idols in Western Australia. As a solitary man, he did, though, suffer allegations of being a detached personality. He was much less involved with players off the field than Shepherd had been before him and also his successor, Inverarity. There was speculation among less than respectful juniors as to the nature of their captain's nocturnal activities.

One writer put forward a more responsible point of view. 'In fairness to Lock,' he said, 'it must be remembered that he was not only from another country, with its very different traditions of English professionalism, but also another generation compared to the majority of players under his command.'

The wide-eyed boys looked on with mingled amazement and amusement at the pre-match preparations undertaken by Lock. It involved interminable rolls of strapping for the forty-year-old muscles and joints. Ian Brayshaw vividly remembers the bandaging routine. 'Lockie really had to prop himself up to get out on the field, especially in the later stages of his career.'

Brayshaw was probably one of the few players who made the connection between the evidence of the wear and tear of decades of cricket and a man disinclined to socialise after a day's play. 'Lockie was often shattered by the end of the day. He had bowled a lot of overs. He just wanted to relax quietly with a beer and a cigarette.'

As Lock's regular roommate on tour, Brayshaw could appreciate another side to a man operating on a different social schedule to his youthful companions. 'We youngsters would celebrate big time but not Lockie. One evening I looked into our room. The television and lights were on but Lockie was stretched out on the bed fast asleep. I could understand his need for rest because he was double our ages.' Refreshed after his slumbers, Lock belied his reputation as a hard-bitten English professional. The man, who had initially instructed his charges to call him either 'Skipper' or 'Mr Lock', would regularly fuss over Brayshaw with a morning cup of tea in bed.

The decline in physical powers did not lessen Lock's ability as a fieldsman. John Inverarity remembers the astonishing reflexes displayed by his captain. 'All the time I've played cricket I've never seen a better catcher. He was phenomenal despite his rickety knees. He always fielded close to the wicket. I would put Tony in the same category as our great Australian close fieldsmen – Bobby Simpson and Mark Waugh.'

There is a remembrance, too, from Ian Brayshaw, of Lock's fielding off his own bowling. 'If someone was driving him – and that didn't happen too often – it had to be fairly wide of him to evade his reach.'

Tony Mann, always an exuberant hitter, provides another anecdote about the 'sensational catcher'. He was in his last year at university in Perth and opposed to Lock in the Midland-Guildford team. His batting partner was his close friend, John Inverarity. 'We had lost three or four wickets for around 150 when I came in to bat. I told Inver: "We'll have to get after Lockie today."' Mann was as good as his word. He capered down the wicket and struck Lock's first ball for a steepling six far into the crowd. The veteran looked quizzically down the wicket at the impertinent youngster. He now dropped his next ball a little shorter. Mann was alert to the danger and stopped in his stride to crack the ball through the covers for four.

Lock was not to be denied by the audacious hitting. He had, after all, had the last laugh on more serious occasions and against all the great batsmen of the time. The next ball was still tossed up, a little higher and marginally shorter, to provide yet more temptation. Mann recalls: 'I hit it straight back at him like an Exocet missile. Lockie rocked back on his heels to cling on to a magnificent catch.' In his postscript to the duel, he says: 'But I had struck the great man for two boundaries before he rolled me over.'

Lock, with ample justification, took special pride in his batting. His natural pugnacity came boisterously into play, especially in moments of crisis. He was, however, by this time, unequal to the demands of swift running between the wickets. Ian Brayshaw remembers batting with Lock in one match against Victoria at Melbourne. 'We were chasing a target and needed quick runs.' The yawning gulf of unguarded territory in the vast arena offered the prospect of bolstering the total.

Guarding the on-side were just two fieldsmen, a bat-pad catcher and a fine leg. 'I pushed one firmly past the short leg into the wide-open spaces. The solitary close fielder had to get up from his haunches to retrieve the ball. We ran five!' At the end of the over Lock was perspiring profusely and highly indignant at the toll on his energy. 'Brayshaw,' he said, 'If you ever do that again, I'll kill you.' Brayshaw now concedes that he was expecting too much of the veteran. 'It really was an effort for him. But if I'd been batting with Ross Edwards or Rod Marsh we'd have run six.'

Another batting anecdote illustrated the vein of eccentricity in Lock's make-up. It also marked an abhorrence of bad decisions. There was one period when he seemed to be jinxed as a batsman. One after the other the innings were curtailed by marginally valid lbws and catches behind the wicket. Lock was always proud of his accomplishments as a batsman. He had been given out more times than he liked.

At this time Lock was the owner of a lovely grained new bat. It had only a small scar on the edge, which he pointed out to his teammates after one lbw decision went against him. Over in Melbourne he had two more setbacks and suffered a 'pair' in the match. Brayshaw knew that the captain was now seething with anger at the succession of reverses. 'We all thought we had better steer clear of the skipper until he cooled down. Two players cowered in a locker and the others were in the toilet when Lockie marched back in high dudgeon. We all expected him to fling his precious bat across the room. Instead, he went to his own locker, pulled out a cigarette lighter, turned it up to full blaze, and set fire to the bat.'

Overshadowing all else in the 1970/71 season, Lock's last as West Australian captain, were the exploits of South African Barry Richards. Richards was in such dominant form that he often took the limelight away from England's tour of Australia. *Wisden* reported: 'The Australians saw in the South African globetrotting professional a complete batsman, combining grace and power with great technical skill.'

South Australia, exalted by Richards's mastery, were almost inevitably Sheffield Shield champions, ten points clear of their nearest rivals, Victoria. By mid-January Richards had reached 1,000 runs. In 13 innings (twice not out) he amassed 1,145 runs in the competition. He headed the Australian first-class batting with an average of 109.86.

Tony Lock, for once, had to take a back seat as Richards went on the rampage at Perth. He reached his highest first-class score: 356 runs, including a six and 48 fours. All but 31 of the runs came on the first day. Richards' score was only three runs short of the highest individual score in Australian post-war cricket: 359 by Bobby Simpson for New South Wales against Queensland at Brisbane during the 1963/64 campaign. He shared a second-wicket partnership with Ian Chappell of 308 in two hours and fifty minutes. Richards reached his first hundred in two hours and five minutes; in just over another three hours he had hoisted a triple century. He scored 137 between lunch and tea.

It was a day of complete annihilation. The heady batsmanship produced other centuries rolling up inexorably as debits against the West Australian bowlers. Two present and future Test bowlers, Graham McKenzie and Dennis Lillee, each conceded over 100 runs with only one wicket between them. Lock and his fellow spinner, Tony Mann, shared seven wickets to console them in their labours.

Ian Brayshaw, as the most economical bowler amid the onslaught, recalls that his captain rationed his workload. 'We all had a good laugh about the reasons why Lockie didn't prefer bowling on that day. Bo didn't bowl much. Richards was caning us to all parts of the ground. I conceded 69 in eleven overs – six and a half an over. The rest of us were going for seven, eight, nine and ten runs.'

Brayshaw remembers discreetly averting his eyes away from Lock after failing to hold on to a catch offered by Richards. He was fielding at mid-on when his captain came on to bowl at the Southern End. 'Barry came down the wicket and "creamed" one straight at my midriff. I didn't know whether to get my arms up or down and I dropped it.'

It was now a case of deciding how best to hide his embarrassment at the lapse. 'I knew that I must not look at Lockie. He gave you a withering look if you did something wrong.' The hapless fieldsman turned his back to examine the scoreboard. By way of an apology, offered more in hope than expectation, he told Lock: 'He's on 169; he won't make many more.' But there were more runs in Richards' locker. Great batsmen capitalise on mistakes; the bowling toils continued as he more than doubled his score.

Tony Lock had been dragged out of a greater despair when he arrived in the welcoming fold in Western Australia. One of the best indicators of the esteem in which he was held in Perth came in a tribute from Jack Lee in the *West Australian*. Lee said that the expatriate Englishman would have been the first man to be picked in the Australian side for the tour of New Zealand in 1967 if merit had been the sole consideration.

Lock had now enriched the Australian cricket scene for five years, setting records in the past two seasons for the number of wickets taken by a West Australian bowler. An auspicious beginning in the 1962/63 season was noted in an extract from the *WACA Annual Report*. 'The inclusion of English Test player Tony Lock in the West Australian team added greatly to the standard and variety of our attack. He took 32 wickets in the Sheffield Shield competition at an average of 27.59 off 276 overs and (those) figures included a splendid 7-53 against Victoria at Melbourne ... This very experienced cricketer was an inspiring team man. The Association was delighted when arrangements were made for him to return to West Australia next season.'

In his first three seasons Lock achieved a total of 64 wickets in the Sheffield Shield at an average of 29.48 and in all first-class matches for Western Australia he captured 72 wickets at a near identical average. A signal of his impact on the fortunes of the state was reinforced in the 1965/66 season when Western Australia were runners-up to New South Wales. The mighty eastern states now had to take notice of their hitherto undistinguished rivals across the Nullabor Plain. Lock, along with Graham McKenzie, reached the target of 100 wickets in the competition. Another milestone for Lock was his season's aggregate of 41 wickets at 22.36 runs each. He headed the bowling averages for the first time and surged ahead of Ray Strauss, the previous highest Western Australia wicket-taker with 33 wickets in the 1956/57 season. Lock held sway as a bowler in his last triumphant phase alongside Australian Test bowlers Laurie Mayne, Des Hoare and Keith Slater. Others to be introduced into his august company were the youthful Bob Massie and, briefly, Terry Jenner, two others who gained Test promotion. By

1966/67, while still dividing his cricket seasons in Perth and English county championship action at Leicester, Lock was close to scaling the peak of his endeavours.

The stamina of the veteran was severely stretched by the regime of eight-ball overs operating in Australia at the time. Yet he still bowled magnificently to take 51 wickets at an average of 21.29. The charge on his energies amounted to 398.4 overs, 105 of which were maidens. On three occasions Lock took five or more wickets in an innings and he became the first West Australian bowler to take 50 wickets in a Sheffield Shield season.

Tony Mann, one of Lock's admiring companions, speaks of how his captain, like a true professional, set himself ever more imposing targets. The ensuing challenge, which culminated in glory and wild glee in the torrid heat of Melbourne, was one that Lock relished to the utmost. After a long career in England as one of the troops, he must have done one of his jigs of joy as captain of a young company on that day.

Lock had won the veneration of his boys in the maelstrom of competition in what was, for him, the land of his dreams. He had brought his own bullying voice to endorse one of the Australian maxims of cricket. An acceptance of being a jolly loser was a state of mind for which one should be certified. 'We had a good discipline without strain and without any sort of parade ground stuff,' was how he mildly summed up his relations with his team. The celebrations soon to engulf them would lead to an approving media accolade. They were named, one and all, as 'Lockie's mob'. 'It sounded great,' said the proud captain, 'because I knew then that we were a real team.'

TWELVE

The Legacy of an English Lord

'The sporting links between England and Australia were given firm roots amid the ravishing dells and glades of Sheffield Park.'

The adulation accorded to Tony Lock when he raised the Sheffield Shield aloft in the ultimate triumph of his career was also a salute to one of the great benefactors of the game. Modern cricket owes an immense debt to Henry North Holroyd, the Third Earl of Sheffield. He was in many ways the godfather of Test cricket, a man who brought an international dimension to a hitherto largely national game. The long-standing Anglo-Australian tradition and link between the two countries stems from the generosity of a dedicated enthusiast. The monumental silver trophy bearing his name and the Sheffield and Australian coats of arms was the coveted prize in inter-state competition in Australia for over a century.

An article in *The South Australian Register* on 16 July 1894 referred to the presentation of the trophy to Sir E.T. Smith, the President of the South Australian Cricket Association. 'Our cricketers gained temporary custody of it by brilliant cricket last season ... The Shield is a beautiful and handsome trophy worthy of the noble donor and of the inter-colonial matches, supreme skill in which is the requisite for possession of it. It measures forty inches by thirty inches. The centre-piece represents the charming cricket ground, with its pretty pavilion, which is on the domain of the Earl of Sheffield at Fletching in Sussex.'

'On each side of the centrepiece are eight golden tablets, on which are to be inscribed the names of the winning teams, while on both sides of these again are a batsman and bowler, the former with his bat upraised over his shoulder preparatory to a big hit, and the bowler with his right arm raised just prior to delivering the ball. Above the centrepiece in gold are a wicket, a bat and a ball; over these the Sheffield and Australian Arms, with beneath them respectively the Earl's motto, *Quem to Deus Esse* and Advance Australia. The whole is surmounted by a miniature statue of the Goddess of Liberty.'

The Sheffield Shield had first been awarded for competition in 1892. The first contestants were Victoria, South Australia and New South Wales. It followed one of the Earl's splendid cricket adventures. He funded, at a personal cost of £16,000, a full England tour of Australia in 1891/92. His loss of £2,700 did, as one observer remarked, make the tour quite an expensive gesture of goodwill.

The tour plan had first been aired during the Australian tour of England in 1890. After the match at Sheffield Park, the Earl remarked: 'that he must take a team to Australia, and give battle to the colonists on their own ground.' It was also a recuperative trip for Sheffield. He explained his mission in a letter published in an Australian newspaper. 'I have long wanted to see your country and your cricket, and as I was compelled by failing health to decide upon taking a long sea voyage and spending a winter away from England, it occurred to me that I could combine a voyage for health with a visit of English cricketers.'

The previous decade had brought a growing American investment in Australia, a development which, since the last English cricket tours in 1887/88, had included a well-funded visit of a USA team of baseballers. Sheffield's cricket tour was seen as a counter to this intrusion. The Earl considered the time was ripe to use the weight of cricket once more to support British influence in the colonies, stimulating with it the growth of Australian national sentiment and the moves for federation.

One Australian observer described their benevolent visitor as a 'genial, jovial and hearty soul.' He also noted the strain of eccentricity: 'He cares little about the vanity of wearing apparel, but dresses himself in comfort, and a style all his own. He wore an alpine hat with the colours of his eleven (yellow, red and dark violet) as a band, dark blue shooting coat and roomy nankeen trousers. A newspaper parcel was in one pocket, and a warm-tinted kerchief in the other.'

W.G. Grace had been specially recruited by Sheffield as captain for the tour as the star attraction for a new generation of Australian supporters. At forty-three and increasingly portly, the great man was past his peerless best. He did, though, remain the greatest identity in the game. His batting record was unsurpassed: in the twenty-seven seasons before 1891, he had scored 36,942 runs at an average of 42.65. He had also taken 2,291 wickets at 16.30. Some argued that, by going to Australia, he was putting his reputation 'needlessly at risk.' W.G. was given the incentive of a tour fee of £3,000 to compensate him for the long absence from his medical practice. The enormity of the payment did have an adverse effect in hampering Lord Sheffield's efforts to recruit a team – esteemed professionals like George Gunn and Arthur Shrewsbury, for instance, were not attracted by an offer that was only 10 per cent of Grace's fee as an amateur. It was still a strong contingent in Australia: the party included other professionals, Bobby Abel of Surrey and Yorkshire's Bobby Peel. Others in the distinguished assembly included Andrew Stoddart, George Lohmann and the Scottish amateur wicketkeeper, Gregor MacGregor.

The series in Australia was marked by closely fought games. Australia won the first Test by 73 runs and repeated the success in second Test following an England batting collapse and the loss of three wickets for eleven runs. The revered Grace was reportedly severely criticised for batting in poor light in an unavailing bid to overhaul a target of 230. There was a belated England triumph in the dead rubber when they forced Australia to follow-on in the third Test but by then the delighted hosts had already won the series with two victories.

Before leaving Australia, Sheffield made a donation of £150. His first suggestion was to present three trophies at a value of fifty guineas each (to Victoria, New South Wales and South Australia). Victoria favoured this division of the monies. Eventually, ten months after the first news of the gift, the Australasian Cricket Council decided, by one vote, 'to devote the whole sum to the establishment of the Sheffield Shield, by way of a permanent commemoration of Lord Sheffield's visit.' Apart from the two World Wars, the Sheffield Shield was competed for by the leading colonies (later states) including Queensland from 1926/27, Tasmania on a provisional basis in 1977/78 and Western Australia (on a limited basis) in 1947/48.

There was great regret among the traditionalists when sponsorship demands in the form of the Pura Cup intervened in the late 1990s. Western Australia were the last winners of the historic trophy in the 1998/99 season.

Of all the private patrons of cricket, few, if any, exceeded the passionate devotion of the Sussex Lord. Born in 1832, the young Viscount Pevensey, as he was then known, had a gentleman's upbringing. He went to Eton College and then travelled through Europe with the Prince of Wales as his companion. He served in the Army in India and sat as a Conservative MP for Sussex East in the House of Commons. In 1876, on the death of his father, he succeeded to the title of Lord Sheffield.

Cricket was to remain a consuming interest throughout his life. The humble benefactor was completely disinterested in personal prestige. He disdained self-promotion and was famously reluctant to pose for photographs. His considerable wealth brought succour to the Sussex County Cricket Club, which might have had to withdraw from competition without his financial support. The liberality was unbounded in Sussex. There were also generous contributions to the professionals at Hove and the employment of Alfred Shaw of Nottinghamshire, and William Mycroft of Derbyshire, in the quest to foster local talent.

Unlike his fellow peer, Lord Harris in Kent, Sheffield never gained fame as a player but he was good enough to regularly represent the Gentlemen of Sussex XI. His one first-class appearance was for the Sixteen of Sussex against a United All-England XI at the delightfully named Dripping Pan ground at Lewes in 1854. He failed to score in either innings, being twice dismissed by Jemmy Dean. Sheffield held the county presidency for three periods, first as the Viscount Pevensey from 1857/58, and then from 1879 to 1896 and finally in 1904, five years before his death in Beaulieu, France, at the age of seventy-seven. He was buried in the family vault inside the village church at Fletching, a few miles from his cricket ground at Sheffield Park. The association with other influential patrons in Yorkshire in the next century was established on his mother's side of the family. Lady Harriet was the daughter of Henry Lascelles, the Second Earl of Harewood.

The sporting links between England and Australia were given firm roots amid the ravishing dells and glades at Sheffield Park in a picturesque little corner of Sussex. The then-Viscount Pevensey was a thirteen-year-old Eton schoolboy at the time of the first recorded match at the park in 1845.

The transition to the ground that was to become Sheffield's pride went through several stages over the next thirty years. Charles Payne, the Sussex professional and a member of the cricketing family from East Grinstead, remembered scoring a century on another ground, soon to be disused, on the estate before being bowled out by the Lord Sheffield.

In 1876 it was reported that Sheffield was determined to commission a private ground, designed to the highest possible standards, at his park. Another Sussex professional, Charles Ellis, had previously made extensive alterations to the site and this was complemented by a massive operation involving 16,000 tons of earth to fill in a depression on the northern part of the ground. The vast improvements made in the succeeding years led one contemporary to observe that it was unrivalled as a pleasure ground for cricketers.

The sylvan splendours of Sheffield Park would soon rival its modern counterpart – aristocratic Arundel – as the gateway for Australians and other tourists to an English cricketing summer.

The idyllic reign of Sheffield Park at its Victorian heyday lasted but fifteen years from 1881 to 1896. It could, however, boast an international cricket guest list of household names at the time. The representative matches between Lord Sheffield's team and the Australian tourists, five of them in the 1880s and '90s, were played on a ground described as 'good if a trifle fiery in dry weather and, like all wickets, apt to crumble.' One may surmise that the 'cordial happiness', as one writer described the atmosphere at Sheffield Park, was muted after the Australians won by an innings and 34 runs in the fixture in 1890.

Sheffield's men were dismissed for 27 in an humiliating debacle. Matters would have been even worse but for the customary resolution of the champion, W.G., who scored 20 of the total. The torture on this day was inflicted by one of the most famous of Australian bowling partnerships. The fear in the hearts of the demoralised batsmen was a familiar sight for Charles Turner, aptly named the 'Terror', and the successor to another demon bowler, Fred Spofforth. He took 4-9 and his left-handed ally, John Ferris, mingled pace and spin in his return of 4-18. Billy Murdoch, who had first appeared at Sheffield Park in 1884, was the Australians' top scorer with 93 out of a match-winning total of 191.

Murdoch was a renowned Australian captain who took the opposite course to Tony Lock in transferring his allegiance to England and Sussex. He was born at Sandhurst, Victoria, but his cricket as a young man was exclusively identified with New South Wales. The first official indication of Murdoch's intentions came in a letter published in the *Sussex Daily News* from Lord Sheffield on 16 February 1891. He enclosed a note for publication from Murdoch and said: 'All those who are interested in Sussex cricket will read its contents with the greatest satisfaction.' Murdoch had promised the Earl that he would advise him, presumably in the context of an earlier discussion, about a move to Sussex.

The 'good tidings' referred to by Sheffield in the newspaper, were contained in the letter from the Australian. 'I am writing to let you know that very shortly I shall be resident of your county. I need hardly say how very pleased I shall be to represent Sussex on the cricket field as soon as ever I'm allowed to do so, which I am afraid cannot be before the season of 1893.' Murdoch's debut was eagerly awaited. Eleven years earlier Sussex had had to watch and wonder at his mastery when he scored an unbeaten 286 against them at Hove.

Murdoch played in 18 Tests for Australia and was the first player from any country to score a double century in Tests. For some time he shared with W.G. Grace the distinction of being the only batsman to score over 300 in a first-class match – for New South Wales against Victoria. Six years earlier, Grace had twice hit a triple century for Gloucestershire against Yorkshire at Cheltenham and for the MCC against Kent at Canterbury. Murdoch toured with five Australian teams from 1878 to 1890 and topped the batting averages on all apart from the first trip.

He was dropped by Australia, supposedly on the count of age, after the last tour and migrated to England. At thirty-six he countered the snub of his home selectors when he was capped by his adopted country against South Africa at Cape Town on the 1891/92 tour.

C.B. Fry, one county colleague, was a staunch admirer of the Australian who went on to captain Sussex for seven seasons. 'Every dressing-room he entered was full of fun,' he said. 'Mark him now,' continued Fry. 'A square-round – the double term applies – a powerful, well-knit figure as active as most men half his age and every bit as keen.' As Fry also remarked, nothing about Murdoch was commonplace. 'He drank, smoked, talked and wore a hat distinctively and did nothing by formula.'

The tables were turned against Australia in Lord Sheffield's parish in 1893 when the combined batting forces of Grace, Arthur Shrewsbury and William Gunn, supported by nine wickets for Bill Lockwood, brought victory by eight wickets. Sheffield had thoughtfully strengthened his ranks on this occasion; they included ten Test players, nine of whom had played in the series against Australia that season.

The hospitality at Sheffield Park at its Victorian zenith lingered long in the memories of cricketing visitors. There was a compulsion to accord the best possible entertainment for guests at the park. All were well wined and dined. It was the perfect overture to a tour, brimful of camaraderie in post-match revelry at the nearby Sheffield Arms. The social scene reached its height at the park with the visit of the Prince of Wales (later King Edward VII) to watch the Australians in 1896. Genuflecting in the customary approval were the remarks of one observer: 'The great Australian colonies cannot fail to appreciate the compliment paid to their representatives by the Heir Apparent to the Crown of the British Empire, and the people of Lord Sheffield's native county rejoice in the recognition which has thus been given to the noble earl's patriotic endeavours to strengthen the ties which bind the colonies to the Mother Country.'

The report in the *Sussex Agricultural Express* described the glittering May Day occasion: 'The sun shone and the beautiful cricket ground, the lakes below with their grand cascades, the parterres radiant with spring flowers, and the noble trees in the first flush of their garb of tender green, with the mansion at a distance above the water-system, made the picture, or rather a series of pictures, worth going miles to see.'

Lord Sheffield must have taken pride in this lovely setting, the cricket ground on its high plateau overlooking his home and 'environed with a belt of venerable trees whose branches almost speak the age they took to grow.'

Sheffield Park is one of the oldest estates in the country. It is on record that the land was, at one time, the property of the Godwin, the Earl of Kent, and was later bequeathed by William the Conqueror to his half-brother, the Earl of Cornwall. During the previous thousand years it had constantly changed hands through many distinguished families. One of the curious and interesting features of the mansion was the frieze running round the house. These included the arms of all its various owners since and before the Norman Conquest.

The elaborate preparations for the visit of the Prince of Wales in 1896 included the erection of seven triumphal arches. The first at the station entrance to the park was composed of evergreens – bay, yew and box – and studded with bunches of wild flowers, bluebells, primroses and cowslips. Another larger arch, particularly beautiful, was a masterpiece of floral design. The base was the dark blue of the Australian colours, as were the pillars wreathed with flowers and interlaced with Lord Sheffield's colours – red, yellow and purple – and tied with silk ribbons. At the summit was the Australian coat of arms, flanked by the Earl's flag and that of Australia.

The arrangements at the cricket ground were of similar opulence. On the east side a space was set apart for the Prince's pavilion and dining saloon. The front was shielded with Japanese bead curtains. Inside it was fitted with Axminster carpets, with panelled and decorated walls, hung with pictures and rare trophies and costly ornaments, brought home by Lord Sheffield from his travels in the East.

It was estimated that a crowd of 25,000 was present on the opening day of the match against the Australians. Admission was free and the Earl had thoughtfully allocated places for his tenants and local children from Fletching and Danehill in spaces roped off behind his private pavillion. By early morning the spectators were flocking in by road and rail. Scores of carriages took up positions in the welcome shade of the trees on the route to be taken by the Prince. He arrived at 11.30 a.m. and was greeted by his host at the station. The 1st Sussex Engineers were the guard of honour and its band played the national anthem as the royal party entered the state carriage drawn by 'four greys with postillions and outriders' and drove to the park.

Two illustrious Sussex and England amateurs, K.S. Ranjitsinhji and C.B. Fry, were in Sheffield's XI for this last first-class fixture at Sheffield Park. But the match was conspicuous for the brilliance of F.S Jackson, the elegant Yorkshire stylist. He drove handsomely in an innings of 95 not out. Jackson would reach the pinnacle of his career in 1905 when, as England's captain, he dominated the series against Australia. He won every toss, headed both the batting and bowling averages, and retained the Ashes.

Jackson and Fry related that the Sheffield Park match was the occasion of the memorable encounter between W.G. Grace and Ernest Jones, a fiery opponent. At the start of the home side's first innings Jones had bowled a vicious bouncer which brushed or passed through the Doctor's famous beard. 'Whatever are ye at?' called out W.G. in his high-pitched voice. 'Steady, Jonah,' was the warning from George Trott, the Australian captain. The offender thereupon uttered his celebrated apology: 'Sorry Doctor, she slipped.' Grace, then aged forty-seven, massive in build and less mobile than in his prime, had suffered several bruises on the chest from Jonah's express deliveries. He was asked later how he had withstood such a dreadful barrage. W.G. made the classic reply: 'Well, he did rap me a bit sharp but I don't mind even now how fast they bowl to me; it's the slow ones I don't like, I can't get at them as I used to!'

The programme at Sheffield Park at the turn of the twentieth century included numerous minor matches. In 1885 during a match against Birch Grove (later the country estate of the British Prime Minister, Harold Macmillan) one Sussex stalwart of the time, W.A. Humphries, scored 239 not out, the highest individual innings on the Sussex ground. Around the same time a match was staged between Sheffield's XI and the Parsees from India. One resident in the neighbouring village of Fletching remembered how the game was abruptly stopped on the stroke of noon for the devotions of Parsee fielders bowing towards Mecca.

The outbreak of the First World War in 1914 lowered the curtain on a great era at Sheffield Park. The old ground was ploughed and put down to wheat as a means of aiding the war effort. Cricket was, though, given another innings with local cricket between the wars on the high plateau above the gardens at Lord Sheffield's ground. Play continued until the Second World War, when the gardens were requisitioned by the War Office and became the headquarters for the Canadian Armoured Division before the D-Day invasion of Europe, and were also used as a prisoner-of-war camp. One relic of the old glories, the foundations of Lord Sheffield's private pavilion, were still to be seen in recent times. The ladies' pavilion, built in 1881/82, was still standing in the 1950s. It was an ornate edifice in an octagonal design, the lavatories having marble floors with gold and blue basins. The spiral staircase from the building can now be viewed in the cricket pavilion at the nearby Forest Row ground.

One of Sussex's finest cricket nurseries will soon be rediscovered to perpetuate the tradition begun by a visionary man. The restoration of the Sheffield Park ground was largely completed in 2006 and a new pavilion is about to be constructed. The inviting prospect of the reopening ceremony and a celebrity match in an idyllic setting beckons.

THIRTEEN

The Shield Goes West

'It has been a long hard struggle for the state's cricketers. Lock's leadership and the ability to make a tough and uncompromising bid for victory was based on teamwork.'
– Leader in *West Australian*, March 1968

The great tradition established by the Sussex Lord was fittingly embellished by another pioneering Englishman. He would, in a fascinating coincidence, ignite an explosion of cricket pride in Western Australia during the 1960s. Tony Lock, in his own inimitable style, complemented the zeal of Lord Sheffield in returning the historic Shield to his adopted state. Twenty years had elapsed since Western Australia last won the trophy in their inaugural season in the competition in 1947/48.

This was Lock's first season as the state captain, having replaced Murray Vernon, and it followed his farewell season in Leicestershire. The march to the title began in an auspicious fashion against Victoria at Perth in October. Ian Brayshaw became the first West Australian to take all ten wickets in an innings in the victory by 136 runs. His victims on a good wicket included eight men who had played Test cricket and seven who had made at least one century in first-class cricket.

Brayshaw's 10-44 runs in 17.6 overs was considered a triumphant recapture of swing by a player who had suffered from an enforced role as an opening bowler in the previous season. Only two other bowlers – Tim Wall for South Australia against New South Wales at Sydney in 1932/33, and Peter Allan for Queensland against Victoria in 1965/66 – had achieved the feat in Sheffield Shield cricket.

Tony Lock recalled that he had played in four games – three of them in one season – in which a bowler took ten wickets in an innings. 'Indeed,' he said, with a rueful backward glance. 'Had it had not been for the solitary first I took in the second of those games (for England against Australia in 1956) I could have witnessed Jim Laker taking all twenty.' In the same year Laker also took ten wickets for Surrey against the Australians at the Oval. The third occasion was when Lock himself took all ten for Surrey against Kent at Blackheath. 'At the end of that magical season I never thought I would see that happen again,' added Lock.

Eleven years later at Perth Ian Brayshaw was the bowler who defied that prediction. He modestly remembers that there was 'something mesmeric about my miserable medium-pace and swinging deliveries and we kept on taking wickets.' Brayshaw took 2-2 on the first evening. The following day, as both he and Lock recalled, there was a capricious wind that kept fluctuating between the east and south-west. According to the West Australian captain, it compelled him to switch Brayshaw to different ends six times during the course of a remarkable bowling feat.

Brayshaw concedes that the tactic did work in his favour. He does, however, contend that at other times it was not a good procedure to establish the required rhythm as a bowler. 'Lockie had this drill of using me in short spells. He made the assumption that it worked better that way.' In a postscript to his performance against Victoria, Brayshaw says that he was not sure whether Lock was keen to bowl himself on that day. 'He and I were vying to bowl from the same end as "into the wind" bowlers.'

Among the charges levelled at Western Australia prior to the season was that the team suffered from an inferiority complex. Richie Benaud, in New South Wales, considered this state of mind to be a barrier to the progress of the Cinderella state. Brayshaw acknowledges the frailty: 'We were following the wake of a not very competitive record in the Shield.'

Lock's response to the allegation was to insist that there would be no room for sentiment under his captaincy. Jack Lee, writing in the *West Australian*, referred to what he described as psychological warfare waged by Lock. It was, he said, designed to inculcate a 'hate-the-opposition' outlook. The measures alluded to by Lee included non-fraternisation with opponents and early nights for his team: 'Lock has pursued a tough policy, starting with an 11.30 p.m. curfew for WA players before each playing day.' Unknown to Lock, his young teammates kept him under scrutiny to see that he observed the curfew. On the night before a match at Sydney, Lock dined with a local cricket writer. At about 11 p.m. he realised that he would have to hurry to be back at the hotel in time. He arrived at 11.28 to be greeted by teammates eagerly scanning their watches.

Western Australia, after gaining a win over Victoria, made it two in a row when they beat New South Wales at Perth. They next gained first-innings points over Queensland in the following home fixture. South Australia were the stumbling block to dispel any notion of complacency. Ironically, it was off-spinner Ashley Mallett, returning to his home city, who took eight wickets in the victory by 95 runs at Perth. In the return match at Adelaide there was an even more humiliating setback as South Australia won by an innings and 29 runs, with a day and a half to spare. Fifteen wickets fell on the opening day, with the honours first going to the visitors in the opening joust. South Australia slumped to 29/5 and Graham McKenzie took the first four wickets. The breakthrough was halted by Greg Chappell (154) and Barry Jarman (113) who shared a sixth-wicket partnership of 215 at more than a run a minute to seal a match-winning revival.

Lock and his team had to wait six weeks without any first-class cricket before beginning their tour of the eastern states. The lull gave time for reassessment and, after the reverse at Adelaide, a happy gain in confidence. The return to the West Australian ranks of former Test bowler Laurie Mayne was widely considered to be the catalyst for the recovery. In the final section of the Shield programme, Mayne proved to be an inspired selection. He and Graham McKenzie were the bowling spearheads who swept aside the top order before Lock consolidated the advantage.

Another powerful factor was the form of John Inverarity, who was Western Australia's most prolific batsman that season with 779 runs at an average of 59.59. Inverarity was the Perth-born son of former Western Australia captain, Mervyn Inverarity. John graduated from the first eleven at Scotch College to the Claremont-Cottlesloe first-grade team and thence to the state side in 1962/63. In all of these teams he was linked with Ian Brayshaw as a colleague and their comradeship blossomed in practices together at the Claremont Oval.

Inverarity's batting was built upon intense concentration. There was general surprise when this security foundered in a match against South

Australia at Adelaide. He missed a simple half-volley from Greg Chappell and was bowled. After Inverarity reached the pavilion gate the body of a swallow, freshly dead, was found on the pitch near the batting end. The umpires agreed that the ball had struck the swallow before it reached Inverarity and he was recalled to the wicket. The bird was subsequently stuffed and mounted in a glass case that is on display in the committee room at Adelaide Oval.

The tide was now turning in favour of Western Australia and it was confirmed in early February with a stunning victory over New South Wales at Sydney. Inverarity and Irvine overcame a parlous position of 8/3. Both hit centuries in a stand of 242, Western Australia's highest for the fourth wicket, and extending over six and half hours. It was achieved with a stoical disregard for injuries; both batsmen had to weather severe handicaps, Inverarity with a bruised right hand and Irvine with a dislocated finger and chipped bone in his right hand.

Wisden reported the ensuing downfall of New South Wales. 'They were humiliated when the visitors, with bowling and fielding of the highest order, and aggressive captaincy by Lock, bundled them out for 121 and 131.'

Mayne richly merited his recall to the team with 6-59 and McKenzie, at the other end, dismissed seven batsmen in the match. Lock was stealthy in support, taking 3-27 in fourteen overs in the second innings. There were another seven wickets for Mayne and nine for Lock when the action moved to Brisbane. Western Australia won by 144 runs but not before Peter Burge scored a century in his last first-class match. It was his twenty-second century in interstate cricket.

Few Australians have ever hit the ball harder than Burge and he is reckoned by his contemporaries to have prospered more than most against the wiles of Lock in Sheffield Shield cricket. By the time of his second visit to England in 1961 Burge had become one of the most dangerous batsmen in the world. His brilliant driving power put England to the sword in the second Test at Lord's. He came to the wicket, with Australia 19/4, requiring a further 52 to win. Statham and Trueman, still feared adversaries, were in opposition but each of them was punished as Burge savagely drove and hooked Australia to victory by five wickets.

The finale to a gladdening season for Western Australia was staged in the mighty citadel at Melbourne and against a formidable Victorian eleven. On paper they appeared to be an infinitely superior combination.

They were led by Bill Lawry and included seven other players with Test experience – Ian Redpath, Bob Cowper, Keith Stackpole, Paul Sheahan, Alan Connolly, Graeme Watson and Leslie Joslin. With only one match to play, only Victoria stood in the way of Western Australia's first full-status victory in the Shield.

Victoria led the table but only so narrowly that the title could be won by either side, not simply through outright victory but with a first-innings win in a drawn game. Western Australia were seeking to exceed their previous success in the first season in the competition in 1947/48. This had been the yield of a modified programme of four matches, fewer than other states, and the win-loss ratio was adjusted to produce an equitable winner.

There had been a prolonged drought in Melbourne before the conclusive match. In the previous week bush fires had raged in the Dandenong Ranges, twenty miles east of the city. Billowing smoke rose as high as an estimated 8,000ft in the hills behind Ferntree Gully and could be seen in the centre of Melbourne. 'Most of Victoria resembled a giant tinderbox,' reported the *West Australian*.

The temperature, soaring into the forties, rendered even more inexplicable the decision by Lawry to put Western Australia in to bat after winning the toss. Tony Mann, twelfth man at Melbourne, believed that Lock 'coddled' his rival captain into making the decision, possibly with the mischievous plea that he had many inexperienced players in his team. 'Lockie was a master manipulator of the opposition. I think Lawry expected to knock over a few of our fellas early.'

Ian Brayshaw recalled: 'It was dusty and baking hot and we had to put up with the clanging and banging of demolition workers on the ground. It was a day to say: "We've won the toss, the wicket is a beauty; let's get out there and bat for two days."' Brayshaw remembers the prayers offered up for the coin to fall in Western Australia's favour. The outcome of the toss was awaited in an atmosphere of feverish anticipation. 'Lockie kept us in suspense. He was po-faced as he walked back to us. He entered the dressing-room and said: "Boys, we've won the Shield."'

Lock, in one post-match television interview, was asked if he would have batted had he won the toss. He was dismissive of the question. 'I called "heads", as I always do. When Bill won he asked for a few minutes to make up his mind. I said that must mean that we would bat and he agreed.' The rival captains moved back to the pavilion. Lock quietly remarked: 'Well, Bill, thanks very much!'

John Inverarity, the 'marathon man' as Western Australia totalled 405, remembers the general disbelief at Lawry's decision. 'The wicket was hard and dry. Tony was weeping with joy when he came back to our dressing-room.' The glee was redoubled on receipt of a long telegram crowded with good luck messages from Perth. It was flourished with delight as an augury of success.

Inverarity was close to exhaustion at the end of the first day. 'It was like a cauldron out there. One of my batting partners, Ron Bowe, was so overcome by the heat that he cramped up in both calves and thighs and had to be carried off the field.' Bowe, the Fremantle club captain, was a newcomer as an opening batsman and playing in only his second Shield match. He hit 86 and was actually associated in two stands, one for the second wicket and the other for the fifth wicket, with Inverarity. In the first before his retirement the total was advanced by 53 and then, on his return, the pair scored another 148 runs. Inverarity's 173, including 142 in just over five hours on the first day, was considered a masterpiece in courage and concentration in the enervating conditions.

Equally praiseworthy was the bowling of Alan Connolly whose return of seven wickets for 100 runs in forty-four overs represented for *Wisden* 'an outstanding effort of perseverance against riskless batting'. His accuracy was such that only thirteen runs were scored in a spell of ten overs. 'It was in this period,' reported the *West Australian*, 'that Inverarity showed his great powers of concentration and it is to his credit that his play was dedicated to the team's cause and not to impress with fluent stroke-making.'

Victoria conceded arrears of 209 runs on the first innings and were asked to follow-on. Bill Lawry valiantly tried to stem the Western Australian advance with a typically obdurate century in the second innings. But the visitors, in the end, required only eighteen runs to win by ten wickets.

Tony Lock, in reaching yet another summit in an amazing career, chose the occasion to express his brilliance as a bowler. At the time of his new conquest the Australian selectors had announced their team to tour England in 1968. It included two West Australian representatives, Inverarity and McKenzie. The *West Australian* regretfully noted the lack of spin claimants for selection. 'The worst feature of the selections was that on Australian form it did not include one slow bowler sure of commanding a Test place.' The correspondent said that there were no specialist contenders playing in any of the five Sheffield Shield teams. The irony of the dilemma was that in their midst was an English exile who was reputed to be one of the finest left-arm spin bowlers – and possibly without equal – to play in Shield cricket.

Throughout his time in Western Australia Lock had duelled with batsmen of Test calibre. He was a beguiling assassin. The guile and nagging length so often had a hypnotic effect. 'His mastery of flight,' commented one colleague, Tony Mann, 'sucked them in time and time again.' Lock could judge precisely when his opponents sought to take the initiative against him and they invariably paid the price with their wicket. It was also a mistake to rile Lock when he was on the warpath.

During the match at Melbourne he was bowling when one Victorian barracker called out: 'Go home, you Pommie bastard.' Richard Lock says that his father knew then that he had beaten them.

The economy of Graham McKenzie kept one end secure as Lock stamped his signature on the crucial match at Melbourne. In just under two hours before lunch McKenzie sent down twelve overs for 35 runs and one wicket – that of Lawry who was brilliantly caught by Inverarity. Laurie Mayne, McKenzie's partner, sealed his comeback to the team with five wickets, including four of the top order, in Victoria's first innings. It brought his tally to twenty wickets at an average of 20.26 in the last three matches of the season. His lion-hearted bowling led the *West Australian* to demand the inclusion in the touring party to England of this 'almost forgotten figure of Australian cricket.'

Lock did profit from the dedication of his fellow bowlers but none of them would deny that it was his supremacy which tilted the match in Western Australia's favour. He finished with a match return of 9-119 and they included the key scalps of Test players Paul Sheahan and Keith Stackpole. He was close to being the leading wicket-taker for the third successive season. Only Alan Connolly, his Victorian rival, with 46 wickets, exceeded Lock's aggregate of 42 wickets at an average of 17.19.

The Sheffield Shield results at the end of the season put Western Australia in the lead with 54 points, eight ahead of Victoria. The record in the eight-match programme included five outright victories. There was also one win on the first innings and two losses both at the hands of South Australia, whose five successes included two outright wins after being behind on the first innings. Befitting a title-winning season, the Western Australia averages reflected a stellar year for bowlers. Despite Lock's stunning performance, he had to settle for second place behind Laurie Mayne's 20 wickets gained at the superior average of 15.10. Even the great Graham McKenzie, in arguably his finest season for the state, had to settle for sixth place in the averages. McKenzie's 37 wickets at 23.02 would, in most seasons, have been good enough for him to head the table.

'The Shield Comes Back' was the headline above the leader article in the *West Australian* on 1 March 1968. 'It has been a long hard struggle for the state's cricketers. The reward has come this season in what was a consistently impressive performance of five victories out of eight and culminating in an outright win against Victoria on a ground that has often put our cricketers and footballers at a disadvantage. West Australian cricket has grown up. It might have reached maturity when the standard in the bigger states has declined but this does not detract from the patient administrative and coaching efforts of the association.'

The article enthused about Lock's leadership and commended teamwork as the prime reason why the team were able to make a tough and uncompromising bid for victory. It expressed its satisfaction that the fruits of this success were the inclusion for the first time of two West Australians in an Australian touring party to England. 'We will all be barracking for Australia soon and it is gratifying as we bask in our Sheffield Shield achievement, to know that we are sending away a great fast bowler and a batsman of high promise, both of them local products.'

There was a delicious frenzy about the celebrations following the triumph in Melbourne. A drinks rendezvous was arranged when the plane carrying the team landed to refuel in Adelaide. Ian Brayshaw recalled: 'We flew home that night after the victory. Tony Mann was in our side. His own family vintners knew Eileen Hardy, the doyenne of the famous South Australian winemaking family. She was in Adelaide when we stopped before travelling on to Perth. She arranged for a special room to be put at our disposal at the airport.'

The celebrants remember scenes of great conviviality. Their hostess had supplied a truckload of wines. The glasses were raised in toast after toast before the happy party resumed their journey home. 'There was this telegram – several feet long – awaiting us and bearing the signatures of thousands of our supporters from a Perth radio station,' recalls Ian Brayshaw. Despite this, he says, the team was unaware of the hullabaloo raised in their honour. 'I estimate that there were 5,000 people waiting to greet us. A live telecast was organised by Channel 7. Bo Lock was so pissed that he could hardly speak to his West Australian audience. We were celebrating a stunning victory which paved the way for Western Australia to become a cricketing force then and in later years.'

The Shield triumph was one of the great moments in Lock's career, to vie with his championship years with Surrey. Only the most ardent enthusiasts on the western seaboard gave him any chance at all. Victoria had won the Shield twenty times since its inception in 1892/93. The state was riding high in popular esteem and was reputed to be the best state side since Lindsay Hassett's line-up in 1950/51.

Five batsmen – Sheahan, Cowper, both with close on a 1,000 runs, and Lawry, Stackpole and Redpath – between them scored 3,800 runs in the season. Before the opening match against Western Australia at Perth, former Test spinner Doug Ring pronounced the Victorian batting strong enough to beat the world record one-innings score of 1,107 set by their state predecessors against New South Wales in 1927. Ian Brayshaw's ten wickets provided a timely rebuke for the arrogant prediction. The Victorians proceeded to fall short of the record by a margin of 955 runs in their first innings.

The Shield euphoria in Perth in March coincided with a surprise development – Lock's recall by England as a replacement for Fred Titmus who had had four toes sheared from his foot in a boating accident in the West Indies. Lock's two young sons, Graeme and Richard, received the news with extreme disfavour. They firmly announced their own loyalties. It was, to their innocent minds, a betrayal. 'Dad,' they said. 'You're a traitor, how could you play for the Poms!' An ironic cartoon in the *West Australian* was more complimentary about the selection of their father. Two men were shown investigating a heavily padlocked door bearing the sign, 'The best left-arm spinner in the world.' The caption read: 'It's about time that was picked.'

Lock, unlike his sons, was quietly pleased at the recall. Yet he had little time to digest the offering amid the Shield celebrations. He remembered a 'fantastic reception and a Beatles-style welcome.' At one light-hearted reception in Perth, Mr A.D. Drew, the team manager, said that among the congratulatory messages received in Melbourne was one from the WA National Football League. It read: 'Congratulations, you have done what we have been trying to do for years.' It was a reference to their many unsuccessful attempts to beat the Victorians at football on the MCG.

Lock was constantly the focus of attention from the clamouring television and radio crews. He reflected on a triumph of team spirit. 'We were not a group with a few stars, or eleven individuals, but a team, and this is the greatest compliment I can pay them. It was a real pleasure to lead such a good side.' Lock had to juggle preparations for his journey with many receptions over the next two days. On the Saturday night he returned to Perth airport to start his flight via London to the West Indies.

The globetrotting veteran was just four months short of his thirty-ninth birthday when he played in the last two Tests at Port of Spain, Trinidad, and in Georgetown, Guyana. Pat Pocock, his former Surrey colleague, was reunited with Lock at the England team quarters at the Windsor Hotel in Barbados – owned by former West Indian captain, John Goddard. It was an effusive meeting. Pocock, popularly known as 'Percy', had returned to the hotel after an evening function. 'There was a huge corridor at the hotel and as I entered at one end I heard a tremendous shout from the other side.' 'Percy!' was the cry that echoed down the corridor. 'Lockie was so unpredictable but on this occasion he greeted me just like a long-lost friend.'

The affectionate salutation grew in fervour when Lock and his former pupil were associated in a rescuing ninth-wicket stand in the fifth Test at Georgetown. England held a 1-0 lead in the series by virtue of their win by seven wickets in Trinidad. The West Indies counter-attacked furiously in a bid to retrieve the situation at Georgetown. Starring for them were the irrepressible Sobers and Kanhai who both hit centuries in a stand of 250 for the fourth wicket. England, in their turn, seemed to have reached a position of parity after Boycott and Cowdrey added 172 together in the reply. This earlier dominance was undermined by a middle-order collapse.

At 259/8, reported *Wisden*, 'England were in grave danger. Lock, however, proceeded to bat with typical belligerence, and Pocock with such obduracy that he spent eighty-two minutes before scoring his first runs.' In the history of Test cricket only Godfrey Evans, who took ninety-seven minutes against Australia at Adelaide in 1946/47, had waited longer.

Pocock's resistance was the ideal foil for Lock in his merry innings. In the last hundred minutes of the fourth day the pair added 93, of which Lock drove and slammed 76. The next day the stand advanced to 109,

England's best for the wicket against the West Indies. Lock, batting for two and a half hours, superbly struck 89, his highest score in first-class cricket. Jim Laker, his old bowling partner, later wrote: 'If I know my Tony, that innings in Georgetown probably gave him more satisfaction than any bowling performance in any Test.'

It is certainly true that Lock was pleased and proud as to settle accounts with the bat as with the ball. Of the fulfilling bout of batting fireworks at Georgetown, Pocock recalls: 'It would be an understatement to say that Lockie was belligerent at the crease. He had a bolshie's approach. It didn't matter who was bowling and he had to contend with two formidable fast bowlers in Wes Hall and Lester King in this Test. My job was to avoid taking singles off the last ball of an over. I didn't take them because Lockie was smashing them all round the ground. He was just as aggressive as a batsman as he was as a bowler.'

The West Indies were restricted to a lead of 43 on the first innings but Sobers was again in magnificent form in the second innings. He was unbeaten on 95 and England, trailing by 407, were attempting to save the game on the sixth and final day. It seemed a forlorn hope when they lost five wickets for 41 runs. Lance Gibbs, with his looping off-spin, took four of the wickets at a cost of just twelve runs before lunch.

Alan Knott, the puckish adventurer in this and other rallies, was once again England's saviour. 'All seemed lost when Knott joined Cowdrey but he was to stay there until the end, nearly four hours later,' reported *Wisden*. Seventy minutes still remained for play when Gibbs finally breached Cowdrey's defences. Somehow, Knott extracted enough help from the tail-enders to guide his team to safety.

Crisis, though, did loom when Pocock was given out to a 'first bounce' catch by Clive Lloyd. He had just survived a legitimate dismissal, a faint edge to the wicketkeeper. Jeff Jones, the last man and the worst of 'rabbits', seemed an unlikely candidate to prevent defeat. The Welshman was encouraged by Knott and just managed to scramble through the last over bowled by Gibbs. Knott was determined not to lay waste all the hard toil of a gruelling tour. He called up his trembling partner for a mid-wicket conference. Pocock recalled: 'Knotty put his mouth to Jones's ear and softly crooned: "We'll keep a welcome in the hillsides …"'

The anxieties were not over in the England camp. There was consternation among the bewildered crowd and wild, unruly scenes at the end of the game. 'Frustration had welled up – they couldn't bear losing the series,' says Pocock. An estate car sponsored by a cigarette company was waiting to carry members of the England team back to their hotel. It was emblazoned in the bright yellow and red logo of the company and all too easily recognisable as the visitors' transport. 'There was a mass of people – around 500 – outside the ground and it was impossible to move,' remembers Pocock. 'A police car reversing at improbable speed cleared a path for us. I had two bags, one of which was carried by the bellboy who had asked for a lift back to the hotel.'

It was speedily clear that this was a situation fraught with danger. The waiting players also included John Snow and Tony Lock. Pocock says the riot only lasted a few minutes but that it was unbelievably frightening. 'A shower of stones began landing on the car and hitting us. Suddenly, a big rock hit Lockie on the back of the head and a stream of blood spurted from the wound. Someone picked up a tubular steel chair and threw it at the bellboy standing beside me. Within seconds a posse of mounted policemen, armed with batons, arrived on the scene. They rode their horses straight at the crowd. The angry supporters were bouncing off the chests of the horses like rag dolls.'

'I remember slumping in the back seat of our car speechless with fear. I draped a towel round the stricken hotel boy. We got into the car and the driver with his hand on the horn drove straight through the crowd. They dispersed. We travelled fifty yards and turned right to go back to the hotel only to face another large crowd. They didn't identify us as English cricketers sitting among them and peppered the area from which we had just driven.' The players were mightily relieved to escape the attentions of the unsuspecting mob and find welcome sanctuary at the hotel.

Tony Lock did not wilt on any cricketing battlefront but this was clearly a little out of the ordinary. He was, though, as imperturbable as usual in the affray, wrapping a handkerchief around his bruised head. 'Lockie was completely unfazed by this nasty episode,' declares Pocock.

The interlude in the West Indies was a signal from the English selectors that the achievements in Western Australia of the bowler discarded six years earlier had not gone unnoticed. But Lock, who would take out Australian citizenship in 1982, was now hailed as a kindred spirit in his adopted land. He could forget the injustices of the past. If he was not able to recapture the heady fervour of the Shield-winning season there were still plenty of reasons to smile. The hurrahs still rang out as he approached retirement. Western Australia were twice runners-up to South Australia and Victoria and third to South Australia in Lock's last three seasons as captain. In 1968/69 he won renewed acclaim in taking 46 wickets, including eleven against Queensland, to surpass his record in the Shield victory season. His nearest challenger, Laurie Mayne, claimed 33 wickets and was nearly thirteen runs per wicket more expensive.

Before the curtain fell on his career, Lock presided over the introduction to first-class cricket of three future Test players, Rod Marsh, fresh, young pacemen Bob Massie and Dennis Lillee, who would torment England at Lord's in 1972. He also forged a regular partnership with a late developer, the leg-spinner, Tony Mann. Both Lillee and Mann were prominent in victories over South Australia and Queensland. Lillee gave a foretaste of his menace against South Australia, obtaining steepling lift from the pitch in taking 7-36. Mann gained another kind of purchase with his leg-breaks and deceptive wrong 'un to return figures of 5-65 against Queensland.

Lock's stewardship undoubtedly fostered the enduring strengths of a one-time cricketing outpost. In eleven seasons from 1967/68 Western Australia won the Shield six times and finished second and third twice, and fourth on another occasion. Of the eighty-nine Shield games played in that period, Western Australia won forty-five outright. In two seasons – 1976/77 and 1977/78 – the state won both the Shield and the Gillette Cup. John Inverarity, highly regarded as a shrewd analyst, was a worthy successor to Lock. He was at the helm in another great era and led the team in four successful Shield campaigns.

The credibility of the state as a nursery of Test-match talent was given an impetus in the reigns of Barry Shepherd, Tony Lock and John Inverarity. Seventeen Test players, ultra-competitive and battle-hardened, emerged as proud representatives of the state. Six of them – Marsh, Lillee, Massie, Inverarity, Ross Edwards and Graeme Watson – played for Australia in the fifth Test against England at the Oval in 1972.

Tony Lock's final summer with Western Australia, in 1970/71, coincided with the inaugural Test match at Perth. It was fitting that his farewell should be crowned with a distinction he had done so much to promote with his exploits in the state. The transformation in playing fortunes at the WACA was a direct result of the combined leadership skills of, first, Barry Shepherd and then Lock. Two men, each of them ferociously competitive, had ushered the state into the limelight to bring to an end the years of isolation.

Anthony J. Barker in his book, *The WACA – An Australian Cricket Success Story*, recalled that the decision to pursue the goal of a Test at Perth in earnest was the sequel to the Shield triumph which had confirmed Western Australia's rise as a cricketing power. There was understandable concern about the costs of the necessary ground improvements. But the campaign had been so strongly advocated by political leaders and the community that it was inconceivable that the project would be abandoned. It came down to a matter of state pride and a conviction that it was buttressed by a booming economy in the state.

A December day dawned to plunge Perth into high excitement as its citizens gave a 'fantastic welcome' to Test cricket. There was 'turmoil', reported *The Daily News*, as 'thick queues of people spilled on to the road' hours before the game was due to start. A Narrogin farmer arrived at 7.30 a.m. armed with a movie camera to record the first ball delivered by Western Australia's leading contemporary player, Graham McKenzie. His reputation and the presence in the Australian team of local wicket-keeper Rod Marsh contributed to the fervour of the occasion. 'It is not recorded,' wrote Barker, 'whether the farmer's camera was in focus as McKenzie delivered the famous first ball' – surprisingly into the breeze, rather than downwind – but 'business in the city came to a virtual standstill at 11 a.m. as thousands of workers listened on the radio to the start of an historic game.'

As a prelude to the Test, Western Australia took the honours in the drawn game against the MCC at Perth. Inverarity hit 93 and Tony Mann struck a violent century off 92 balls. It included two sixes and thirteen fours. A second-wicket stand of 108 between Edrich and Fletcher for the visitors was followed by a collapse as the MCC lost four wickets for 42 runs. *Wisden* reported: 'Only the stubbornness of Taylor and Shuttleworth in support of Luckhurst prevented Lock and his enthusiastic side giving WA their first win over the tourists.'

All roads led to the WACA for the eagerly awaited inaugural Test, described by *Wisden* as an outstandingly successful promotion. 'It was perfectly organised and 85,000 watched play over the five days.' The attendance was nearly twice that at the preceding Test at Brisbane and the gate receipts in the region of £50,000 were almost three times larger.

The excitement was tinged with sadness at the impending retirement of Tony Lock. 'The state was very fortunate in having Tony's services in the last years of his career. He leaves cricket as captain of the state side that he has led to wonderful achievements,' was part of an extensive tribute paid to Lock in the *WACA Annual Report*. In Western Australia, Lock took 326 wickets in first-class cricket at an average of 24.77 and scored over 1,500 runs. His Sheffield Shield record was 302 wickets at a cost of 23.87 runs each in 66 matches. The report added: 'These figures represent a remarkable achievement for a slow left-arm spinner under Australian conditions.'

The survey was even more remarkable when posited against the fact that at least half of the matches in which Lock played were on the less than friendly WACA pitches of the time. The passage of years reinforces his prowess, newly won, as a veteran who rose above adversity. Even to this day only Jo Angel (419 wickets in 105 matches), Terry Alderman (384 wickets in 97 matches) and Dennis Lillee (323 wickets in 70 matches) have taken more Sheffield Shield wickets for Western Australia. None but Lillee played in far more matches than Lock to give further proof of a career that resisted the march of time.

Richie Benaud, an opponent cast in a similar mould, was the spokesman in another fine tribute to a great cricketer. 'We could do with a few more characters of his style in the game today. I hope his retirement brings him some repayment for the thousands of hours of entertainment he has provided for the people who pay money at the turnstiles.'

There was one final act of homage on the last day of the final match against Victoria. Mr C.R. Bunning, the President of the WACA, conducted the retirement ceremony. He presented Lock with a clock and the ball with which he took his 300th wicket in the Sheffield Shield competition. The exile was now an Australian hero. He was unmistakably one of them. As someone wittily put it, 'In Perth, you clap yourself on.' The applause still rumbles on his memory.

FOURTEEN

Shadows Across His Name

'My reputation has been destroyed, but I'm lucky [that] I've got friends who won't give a stuff and they're the only people who matter.'
– Tony Lock

'Lockie's dead,' announced the voice on the telephone on an evening in March 1995. The recipient of the call was Ian Brayshaw, the former West Australian cricket colleague and then an ABC radio and television commentator. 'I was reading the Channel 10 sports news that night. I didn't bother taking the make-up off and drove straight to the hospital.'

It was a sad moment for Brayshaw, one of Lock's closest friends in Australia. They had shared so much fun on and off the cricket field over the years and he revered his old captain. At the hospital he joined the distraught family group waiting in an anteroom. After a while they were admitted to the ward. Brayshaw remembers: 'Lockie was lying on the bed in full cricket regalia. He had joggers on instead of boots but that was the only item missing.' It was an astonishing and poignant moment to look down on his friend in repose but still arrayed in cricket garb. He was immaculately clad in a long-sleeved cream shirt bearing the monogram 'TL' and flannels.

The eeriness of the scene in the hospital room was accentuated by the display of Lock holding a cricket ball in his left hand. 'Someone must have watched him closely during his playing days,' recalls Brayshaw. 'I could exactly picture Lockie as a bowler even to the extent of his fingers on the ball. They had got it to perfection.'

The sad tidings of the death of a great cricketer were flashed across the world. Two Ashes winners had fallen inside three months. The passing of Lock had been preceded by the loss of Peter May, his former Surrey and England captain during another series in Australia. The Charterhouse School prodigy, unfailingly courtly in manner, matched Lock in the steel of his cricket. The two players, socially divided but once united in Surrey's great years, were still only in their mid-sixties. At Kennington Oval the flags fluttered at half-mast in homage to Lock, just as they had been in Melbourne on Boxing Day to salute another peerless cricketer.

The last years of Lock's own life had been beset with troubles that gathered with hurricane force. The cancer, which eventually killed him, brought release from a relentless persecution. Casting a deep shadow were the sexual abuse allegations. 'We were all devastated when we heard the news,' said Julia White, a friend of the cricketer from girlhood. 'I never believed it for a moment. I knew him far too well.'

Julia White was not alone among other friends, cricketing wives and supporters, who remain incredulous about unproven allegations. For them, the events unfolded in a poisonous atmosphere. The charges of indecent assault purportedly involving the ten-year-old daughter of a close friend, were first laid in February 1993. Lock was arrested but acquitted by ten votes to two after the jurors had deliberated for more than eight hours. In an interview with Australia's *Sunday Times* newspaper, Lock related the shock of the first arrest. 'I was photographed, given a number, fingerprinted and chucked in a locked cell. It was embarrassing and very, very frightening.'

Lock was re-arrested two days later on a second offence said to have taken place nearly fourteen years earlier. The girl in question alleged that the abuse had occurred at Lock's home. She, or her advisers, ignored the fact that he had not moved into the house at the time. Lock was remanded on this offence until December and then further remanded until a preliminary hearing the following February.

There were further postponements until June and the following month it was discovered that Lock had been diagnosed with an inoperable cancer between his shoulder and collarbone. The treatment involved a round trip of eighty miles for exposure to radiotherapy. Lock and his wife, Audrey, moved to a smaller house to be nearer their son, Richard. They were barely settled there when Audrey suffered a stroke brought on by the stress of the court proceedings. She died in September.

The headlines in the Australian tabloid newpapers paraded the sombre news: 'Lock for trial – Only three months to live.' At the next court hearing, on 22 December, the jury were unable to reach a verdict. Six defence witnesses testified that Lock was not living in the house at the time of alleged offence. Julia White related: 'Eventually, and unbelievably, the judge told the jury that the exact date was not vital to their deliberations. They could convict, he said, if they believed the incidents followed closely on the dates between April 1980 and February 1981.'

There was some good cheer for the besieged Lock from an old cricket friend in Surrey. Dave Sydenham had invited him to attend the 150th anniversary celebrations in July of the following year. It was a much-appreciated gesture at a critical time. Julia White knew that there was little or no chance that her friend could make the long journey but agreed to accompany him to the function.

The following extracts from the diary of Julia White convey mingled relief and distress at the trauma of the last days:

> 1 February: Tony phoned me at 6.55 in the morning to say that all the charges had been dropped. They had been dropped after the questioning of the child and because of his failing health and the expense to the state of a retrial. I thought at least Tony wouldn't die with the charges hanging over him. Micky (Stewart) said that he and other Surrey cricket friends, including Ron Tindall, who lived in Perth, would now aim to 'kick start' Tony back into a normal life again.

> 14 March: Tony has become very introvert and frightened to go out.

> 26 March: Jackie (the Locks' adopted daughter) phoned to say that her father was going into an hospice on the following day. He died on 29 March.

After the hearing in his favour Lock had said: 'It is gratifying to know that my fight for justice has been won. I will never forget what I've been through. At least I can hold my head a bit higher when I walk down the street. My reputation has been destroyed but I'm lucky that I've got friends who won't give a stuff, and they're the only people who matter.' He had borne this harrowing ordeal stoically but it brought him close to financial ruin. His son, Richard, had mortgaged his own house to help meet his father's legal fees, and precious items of cricket memorabilia had had to be sold.

One of the tragedies of the affair was that it ended any association with minors. Lock had always enjoyed an affinity with children, boys and girls. Encouraging their interest in cricket was a special pleasure. His coaching in West Wales in the 1980s had earned him warm approval from the parents of his pupils. 'Dad liked nothing better than going down to work with autistic children, teaching them hand-to-eye coordination,' remembers his son, Richard. 'He had untold patience with these kids. His rapport with children was, I think, because he responded to their innocence.'

Before the darkness of his nightmare, Lock had lived quietly in Gidgegannup in the hills east of Perth. He had been accorded the honour of life membership at the WACA. He swaggered happily like a true countryman around the vast acres of his property. There were horses in the paddock for his equestrian daughter, Jackie, and quarters for his beloved dogs. Richard Lock remembers that his father was never happier in these years, walking around his estate in the hills and sporting a large bush hat, its rim dipped against the sun. 'We always had dogs at home. Dad taught one of them to bring his morning paper.'

The droll humour surfaced in the company of his family. Pet names seemed to amuse him and were freely distributed among his grandchildren. One of them, Brendan, was called 'hunkynuts' after the fruits that dropped from the gum trees. His brother, Ryan, was known as 'Huckleberry', twinning him with Mark Twain's fictional urchin. Their mother, Wendy, was rechristened 'Liz'. 'If he called you by your proper name, you knew you had done something wrong,' she says.

Richard Lock, as a seventeen-year-old, played alongside his father in grade competition games. 'It was probably my greatest thrill and a privilege to be in the same team. He treated me, expletives and all, just the same as anyone else.' The reflexes of Lock Senior, then in his mid-forties, were not quite so sharp by this time. 'Dad once dropped two catches off my medium-pace bowling, the only ones he missed in the whole of that season.' One impudent critic sought to make capital of one of the lapses, off a fiercely struck shot, which was really only half a chance. Richard loyally said: 'He is the only player on the field who would have got anywhere near the ball.'

The insistent message conveyed by Lock to his sons, Richard and his elder brother, Graeme, was that they should not play cricket because he was their father. His fear was that comparisons would be made with him. 'You must play cricket because you love it – that must be your motivation.'

'Dad very rarely came to see us play,' says Richard. 'He said that, having played cricket at the highest level, he would be too critical of his sons.' It was a different matter when the sports were Australian-rules football or hockey. 'He would come to these games and yell his head off because he did not know anything about them.'

At cricket, Lock would always express his satisfaction, provided his boys performed to the best of their abilities. There was particular delight when Richard scored a century, a distinction never achieved by his father. Richard scoffed at the praise, saying that it had only happened in a minor sixth-grade game. 'Yes,' said his father, 'but you know it was a hundred and it is something you should cherish.'

Mellowness settled on Lock in his final years; the fieriness had been quelled and he was polite and tolerant towards other people. The diagnosis of cancer, which added to his burden, made him aware of the need to adopt a respectful attitude. A man who had been quick to anger in other years was becalmed amid his trials. On one occasion after a court proceeding, Richard and his father were walking up St George's Terrace, one of the main thoroughfares in Perth. A posse of reporters and photographers accosted them. 'They were trying to take Dad's photo. I was getting very agitated and angry about the intrusion.' His father was unruffled and quietly said: 'They are only doing their job. Just keep walking and don't worry.'

A deeper concern for Lock was the death of his wife, Audrey, after forty-two years of marriage. She had stood firmly by his side and never wavered in her belief in his innocence. One friend tried vainly to comfort Lock. 'You've still got your children and grandchildren to live for.' Lock replied: 'But I've just lost my best friend.' There were other rallying voices among his former West Australian cricket colleagues. Dennis Lillee was especially sympathetic and maintained contact with his friend in the final days. Lock also found great comfort in the support of the Dean of Perth, the Very Reverend Dr John Shepherd, who conducted the funeral services of Tony and his wife at the Anglican Cathedral in Perth.

A Christmas interlude in Melbourne, the occasion of his daughter Jackie's wedding, brought a welcome respite from the turmoil of the protracted court proceedings. Richard remembers the discussions with their father's solicitor. He strongly advised that an appeal should be mounted in the event of a guilty verdict. Richard answered: 'If that happens, let it go.'

Prolonging the agony was, in the view of the son, an unbearable course and bound to inflict further harm. Richard had watched his father deteriorate in health. He added: 'So, if he's found guilty – and I don't believe he is – we're not going to fight it. I want to spend whatever time is left with my father and enjoy his company.' He had already been given an indication that a prison sentence had been ruled out. The mounting legal costs meant that much of his father's cricket memorabilia had to be sold. 'We lost things that we can never replace. The trophy cabinet was Dad's pride and joy.'

Tony Lock had apologised to his family for having his name dragged through the gutter because of the criminal charges, none of which were proven. The private hell into which he was thrown caused immense emotional strain. In the final weeks of his life he became a virtual recluse. 'Towards the end there would be days when Dad never left the house,' says Richard. 'I would go round to see him. The temperatures would be in the forties. The house would be locked up and he would be sitting there watching television. He was too scared to go out in case someone recognised him and would want to know what was going on in the court case.' Richard attempted to bolster his father's dwindling morale at this sad time: 'Regardless of what the outcome is in the trial, our love for you is unconditional.'

The life of a demoralised man ended two days after being admitted to a Perth hospice. His ashes, along with those of his wife, were given a temporary abode in the lounge at his home before being transferred to the custody of his daughter Jackie in Melbourne. A flowering plum tree was one of her father's favourites. The ashes were to be laid beside the tree in Jackie's garden.

Richard had joined his sister for the final parting. 'It was an emotional time. Jackie and I couldn't look at each other without crying.' Brother and sister were united in grief as the days went by, but at last the ceremony could be delayed no longer. The farewell to their father was left until the last morning on the day that Richard and his family returned home to Perth.

The passing of a great cricketer in such tragic circumstances drew a line under years of persecution. Tony Lock had lived in the public eye all his life and had always found the resilience to bounce back from cricketing setbacks. He was hugely protective of his reputation and the family name. In the end he was consumed with worry. There was a bitter exclamation that he would be remembered only for the charges against him and not for his cricket achievements. All who had admired him in happier times knew that he was wrong. The proud, volatile and vulnerable man was an astonishingly durable cricketer and it is this memory that will endure.

Epilogue: Memories of the Born Winner

Tony Lock was the stout-heart who typified Surrey's approach in their great years in the 1950s. The big man, with his bald pate glinting in the sunshine and his sleeves buttoned down as he bowled, was endowed with a boundless fury. It was said of him that he possessed the mindset of a fast bowler.

Jim Laker: 'Over a period of twenty-five years Tony Lock's career has not, in my view, ever been truly appreciated. He was just about the greatest competitor I ever saw, he never shirked an issue and never failed to give his best. I have seen him bowl a thirty-over spell with knees and ankles strapped up to such an extent that many would not have attempted to walk down the pavilion steps.'

John Arlott: 'As a cricketer, he is the ultimate enthusiast, cricket mad, a furious and never-flagging trier and as absorbed in the game as any man who played it.'

David Foot: 'The impassioned competitive persona was Lock's strength as a team man. He could win games on his own and was an integral part of Surrey's pre-eminence as they kept on winning the championship.'

Brian Chapman: 'Above all, the man who wears his bald pate like a warrior's helmet will go down as cricket's supreme fighter.'

Neville Cardus: 'Lock is still the only left-arm spinner who can be mentioned without some blasphemy in the context of the names of Charlie Parker and Hedley Verity. He is at the moment the last of a great and fascinating line.'

Trevor Bailey: 'He has left me with a host of wonderful memories: there was that catch he took off my bowling at Sabina Park, Jamaica, which removed the opening batsman for nought and started a collapse; the many times we batted and chatted together as we fought to escape defeat. I have watched him prepare to take the field, his whole body encased in a mystifying collection of bandages plus elastic stocking supports, while his spinning finger was treated by a formula intended to harden the skin and heal the cuts. Then there was the exuberant cry when we were back in our hotel, "a G&T would go down very well."'

Colin Cowdrey: 'In his own mercurial and somewhat autocratic way, he became an outstanding leader. At the same time he became an even more effective bowler than he had been in earlier years. It is astonishing to reflect that he has been the most successful slow left-arm bowler ever to have played in Australian cricket … His fielding will never be forgotten. If you were choosing the five greatest catchers of all time, Tony Lock has to be one of them. If there had been a "Catch of the Month" competition, his mantelpiece would be full of trophies.'

Micky Stewart: 'Lockie played in all of Surrey's seven consecutive championship victories and I was fortunate to play with him in the last five of them. I don't think in all the fifty years I have known the first-class game that I have come into contact with a more inspirational cricketer.'

On fielding: 'The spectacular ones, the sudden full-length dives were the easy ones. His best were when he took the rockets close in, without anyone noticing.'

Jim Parks: 'In his early bowling phase he had a nice straight arm and was a bowler with flight. Suddenly, the arm bent a little and he became absolutely lethal. He had an enormous drag, too, and he hurled the ball at you from about twenty yards. He had a toe plate and wore that out over the course of a season. I scored a few runs against him but you had to fight when the wicket was doing a bit. It was quite a contest.'

Sir John Major: 'He was one of our greatest bowlers and a close fielder of breathtaking brilliance.'

Pat Pocock: 'The remarkable thing about Tony Lock is that when he "threw" he was an Underwood type of bowler – by far the best bowler in the world on uncovered wickets. He went from being the best bad-wicket bowler to the best hard-wicket bowler in the manner of Bishan Bedi.'

Raymond Illingworth: 'Lockie was totally unplayable on a wet wicket. Others have likened him to Derek Underwood, who bowled at a similar pace, but Lockie was a genuine spinner of the ball even though he bowled it quickly. Even with a small target you were never safe against him.'

Peter Loader: 'I reckon you could wake Lockie up in the middle of the night, hand him a cricket ball to bowl by moonlight, and he'd drop it straight onto a length … His flight and drift was extraordinary. There was only one Australian batsman he couldn't bowl to, Peter Burge in Queensland. Lockie was an instinctive bowler. He was unable to analyse it – the bowling had to be worked out in practice with others.'

Jack Pollard: 'He was colourful and foxy in all that he did, arousing spectators with raucous appeals, stretching vocal chords to their limits and continually plotting the downfall of the opposition.'

Kirwan Ward: 'There was much in his character that was more typical of Australia than of England. He has the old, prickly, competitive attitudes that communicate themselves so quickly to Sydney's notorious "Hill". An unrelenting attacker, he bowls over after over with never a hint that his spinning finger is coated with Friars Balsam, or that his left knee is strapped with two yards of crepe bandage.'

Ted Dexter: 'The Perth wicket was one of the fastest and bounciest pitches in the world, yet here was by now an orthodox left-arm spinner being particularly successful. There was not another spinner in Australia nearly as effective as he was.'

John Inverarity: 'Tony Lock was a wonderful cricketer. He was an outstanding bowler and reinvented himself as a cricketer in Western Australia. In 1958/59 (Lock's only tour of Australia) he had bowled medium pace, with a very dodgy action. In WA he was a classic left-arm flight and spin bowler. His record in Sheffield Shield cricket was of the highest calibre. As a measure of his success it needs to be stressed that part of his bowling was on our wicket at Perth which was not really conducive to spin.'

On fielding: 'All the time I've played cricket I've never seen a better catcher. He was phenomenal despite not being too mobile because of his rickety knees. I would put Tony in the same category as our great Australian close fieldsmen – Bobby Simpson and Mark Waugh.'

Dennis Lillee: 'He taught me the need for a "hold-no-quarter" approach to playing the game. I had a lot of that in my make-up but to see my captain with the same attributes endorsing this was very important for a young player like myself. Lockie was happy with my attitude. It was what he wanted as, day by day, he revved up his troops.'

Ian Brayshaw: 'Lockie may not have been the best captain in the history of WA cricket, but, by golly, he taught a lot of young greenhorns how to be a lot harder and hungrier and, most importantly, how to win. His uncompromising approach gave a new dimension to our game and did most of all to pave the way for the golden decade that was to follow.'

Anthony J. Barker (Author of *The WACA – An Australian Cricket Success Story*): 'There is no doubt that Lock made a tremendous contribution to the success of the state team on the threshold of a fabulous era when he retired. Nobody could challenge his credentials as a great bowler who captured a record 326 wickets. While some would question his reputation as a captain, nearly all would recognise that he had real qualities of on-field leadership.'

Statistical Appendix

Compiled by Paul E. Dyson

A Brief Chronology

Born: 5 July 1929, Limpsfield, Surrey

Debut in first-class cricket: 13 July 1946, Surrey *v.* Kent, the Oval

County Cap for Surrey: 1950

Debut in Test cricket: 17 July 1952, England *v.* India, Old Trafford

One of five '*Wisden* Cricketers of the Year': 1953

County Cap for Leicestershire: 1965

Appointed captain of Leicestershire CCC: 1966

Appointed captain of Western Australia: 1967

Final day in Test cricket: 3 April 1968, England *v.* West Indies, Georgetown

Final day in first-class cricket: 1 March 1971, Western Australia *v.* Victoria, The WACA, Perth

Died: 29 March 1995, Perth, Western Australia

First-Class Cricket

Batting and Fielding

Season by season

Year	M	I	NO	Runs	HS	Ave.	50	Ct
1946	1	1	1	1	1*	–	–	1
1947	2	2	0	8	8	4.00	–	1
1948	2	3	2	20	14*	20.00	–	2
1949	25	33	14	212	29	11.15	–	28
1950	26	34	7	223	23	8.25	–	33
1951	32	38	17	192	31	9.14	–	33
1952	32	27	15	170	24*	14.16	–	54
1953	19	22	7	274	40	18.26	–	36
1953/54	9	12	2	105	40*	10.50	–	6
1954	32	35	7	353	46	12.60	–	42
1955	33	41	9	669	55	20.90	2	48
1955/56	11	15	2	237	62*	18.23	1	9
1956	26	33	6	338	43	12.51	–	44
1956/57	14	18	4	229	39	16.35	–	11
1957	31	32	6	464	46	17.84	–	63
1958	29	31	2	610	66	21.03	5	46
1958/59	15	18	1	191	44	11.23	–	9
1959	28	38	4	521	64*	15.32	1	34
1959/60	2	4	0	75	40	18.75	–	6
1960	34	41	6	474	60	13.54	1	37
1961	31	46	9	621	67*	16.78	1	48
1961/62	15	17	5	182	49	15.16	–	20

Year	M	I	NO	Runs	HS	Ave.	50	Ct
1962	32	36	2	563	70	16.55	3	33
1962/63	10	18	3	264	48	17.60	–	14
1963	28	36	5	656	60	21.16	5	19
1963/64	5	9	1	194	53	24.25	1	5
1964/65	8	13	2	208	41	18.90	–	8
1965	8	8	0	64	40	8.00	–	8
1965/66	10	13	3	215	44	21.50	–	17
1966	29	43	6	658	56	17.78	3	38
1966/67	8	13	2	136	66	12.36	1	9
1967	28	33	5	603	81★	21.53	2	33
1967/68	12	17	2	242	89	16.13	1	11
1968/69	10	11	0	153	37	13.90	–	13
1969/70	7	9	2	116	39	16.57	–	4
1970/71	10	12	2	101	24★	10.10	–	7
Totals	654	812	161	10,342	89	15.88	27	830

For Each Team

	M	I	NO	Runs	HS	Ave.	50	Ct
Surrey (Championship)	328	383	87	4,529	68	15.30	15	449
Surrey (other matches)	57	68	13	862	70	15.67	1	84
Leicestershire (Championship)	61	80	11	1,274	81★	18.20	5	68
Leicestershire (other matches)	4	4	0	51	21	12.75	–	9
Western Australia (Sheffield Shield)	66	97	14	1,271	66	15.31	1	80
Western Australia (Other matches)	8	11	3	196	53	24.50	1	4
MCC (in UK)	2	2	0	3	2	1.50	–	2
MCC (overseas)	46	54	9	704	62★	15.64	1	36
England XI	9	16	5	254	38	23.09	–	9
Players	5	8	3	107	34	21.40	–	8
The Rest (of England)	5	9	2	160	44★	22.85	–	5
South	3	5	2	38	16★	12.66	–	4
North	1	–	–	–	–	–	–	–
Combined Services	2	3	2	20	14★	20.00	–	2
A.E.R. Gilligan's XI	2	4	0	66	26	16.50	–	2
T.N. Pearce's XI	1	–	–	–	–	–	–	–
MCC All England XI	1	–	–	–	–	–	–	–

A Surrey XI	I	I	I	O	O★	–	–	I
Combined XI								
(Australia)	3	3	O	64	32	21.33	–	2

Summary

	M	**I**	**NO**	**Runs**	**HS**	**Ave.**	50	**Ct**
Surrey	385	451	100	5,391	70	15.35	16	533
Leicestershire	65	84	11	1,325	81★	18.15	5	79
Western Australia	74	108	17	1,467	66	16.12	2	84
Others	81	106	24	1,417	62★	17.48	1	75
England (Tests)	49	63	9	742	89	13.74	3	59
Totals	654	812	161	10,342	89	15.88	27	830

Against Each Opponent

(excluding Tests, listed by country)

	M	**I**	**NO**	**Runs**	**HS**	**Ave.**	50	**Ct**
Derbyshire	19	22	3	III	25	5.84	–	23
Essex	27	28	4	312	57	13.00	I	36
Glamorgan	25	29	5	439	66	18.29	2	27
Gloucestershire	22	32	7	465	81★	18.60	3	29
Hampshire	23	25	6	401	60	21.10	2	32
Kent	29	35	8	395	57	14.62	I	41
Lancashire	27	30	9	424	68	20.19	2	41
Leicestershire	22	21	4	242	60	14.23	I	27
Middlesex	30	38	7	507	56	16.06	I	36
Northamptonshire	22	28	6	338	56	15.36	I	33
Nottinghamshire	28	23	4	207	43	10.89	–	46
Somerset	22	24	5	357	46	18.78	–	28
Surrey	4	7	2	43	16	8.60	–	4
Sussex	21	26	2	372	67★	15.50	2	23
Warwickshire	21	27	10	382	57★	22.47	2	29
Worcestershire	24	29	7	312	43	14.18	–	26
Yorkshire	31	49	12	606	59	16.37	2	45
Cambridge University	16	15	2	240	70	18.46	I	26
Oxford University	10	13	2	154	29	14.00	–	14
MCC	16	18	6	242	34	20.16	–	13

MCC Australian Touring Team	1	2	1	19	10*	19.00	—	1
Gentlemen	5	8	3	107	34	21.40	—	8
North	3	5	2	38	16*	12.66	—	4
South	2	2	0	17	16	8.50	—	5
South of England	1	2	0	45	26	22.50	—	1
The Rest	3	4	2	67	38	33.50	—	3
Combined Services	1	1	0	0	0	0.00	—	3
Australians	8	12	1	199	53	18.09	1	13
Indians	6	7	3	63	30	15.75	—	11
New Zealanders	2	2	0	22	16	11.00	—	2
Pakistanis	3	2	0	10	6	5.00	—	—
South Africans	5	7	1	94	38	15.66	—	3
West Indians	5	8	0	83	35	10.37	—	8
Commonwealth XI	8	14	5	244	38	27.11	—	9
Australian XI	1	1	0	0	0	0.00	—	—
New South Wales	18	24	4	365	44	18.25	—	22
Queensland	16	19	5	296	66	21.14	1	20
South Australia	19	34	3	481	48	15.51	—	22
Victoria	17	25	2	235	44	10.21	—	16
Western Australia	1	1	0	7	7	7.00	—	1
Bombay	1	1	1	9	9*	—	—	2
North Zone	1	1	0	1	1	1.00	—	—
President's XI (I)	1	1	0	4	4	4.00	—	—
Punjab CA	1	1	0	19	19	19.00	—	2
Rajasthan	1	—	—	—	—	—	—	3
Services XI	1	1	0	11	11	11.00	—	—
West Zone	1	1	1	1	1*	—	—	1
Northern & Central Districts	1	1	0	0	0	0.00	—	1
Otago	1	1	0	3	3	3.00	—	—
Wellington	1	—	—	—	—	—	—	2
Amir of Bahawalpur's XI	1	1	0	41	41	41.00	—	2
Combined XI (P)	1	1	0	6	6	6.00	—	—
Combined Railways and Baluchistan	1	1	0	22	22	22.00	—	2
East Pakistan	1	1	0	36	36	36.00	—	—
Governor-General's XI Pakistan	1	2	0	13	11	6.50	—	—
Services XI	1	1	1	62	62*	—	1	—
Pakistan (non-Test)	4	7	1	38	20	6.33	—	3
President's XI (P)	1	2	0	44	25	22.00	—	2
Border	1	1	0	6	6	6.00	—	1

Combined Universities	I	I	0	8	8	8.00	—	2
Eastern Province	I	I	0	5	5	5.00	—	I
Griqualand West	I	I	I	12	12★	—	—	I
Natal	2	4	I	82	29	27.33	—	—
North-Eastern Transvaal	I	—	—	—	—	—	—	—
Rhodesia	4	6	0	75	40	12.50	—	7
South African XI	I	2	0	5	5	2.50	—	I
Transvaal	I	I	0	24	24	24.00	—	2
Western Province	2	3	2	61	39	61.00	—	2
Barbados	I	2	0	22	18	11.00	—	I
British Guiana	I	I	0	4	4	4.00	—	—
Jamaica	I	I	I	40	40★	—	—	—
Trinidad	I	I	0	8	8	8.00	—	I
Windward Islands	I	I	0	4	4	4.00	—	—
All Ceylon	I	I	0	0	0	0.00	—	2

Summary

	M	I	NO	Runs	HS	Ave.	50	Ct
British Teams	454	542	119	6,836	81★	16.13	21	603
Overseas Teams	151	207	33	2,764	66	15.94	3	168
Test matches	49	63	9	742	89	13.74	3	59
Totals	654	812	161	10,342	89	15.88	27	830

On Each Ground

a) in England and Wales, listed by county

	M	I	NO	Runs	HS	Ave.	50	Ct
Chesterfield	3	3	I	30	25	15.00	—	5
Derby	3	4	0	26	15	6.50	—	4
In Derbyshire	6	7	I	56	25	9.33	—	9
Brentwood	I	I	0	3	3	3.00	—	I
Clacton-on-Sea	4	6	I	49	19	9.80	—	6
Colchester	I	I	I	0	0★	—	—	—
Ilford	4	4	I	41	24★	13.66	—	5
Leyton	I	I	0	40	40	40.00	—	I
Romford	I	2	0	6	5	3.00	—	I
Southend-on-Sea	2	2	I	27	26	27.00	—	3
In Essex	14	17	4	166	40	12.76	—	17

Cardiff	3	4	1	39	28	13.00	–	2
Ebbw Vale	1	1	0	1	1	1.00	–	–
Llanelli	2	2	1	29	22	29.00	–	–
Pontypridd	2	2	1	46	44	46.00	–	3
Swansea	4	6	0	163	66	27.16	2	5
In Glamorgan	12	15	3	278	66	23.16	2	10
Bristol	3	3	0	51	51	17.00	1	–
Cheltenham	3	4	2	93	81★	46.50	1	2
Gloucester	4	6	0	58	17	9.66	–	12
Stroud	1	2	1	7	6	7.00	–	1
In Gloucestershire	11	15	3	209	81★	17.41	2	15
Bournemouth	2	3	1	88	51★	44.00	1	4
Portsmouth	5	7	2	131	46	26.20	–	8
Southampton	6	5	1	107	60	26.75	1	5
In Hampshire	13	15	4	326	60	29.63	2	17
Blackheath	13	16	5	183	57	16.63	1	24
Canterbury	2	4	0	67	42	16.75	–	–
In Kent	15	20	5	250	57	16.66	1	24
Old Trafford	17	20	9	243	68	22.09	1	25
Ashby-de-la-Zouch	2	3	0	21	11	7.00	–	1
Coalville	2	1	0	0	0	0.00	–	2
Leicester	42	54	9	811	60	18.02	4	63
Loughborough	1	2	0	10	10	5.00	–	–
In Leicestershire	47	60	9	842	60	16.50	4	66
Lord's	35	44	10	595	46	17.50	–	38
Kettering	2	3	0	2	2	0.66	–	2
Northampton	7	10	1	196	56	21.77	1	9
Peterborough	1	–	–	–	–	–	–	–
Rushden	1	2	1	13	13★	6.50	–	1
In Northamptonshire	11	15	2	211	56	16.23	1	12
Newark	1	–	–	–	–	–	–	2
Trent Bridge	13	10	1	86	43	9.55	–	23
In Nottinghamshire	14	10	1	86	43	9.55	–	25
Bath	1	1	0	24	24	24.00	–	3
Taunton	6	6	0	105	46	17.50	–	5
Weston-super-Mare	2	3	0	71	36	23.66	–	6
In Somerset	9	10	0	200	46	20.00	–	14
Guildford	18	21	8	171	40	13.15	–	24
Kingston-on-Thames	4	6	4	21	13★	10.50	–	6
the Oval	200	227	46	2,481	70	13.70	6	285
In Surrey	222	254	58	2,673	70	13.63	6	315
Hastings	12	20	3	315	31	18.52	–	11
Hove	8	11	2	171	67★	19.00	1	7
In Sussex	20	31	5	486	67..	18.69	1	18

	M	I	NO	Runs	HS	Ave.	50	Ct
Coventry	1	2	0	25	17	12.50	—	—
Edgbaston	9	10	2	116	56	14.50	1	12
Nuneaton	1	2	1	43	25*	21.50	—	—
In Warwickshire	11	14	3	184	56	16.72	1	12
Dudley	1	1	1	0	0*	—	—	—
Kidderminster	1	1	0	7	7	7.00	—	1
Worcester	10	15	3	118	36	9.83	—	7
In Worcestershire	12	17	4	125	36	9.61	—	8
Bradford	2	3	1	34	19	17.00	—	2
Headingley	10	13	3	276	55	27.60	2	12
Scarborough	4	3	2	30	28*	30.20	—	4
Sheffield	6	10	1	123	32	13.66	—	8
In Yorkshire	22	29	7	463	55	21.04	2	26
Fenner's	11	11	1	134	36	13.40	—	17
The Parks	1	1	0	21	21	21.00	—	5
Torquay	5	8	1	146	38	20.85	—	8

b) Overseas, listed by country

	M	I	NO	Runs	HS	Ave.	50	Ct
Adelaide	11	20	2	247	48	13.72	—	12
Brisbane	9	12	2	131	66	13.10	1	8
Melbourne	9	13	1	119	44	9.91	—	11
Perth	47	66	9	997	53	17.49	1	48
Sydney	10	13	3	202	44	20.20	—	9
Sydney No 2	1	2	1	8	8	8.00	—	—
In Australia	87	126	18	1,704	66	15.77	2	88
Colombo, Ceylon	1	1	0	0	0	0.00	—	2
Ahmedabad	1	1	1	1	1*	—	—	1
Bombay	2	3	2	54	23	54.00	—	3
Calcutta	2	3	1	14	11	7.00	—	2
Delhi	1	—	—	—	—	—	—	—
Hyderabad	1	1	0	4	4	4.00	—	—
Jaipur	1	—	—	—	—	—	—	3
Jullundur	1	1	0	1	1	1.00	—	—
Kanpur	1	1	0	49	49	49.00	—	1
Madras	1	2	0	11	11	5.50	—	2
In India	11	12	4	134	49	16.75	—	12
Auckland	1	—	—	—	—	—	—	—
Christchurch	1	1	0	15	15	15.00	—	4
Dunedin	1	1	0	3	3	3.00	—	—
Hamilton	1	1	0	0	0	0.00	—	1

Wellington	I	—	—	—	—	—	—	2
In New Zealand	5	3	0	18	15	6.00	—	7
Bahawalpur	I	I	0	41	41	41.00	—	2
Chittagong	I	I	0	36	36	36.00	—	—
Dacca	2	3	0	4	4	1.66	—	3
Karachi	3	5	2	31	18*	10.33	—	3
Lahore	I	I	0	0	0	0.00	—	—
Lyallpur	I	I	0	19	19	19.00	—	2
Multan	I	I	0	22	22	22.00	—	2
Peshawar	I	2	0	20	20	10.00	—	I
Rawalpindi	I	2	0	44	25	22.00	—	2
Sargodha	I	I	I	62	62*	—	I	—
Sialkot	I	I	0	6	6	6.00	—	—
In Pakistan	14	19	3	285	62*	17.81	I	15
Benoni	I	—	—	—	—	—	—	—
Bulawayo	2	3	0	33	24	11.00	—	I
Cape Town	3	4	2	69	39	34.50	—	4
Durban	I	2	0	51	29	25.50	—	—
East London	I	I	0	6	6	6.00	—	I
Johannesburg	I	I	0	24	24	24.00	—	2
Kimberley	I	I	I	12	12*	—	—	I
Pietermaritzburg	I	2	I	31	21*	31.00	—	—
Port Elizabeth	2	3	0	31	14	10.33	—	I
Pretoria	I	2	0	5	5	2.50	—	I
Salisbury	2	3	0	42	40	14.00	—	6
In Rhodesia & South Africa	16	22	4	304	40	16.88	—	17
Bridgetown	2	4	I	22	18	7.33	—	I
Castries	I	I	0	4	4	4.00	—	—
Georgetown	3	4	0	108	89	27.00	I	2
Kingston	3	4	I	48	40	16.00	—	3
Port of Spain	3	3	0	21	10	7.00	—	2
In West Indies	12	16	2	203	89	14.50	I	8

Summary

	M	I	NO	Runs	HS	Ave.	50	Ct
United Kingdom	508	613	130	7,694	81*	15.92	23	681
Overseas	146	199	31	2,648	89	15.76	4	149
Totals	654	812	161	10,342	89	15.88	27	830

Highest scores

89   England *v.* West Indies at Georgetown, Guyana, 1967/68

81★   Leicestershire *v.* Gloucestershire at the College Ground, Cheltenham, 1967

70   Surrey *v.* Cambridge University at the Oval, 1962

68   Surrey *v.* Lancashire at Old Trafford, 1962

67★   Surrey *v.* Sussex at Hove, 1961

66   Surrey *v.* Glamorgan at St Helens, Swansea, 1958

66   Western Australia *v.* Queensland at the Gabba, Brisbane, 1966/67

64★   Surrey *v.* Gloucestershire at the Oval, 1959

62★   MCC 'A' *v.* Pakistan Services XI at Sargodha, Punjab, Pakistan 1955/56

60   Surrey *v.* Leicestershire at Grace Road, Leicester, 1960

60   Surrey *v.* Hampshire at the County Ground, Southampton, 1963

60   Surrey *v.* Lancashire at the Oval, 1963

Two Half-Centuries in a Match

66 & 56   Surrey *v.* Glamorgan at St Helens, Swansea   1958

Note: Lock followed this with 5 & 57 against Kent at Blackheath, thus scoring three half-centuries in four innings – his best sequence.

Pairs

Surrey *v.* Gloucestershire at the Oval, 1949
MCC *v.* Pakistan at Dacca, East Pakistan, 1955/56
Western Australia *v.* Victoria at the MCG, Melbourne, 1966/67

Notes: a) At Dacca, Lock was bowled by Khan Mohammad in each innings.
           b) Melbourne began a sequence of four ducks in six innings.

10,000th run

28th run during innings of 35, Western Australia *v.* West Indians at WACA Ground, Perth, 26 October 1968.

Century Partnerships

119   For the eighth wicket with J. Birkenshaw, Leicestershire *v.* Gloucestershire at the College Ground, Cheltenham, 1967

109   For the ninth wicket with P.I. Pocock, England v. West Indies at Georgetown, Guyana, 1967/68

Note: The stand with Pocock is still the record for England's ninth wicket against the West Indies.

Bowling

Season by season

	Overs	M	Runs	Wkts	Ave.	BB	5wi	10wm
1946	10	2	24	0	–	–	–	–
1947	56	15	128	4	32.00	2-52	–	–
1948	64	12	168	11	15.27	6-43	2	–
1949	754.5	287	1,672	67	24.95	4-27	–	–
1950	919.2	371	1,762	74	23.81	6-40	3	–
1951	1,155.4	448	2,237	105	21.30	6-32	5	–
1952	1,109.4	416	2,237	131	17.07	6-15	6	1
1953	732.2	284	1,590	100	15.90	8-26	8	2
1953/54	490.1	158	1,178	28	42.07	5-57	1	–
1954	1,027.1	412	2,000	125	16.00	8-36	7	2
1955	1,418.4	497	3,109	216	14.39	8-82	18	6
1955/56	557	296	869	81	10.72	8-17	10	4
1956	1,058.2	437	1,932	155	12.46	10-54	15	5
1956/57	+352.7	120	833	56	14.87	6-14	4	2
1957	1,194.1	449	2,550	212	12.02	7-47	21	9
1958	1,014.4	382	2,055	170	12.08	8-99	14	3
1958/59	+335.1	65	1,328	57	23.29	6-29	4	1
	166.5	64						
1959	972.5	287	2,374	111	21.38	7-66	8	1
1959/60	93.3	31	210	15	14.00	6-76	2	1
1960	1,183.4	352	2,976	139	21.41	9-77	10	2
1961	1,266.1	363	3,618	127	28.48	6-54	8	–
1961/62	695.3	287	1,405	59	23.81	6-65	2	–
1962	1,115.1	390	2,840	108	26.29	6-32	7	1
1962/63	+321.5	55	1,088	39	27.89	7-53	1	–
1963	874.2	302	2,149	88	24.42	6-39	3	1
1963/64	+110.6	31	344	8	43.00	4-49	–	–
1964/65	+273.2	85	718	25	28.72	5-90	1	–

1965	324.1	113	665	35	19.00	5-8	3	—
1965/66	+406.6	84	1,133	44	25.75	5-61	3	—
1966	954.1	328	2,132	109	19.55	8-85	9	2
1966/67	+398.4	105	1,086	51	21.29	6-85	3	1
1967	1,154.1	431	2,319	128	18.11	7-54	10	5
1967/68	+261.6	60	999	51	19.58	5-36	4	—
	97	18						
1968/69	+385.7	66	1,293	53	24.39	7-61	3	1
1969/70	+256.2	43	723	27	26.77	5-53	1	—
1970/71	+323	62	965	35	27.57	4-22	—	—
Totals	20,459.3	7,432	54,709	2,844	19.23	10-54	196	50
	+3,425.6	776						

+ = 8-ball overs

Phase by phase

	Runs	Wkts	Ave.	BB	5wi	10wm
1946-51	5,991	261	22.95	6-32	10	—
1952-58/9	19,681	1,331	14.78	10-54	100	35
1959-70/71	29,037	1,252	23.19	9-77	86	15
Totals	54,709	2,844	19.23	10-54	196	50

For each team

	Overs	M	Runs	Wkts	Ave.	BB	5wi	10wm
Surrey (Championship)	11,775.3	4,308	25,255	1,458	17.32	10-54	106	26
Surrey (other matches)	2,102.5	750	4,580	255	17.96	7-47	17	5
Leicestershire (Championship)	2,295.2	826	4,816	254	18.96	8-85	21	7
Leicestershire (other matches)	137.1	46	300	18	16.66	5-51	1	—
Western Australia (Sheffield Shield)	+2,513.3	556	7,210	302	23.87	7-53	16	2
Western Australia (other matches)	+138.4	21	560	14	40.00	4-68	—	—
MCC (in UK)	54	22	197	3	65.66	2-117	—	—
MCC (overseas)	1,093.2 +535.6	489 149	3,426	218	15.89	8-17	18	6

	Overs	M	Runs	Wkts	Ave.	BB	5wi	10wm
England XI	305.3	42	1,309	41	31.92	6-49	3	–
Players	156	41	502	16	31.37	4-87	–	–
The Rest	160.3	48	484	15	32.26	3-53	–	–
South	115	23	369	25	14.76	6-35	2	1
North	41.4	8	143	6	23.83	4-88	–	–
Combined Services	64	12	168	11	15.27	6-43	2	–
AER Gilligan's XI	68.1	8	354	14	25.28	5-110	1	–
TN Pearce's XI	22	5	89	0	–	–	–	–
MCC All England XI	42.3	11	94	6	15.66	4-36	–	–
A Surrey XI	37.5	10	97	4	24.25	3-44	–	–
Combined XI (Aust)	+85.7	14	305	10	30.50	4-54	–	–

Summary

	Overs	M	Runs	Wkts	Ave.	BB	5wi	10wm
Surrey	13,878.2	5,058	29,835	1,713	17.41	10-54	123	31
Leicestershire	2,432.3	872	5,116	272	18.80	8-85	22	7
Western Australia	+2,651.7	577	7,770	316	24.58	7-53	16	2
Others	2,160.3 +621.5	719 163	7,537	369	20.53	8-17	26	7
England (Tests)	1,988.1 +152.2	783 36	4,451	174	25.58	7-35	9	3
Totals	20,459.3 +3,425.6	7,432 776	54,709	2,844	19.23	10-54	196	50

Against Each Opponent

(excluding Tests, listed by country)

	Overs	M	Runs	Wkts	Ave.	BB	5wi	10wm
Derbyshire	758.5	319	1,292	99	13.05	7-31	8	3
Essex	895.1	331	2,016	87	23.17	6-48	6	1
Glamorgan	925	334	1,825	116	15.73	8-36	9	3
Gloucestershire	867.1	342	1,752	123	14.24	6-15	12	1
Hampshire	891.1	346	1,856	96	19.33	8-26	5	2
Hampshire	891.1	346	1856	96	19.33	8-26	5	2
Kent	1,116.3	408	2,454	136	18.04	10-54	13	3
Lancashire	924.1	337	1,910	108	17.68	8-82	8	2
Leicestershire	874.1	315	1,823	111	16.42	6-22	10	3

Middlesex	1,048.4	404	2,154	151	14.26	7-24	11	2
Northamptonshire	804.2	264	1,766	88	20.06	7-75	7	2
Nottinghamshire	1,088.1	343	2,435	128	19.02	8-81	12	3
Somerset	804.1	277	1,787	100	17.87	6-25	4	2
Surrey	100.2	36	242	15	16.13	5-32	1	—
Sussex	823	293	1,856	83	22.36	6-39	6	2
Warwickshire	544.3	185	1,361	71	19.16	8-85	3	1
Worcestershire	799.4	341	1,567	102	15.36	6-20	8	2
Yorkshire	1,044.5	324	2,652	127	20.88	6-18	6	1
Cambridge University	713.5	279	1,377	97	14.19	7-53	7	2
Oxford University	372	142	738	48	15.37	9-77	3	1
MCC	287.5 +137.5	92 22	1,106	48	23.04	7-47	1	1
MCC Aust Touring Team	16	7	47	1	47.00	1-47	—	—
Gentlemen	156	41	502	16	31.37	4-87	—	—
North	115	23	369	25	14.76	6-35	2	1
South	57.4	11	180	7	25.71	4-88	—	—
South of England	50	18	142	4	35.50	3-69	—	—
The Rest	122.5	26	363	19	19.10	4-59	—	—
Combined Services	48	23	74	2	37.00	2-53	—	—
Australians	247.1 +20	66 2	926	31	29.87	7-49	3	—
Indians	15.3 +2.1	7 1	40	6	6.66	4-36	1	—
New Zealanders	10.2 +13	4 3	67	5	13.40	5-9	1	—
Pakistanis	90	29	246	4	61.50	3-66	—	—
South Africans	151.2	43	406	17	23.88	4-87	—	—
West Indians	206.1 +51.5	83 7	632	28	22.57	6-20	1	—
Commonwealth XI	277.3	36	1,218	40	30.45	6-49	3	—
Australian XI	+24	5	54	6	9.00	6-29	1	—
New South Wales	+725.3	160	2,075	74	28.04	5-68	1	—
Queensland	+634.7	167	1,618	85	19.03	7-61	5	2
South Australia	+710.5	120	2,324	81	28.69	5-93	3	—
Victoria	+585.3	132	1,664	80	20.80	7-53	8	—
Western Australia	+42	12	72	4	18.00	2-26	—	—
Bombay	32	17	65	5	13.00	4-49	—	—
North Zone	36	19	48	7	6.85	4-17	—	—
President's XI (I)	44	13	81	2	40.50	2-54	—	—
Punjab CA	41	16	92	10	9.20	5-33	2	1

Rajasthan	32	13	65	1	65.00	1–30	–	–
Services XI	9	4	19	1	19.00	1–12	–	–
West Zone	21	6	45	2	22.50	2–27	–	–
Nrthrn & Central Districts	30	6	61	2	30.50	2–61	–	–
Otago	20	7	60	2	30.00	2–51	–	–
Wellington	42	11	121	7	17.28	4–72	–	–
Amir of Bahawalpur's XI	42	18	75	7	10.71	4–51	–	–
Combined XI (P)	51	31	79	10	7.90	6–46	1	1
Comb Rlys & Baluchistan	41	17	80	9	8.88	5–42	1	–
East Pakistan	27.3	19	17	11	1.54	8–17	1	1
Governor-General's XI	78.4	50	88	11	8.00	6–57	2	1
Pakistan Services XI	41	17	76	4	19.00	4–70	–	–
Pakistan (non-Test)	234.5	128	362	19	19.05	5–44	3	–
President's XI (P)	44	19	102	8	12.75	5–53	1	–
Border	+8	1	14	3	4.66	3–14	–	–
Combined Universities	+39	14	86	6	14.33	4–63	–	–
Eastern Province	+26.4	4	65	10	6.50	6–14	1	1
Griqualand West	+15	6	33	1	33.00	1–33	–	–
Natal	+46.2	12	115	6	19.16	3–29	–	–
North-Eastern Transvaal	+2	0	7	1	7.00	1–7	–	–
Rhodesia	93.3 +38.1	31 18	291	22	13.22	6–76	3	1
South African XI	+39	13	112	5	22.40	4–63	–	–
Transvaal	+24	9	77	3	25.66	3–77	–	–
Western Province	+89	32	205	12	17.08	5–69	2	1
Barbados	73.3	29	176	9	19.55	5–57	1	–
British Guiana	46.5	17	102	2	51.00	1–47	–	–
Jamaica	42	16	89	2	44.50	2–59	–	–
Trinidad	31	8	93	1	93.00	1–58	–	–
Windward Islands	28	7	62	3	20.66	3–62	–	–
All Ceylon	5	1	16	1	16.00	1–8	–	–

Summary

	Overs	M	Runs	Wkts	Ave.	BB	5wi	10wm
British Teams	16,249	5,861	35,646	2,008	17.75	10-54	142	38
	+137.5	22						
Overseas Teams	2,222.2	788	14,612	662	22.07	8-17	45	9
	+3135.7	718						
Test matches	1,988.1	783	4,451	174	25.58	7-35	9	3
	+152.2	36						
Totals	20,459.3	7,432	54,709	2,844	19.23	10-54	196	50
	+3,425.6	776						

On each ground

a) in England and Wales, listed by county

	Overs	M	Runs	Wkts	Ave.	BB	5wi	10wm
Chesterfield	128.1	50	257	16	16.06	7-50	1	1
Derby	116	51	198	8	24.75	3-48	–	–
In Derbyshire	244.1	101	455	24	18.95	7-50	1	1
Brentwood	28.2	8	74	5	14.80	5-74	1	–
Clacton-on-Sea	163.5	49	434	14	31.00	5-45	2	1
Colchester	25	14	28	1	28.00	1-14	–	–
Ilford	117.4	33	329	20	16.45	6-48	2	–
Leyton	30	10	88	2	44.00	2-88	–	–
Southend-on-Sea	44	18	99	3	33.00	3-93	–	–
In Essex	408.5	132	1,052	45	23.37	6-48	5	1
Cardiff	129.1	59	228	13	17.53	7-66	1	–
Ebbw Vale	35.3	2	114	4	28.50	3-56	–	–
Llanelli	55.5	34	88	6	14.66	4-28	–	–
Pontypridd	72	18	165	10	16.50	6-43	1	–
Swansea	178.3	48	391	13	30.07	5-79	1	–
In Glamorgan	471	161	986	46	21.43	7-66	3	–
Bristol	117.3	59	173	13	13.30	6-15	1	–
Cheltenham	134.3	52	268	13	20.61	4-32	–	–
Gloucester	175.4	74	375	29	12.93	5-32	3	–
Stroud	54.4	17	99	8	12.37	5-60	1	–
In Gloucestershire	482.2	202	915	63	14.52	6-15	5	–

Bournemouth	106	48	196	16	12.25	8-26	2	1
Portsmouth	160.3	56	357	21	17.00	6-73	2	1
Southampton	264.5	85	672	26	25.84	5-149	1	—
In Hampshire	531.2	189	1,225	63	19.44	8-26	5	2
Blackheath	550.5	190	1,309	77	17.00	10-54	7	2
Canterbury	79.4	43	121	9	13.44	6-54	1	—
In Kent	630.3	233	1,430	86	16.62	10-54	8	2
Old Trafford	713.5	269	1,452	78	18.61	8-82	8	2
Ashby-de-la-Zouch	48.4	17	113	4	28.25	4-95	—	—
Coalville	91	43	162	10	16.20	4-48	—	—
Leicester	1,701.3	595	3,608	213	16.93	8-85	20	8
Loughborough	49.1	28	49	8	6.12	5-8	1	—
In Leicestershire	1,890.2	683	3,932	235	16.73	8-85	21	8
Lord's	1,004.1	355	2,275	123	18.49	7-46	6	2
Kettering	84	22	173	9	19.22	3-31	—	—
Northampton	255.3	91	503	24	20.95	5-33	1	—
Rushden	13	5	21	0	—	—	—	—
In Northamptonshire	352.3	118	697	33	21.12	5-33	1	—
Newark	49	12	125	0	—	—	—	—
Trent Bridge	644.5	199	1,439	75	19.18	8-81	7	3
In Nottinghamshire	693.5	211	1,564	75	20.85	8-81	7	3
Bath	52	22	95	3	31.66	2-41	—	—
Taunton	193.2	63	481	18	26.72	4-50	—	—
Weston-super-Mare	61.3	15	168	13	12.92	6-49	1	1
In Somerset	306.5	100	744	34	21.88	6-49	1	1
Guildford	691.2	253	1,506	78	19.30	9-77	4	2
Kingston-on-Thames	168.3	39	514	20	25.70	4-88	—	—
The Oval	6,759	2,492	14,218	864	16.45	8-36	61	12
In Surrey	7,618.5	2,784	16,238	962	16.87	9-77	65	14
Hastings	417.2	93	1,486	46	32.30	6-49	2	—
Hove	317.4	122	700	19	36.84	5-75	1	—
In Sussex	735	215	2,186	65	33.63	6-49	3	—
Coventry	45.5	14	116	7	16.57	5-68	1	—
Edgbaston	295.1	131	586	27	21.70	3-20	—	—
Nuneaton	26	7	98	2	49.00	1-33	—	—
In Warwickshire	367	152	800	36	22.22	5-68	1	—

	Overs	M	Runs	Wkts	Ave.	BB	5wi	10wm
Dudley	52	20	99	4	24.75	3-25	–	–
Kidderminster	46	20	94	9	10.44	6-64	1	–
Worcester	347.1	150	700	32	21.87	5-32	2	–
In Worcestershire	445.1	190	893	45	19.84	6-64	3	–
Bradford	52	13	121	9	13.44	4-43	–	–
Headingley	421.3	161	913	40	22.82	7-51	2	1
Scarborough	145.3	29	587	18	32.61	4-59	–	–
Sheffield	115	34	307	14	21.92	5-11	1	–
In Yorkshire	734	237	1,928	81	23.80	7-51	3	1
Fenner's	512.2	203	941	78	12.06	7-53	7	2
The Parks	44	17	86	7	12.28	4-51	–	–
Torquay	173.2	26	738	36	20.50	6-35	4	1

b) Overseas, listed by country

	Overs	M	Runs	Wkts	Ave.	BB	5wi	10wm
Adelaide	+437	70	1,411	43	32.81	5-118	1	–
Brisbane	+339.1	96	817	45	18.15	7-61	3	1
Melbourne	+329.5	62	973	49	19.85	7-53	5	–
Perth	+1,518	339	4,499	179	25.13	6-85	8	1
Sydney	+405.1	85	1,147	39	29.41	6-29	1	–
Sydney No.2	+44	4	201	4	50.25	2-77	–	–
In Australia	+3,072.7	656	9,048	359	25.20	7-53	18	2
Colombo, Ceylon	5	1	16	1	16.00	1-8	–	–
Ahmedabad	21	6	45	2	22.50	2-27	–	–
Bombay	93	48	172	10	17.20	4-49	–	–
Calcutta	91	38	193	7	27.57	4-111	–	–
Delhi	40	15	83	1	83.00	1-83	–	–
Hyderabad	44	13	81	2	40.50	2-54	–	–
Jaipur	32	13	65	1	65.00	1-30	–	–
Jullundur	36	19	48	7	6.85	4-17	–	–
Kanpur	44	15	93	3	31.00	3-93	–	–
Madras	79.3	29	171	7	24.42	6-65	1	–
In India	480.3	196	951	40	23.77	6-65	1	–
Auckland	20.3	12	29	2	14.50	2-29	–	–
Christchurch	54.2	28	84	11	7.63	6-53	2	1
Dunedin	20	7	60	2	30.00	2-51	–	–
Hamilton	30	6	61	2	30.50	2-61	–	–
Wellington	42	11	121	7	17.28	4-72	–	–
In New Zealand	166.5	64	355	24	14.79	6-53	2	1
Bahawalpur	42	18	75	7	10.71	4-51	–	–

	Overs	M	Runs	Wkts	Ave.	BB	5wi	10wm
Chittagong	27.3	19	17	11	1.54	8-17	1	1
Dacca	146	58	315	13	24.23	5-90	1	—
Karachi	199.4	115	280	19	14.73	6-57	3	1
Lahore	77	44	99	3	33.00	3-99	—	—
Lyallpur	41	16	92	10	9.20	5-33	2	1
Multan	41	17	80	9	8.88	5-42	1	—
Peshawar	56.5	32	92	5	18.40	5-44	1	—
Rawalpindi	44	19	102	8	12.75	5-53	1	—
Sargodha	41	17	76	4	19.00	4-70	—	—
Sialkot	51	31	79	10	7.90	6-46	1	1
In Pakistan	767	386	1,307	99	13.20	8-17	11	4
Benoni	+2	0	7	1	7.00	1-7	—	—
Bulawayo	41 +23.2	14 13	131	9	17.88	5-12	1	—
Cape Town	+128	46	291	18	16.16	5-69	2	1
Durban	+21	7	44	2	22.00	2-21	—	—
East London	+8	1	14	3	4.66	3-14	—	—
Johannesburg	+24	9	77	3	25.66	3-77	—	—
Kimberley	+15	6	33	1	33.00	1-33	—	—
Pietermaritzburg	+25.2	5	71	4	17.75	3-29	—	—
Port Elizabeth	+52.4	15	103	12	8.58	6-14	1	1
Pretoria	+39	13	112	5	22.40	4-63	—	—
Salisbury	52.3 +14.7	17 5	160	13	12.30	6-76	2	1
In Rhodesia & South Africa	93.3 +352.7	31 120	1,043	71	14.69	6-14	6	3
Bridgetown	147.3	45	392	10	39.20	5-57	1	—
Castries	28	7	62	3	20.66	3-62	—	—
Georgetown	136.4	43	286	8	35.75	2-60	—	—
Kingston	139	54	272	9	30.22	3-76	—	—
Port-of-Spain	136	27	440	5	88.00	2-178	—	—
In West Indies	587.1	176	1,452	35	41.48	5-57	1	—

Summary

	Overs	M	Runs	Wkts	Ave.	BB	5wi	10wm
United Kingdom	18,359.3	6,578	40,537	2,215	18.30	10-54	157	40
Overseas	2,100 +3,425.6	854 776	14,172	629	22.53	8-17	39	10
Totals	20,459.3 +3,425.6	7,432 776	54,709	2844	19.23	10-54	196	50

Eight or more wickets in an innings

10-54   Surrey *v.* Kent at the Rectory Field, Blackheath, 1956

9-77   Surrey *v.* Oxford University at Guildford, 1960

8-17   MCC 'A' *v.* East Pakistan at Chittagong, East Pakistan, 1955/56

8-26   Surrey *v.* Hampshire at Bournemouth, 1953

8-36   Surrey *v.* Glamorgan at the Oval, 1954

8-81   Surrey *v.* Nottinghamshire at Trent Bridge, 1956

8-82   Surrey *v.* Lancashire at Old Trafford, 1955

8-85   Leicestershire *v.* Warwickshire at Grace Road, Leicester, 1966

8-99   Surrey *v.* Kent at the Rectory Field, Blackheath, 1958

Thirteen or more wickets in a match

16-83   Surrey *v.* Kent at the Rectory Field, Blackheath, 1956

15-182   Surrey *v.* Kent at the Rectory Field, Blackheath, 1958

13-69   Surrey *v.* Hampshire at Bournemouth, 1953

13-82   Surrey *v.* Middlesex, the Oval, 1955

13-116   Leicestershire *v.* Glamorgan at Leicester, 1967

13-118   Leicestershire *v.* Northamptonshire at Leicester, 1967

13-130   Surrey *v.* Lancashire at Old Trafford, 1955

13-144   Surrey *v.* Nottinghamshire at Trent Bridge, 1956

Note: It will be observed that the top two instances in the above table are both against the same opponents. In five consecutive seasons, from 1954 to 1958, G.A.R. Lock took 69 wickets in seven games against Kent, taking five wickets in an innings on ten occasions, ten wickets in a match three times and averaging 9.79 in the process.

Hat-tricks (4)

Surrey *v.* Somerset at Weston-super-Mare, 1955

MCC 'A' *v.* Amir of Bahawalpur's XI at Bahawalpur, Pakistan, 1955/56

MCC 'A' *v.* Combined Railways & Baluchistan, Multan, Pakistan, 1955/56

Leicestershire *v.* Hampshire at Portsmouth, 1967

Note: The last-named on the above list is the first instance of a hat-trick being taken in first-class cricket in England on a Sunday.

Five wickets in an innings in five consecutive innings

(all for Surrey in 1956)

(4-29) & 5-42   *v.* Yorkshire at the Oval
5-36 & 5-24   *v.* Kent at the Oval
6-29 & 10-54   *v.* Kent at the Rectory Field, Blackheath
(31 wickets at an average of 5.96)

Ten wickets in a match in three consecutive matches

(all for Surrey in 1955)

13-130   *v.* Lancashire at Old Trafford
13-82   *v.* Middlesex at the Oval
10-54   *v.* Somerset at Weston-super-Mare
(36 wickets at an average of 7.38)

Fifty wickets in a month

	Runs	Wkts	Ave.	BB	5wi	10wm
May 1955	587	67	8.76	6-25	6	3
August 1955	790	73	10.82	8-82	8	3
July 1958	620	56	11.07	8-99	6	3

Notes: It will be observed that Lock exceeded a total of over seventy wickets in August 1955. No bowler has since passed this total.

The figures for August include two matches against Middlesex when Lock took 22 wickets at an average of 8.63.

Due to the unavailability of close-of-play bowling figures for a match in 1958 the runs and average totals for the relevant month represent a guesstimate. The average has to be between 10.82 and 11.32.

Conceding less than one run per over in an innings (minimum 20 overs)

+20-11-13-0	0.65 rpo	Western Australia *v.* New South Wales at the WACA, Perth, 1965/66
23.5-16-17-8	0.71 rpo	MCC 'A' *v.* East Pakistan, Chittagong, East Pakistan, 1955/56
30-17-22-4	0.73 rpo	Leicestershire *v.* Derbyshire at Grace Road, Leicester, 1967
27.1-17-21-5	0.77 rpo	Surrey *v.* Gloucestershire at the the Oval, 1955
38-26-31-5	0.81 rpo	MCC 'A' *v.* Governor-General's XI at Karachi, Pakistan, 1955/56
22-14-19-0	0.85 rpo	Surrey *v.* Kent at the Oval, 1952
24-16-21-2	0.87 rpo	Leicestershire *v.* Gloucestershire at Grace Road, Leicester, 1967
+25-13-22-4	0.88 rpo	Western Australia *v.* Queensland at the Gabba, Brisbane, 1970/71
24-11-22-6	0.91 rpo	Surrey *v.* Leicestershire at the Oval, 1954
25-15-23-3	0.92 rpo	Surrey *v.* Nottinghamshire at the Oval, 1950
34-21-32-4	0.94 rpo	Surrey *v.* Gloucestershire at Cheltenham, 1954

Note: In the match at Karachi none of Lock's first 17.2 overs (104 balls) were scored from and this is a world record for the start of a bowling spell.

How batsmen were dismissed

Caught	1,786	62.8 per cent
Bowled	579	20.4 per cent
Lbw	342	12.0 per cent
Stumped	131	4.6 per cent
Hit wicket	6	0.2 per cent

Batsmen most frequently dismissed

18   J.M. Parks (Sussex)

16   C.A. Milton (Gloucestershire)

15   D. Bennett, J.T. Murray (both Middlesex)

14   R.N. Harvey (Australia), R. Illingworth (Yorkshire), C.H. Palmer (Leicestershire), F.J. Titmus (Middlesex)

Most fielding dismissals off Lock's bowling

(50 or more – all Surrey)

202	G.A.R. Lock
162 (122 ct, 40 st)	A.J.W. McIntrye
130	M.J. Stewart
107	K.F. Barrington
97 (75 ct, 22 st)	R. Swetman
79	W.S. Surridge
66	P.B.H. May

1,000th wicket

B.A. Langford, c M.J. Stewart b Lock, 8 – Surrey *v.* Somerset, the Oval, 4 June 1956.

2,000th wicket

B.K. Kunderam, lbw b Lock, 5 – England *v.* India, Bombay, 15 November 1961.

Highest position in national first-class averages

1st – 1956, 1957

2nd – 1958

Highest position amongst season's leading wicket aggregates

1st – 1955, 1957, 1958
3rd – 1956

Highest position in own county's championship averages

1st – 1953, 1956, 1957, 1958, 1965, 1966, 1967

Note: Lock was first or second in Surrey's Championship averages in every season from 1952 to 1960.

Highest position in own county's leading wicket aggregates in championship

1st – 1952, 1955, 1956, 1957, 1958, 1960, 1961, 1966, 1967

Fielding

Four or more catches in an innings

5	Surrey *v.* Lancashire at Old Trafford, 1953
4	Surrey *v.* Glamorgan at the Oval, 1955
4	Surrey *v.* West Indians at the Oval, 1957
4	Surrey *v.* Warwickshire (1st inns) at the Oval, 1957
4	Surrey *v.* Warwickshire (2nd inns) at the Oval, 1957
4	Surrey *v.* Hampshire at Portsmouth, 1959
4	Surrey *v.* Australians at the Oval, 1961
4	Leicestershire *v.* Oxford University at The Parks, 1966
4	Leicestershire *v.* Yorkshire at Leicester, 1967

Five or more catches in a match

8	Surrey *v.* Warwickshire at the Oval, 1957
7	Surrey *v.* Lancashire at Old Trafford, 1953
6	Surrey *v.* Australians at the Oval, 1961
5	Surrey *v.* Rhodesia at Salisbury, Rhodesia, 1959/60
5	Leicestershire *v.* Oxford University at The Parks, 1966

Players from whose bowling Lock took most catches (20 or more – all Surrey)

202	G.A.R. Lock
124	J.C. Laker
107	A.V. Bedser
50	P. Loader
41	E.A. Bedser
31	W.S. Surrudge

All-Round Feats

A half-century and five wickets in an innings in the same match

57	8-99 & 7-83	Surrey *v.* Kent at the Rectory Field, Blackheath, 1958
56	5-33	Leicestershire *v.* Middlesex at Grace Road, Leicester, 1966

Test Cricket

Batting and Fielding

In each series

Year	Opponents	M	I	NO	Runs	HS	Ave.	50	Ct
1952	India	2	I	I	I	I*	–	–	3
1953	Australia	2	3	0	21	9	7.00	–	3
1953/54	West Indies	5	7	I	31	13	5.16	–	4
1955	South Africa	3	6	I	79	19*	15.80	–	2
1956	Australia	4	4	I	46	25*	15.33	–	10
1956/57	South Africa	I	2	0	26	14	13.00	–	–
1957	West Indies	3	3	0	37	20	12.33	–	4
1958	New Zealand	5	4	I	59	25	19.66	–	6
1958/59	Australia	4	8	I	60	21	8.57	–	I
1958/59	New Zealand	2	I	0	15	15	15.00	–	4
1961	Australia	3	5	0	39	30	7.80	–	I
1961/62	Pakistan	2	2	I	4	4	4.00	–	4
1961/62	India	5	7	2	108	49	21.60	–	6
1962	Pakistan	3	I	0	7	7	7.00	–	2
1963	West Indies	3	6	0	115	56	19.16	2	7
1967/68	West Indies	2	3	0	94	89	31.33	I	2
Totals		49	63	9	742	89	13.74	3	59

Against each opponent

	Tests	I	NO	Runs	HS	Ave.	50	Ct
Australia	13	20	2	166	30	9.22	–	15
India	7	8	3	109	49	21.8	–	9
New Zealand	7	5	1	74	25	18.50	–	10
Pakistan	5	3	1	11	7	5.50	–	6
South Africa	4	8	1	105	19*	15.00	–	2
West Indies	13	19	1	277	89	15.38	3	17
Totals	49	63	9	742	89	13.74	3	59

On each ground in England

	M	I	NO	Runs	HS	Ave.	50	Ct
Edgbaston	4	4	0	61	56	15.25	1	5
Headingley	7	9	0	166	53	18.44	1	9
Lord's	3	4	1	36	23*	12.00	–	2
Old Trafford	4	5	3	69	25*	34.50	–	6
The Oval	8	10	0	72	25	7.20	–	12
Trent Bridge	2	1	0	0	0	0.00	–	4
Totals	28	33	4	404	56	13.93	2	38

Note: Lock's record overseas was 338 runs at an average of 13.52

Half-centuries

89   *v.* West Indies at Georgetown, Guyana, 1967/68
56   *v.* West Indies at Edgbaston, 1963
53   *v.* West Indies at Headingley, 1963

Note: These three scores were made in a spell of seven consecutive Test innings

Fielding

Players from whose bowling Lock took most catches

12   J.C. Laker
8   G.A.R. Lock
7   F.S. Trueman
4   A.V. Bedser, B.R. Knight, F. Tyson

Bowling

In each series

Year	Opponents	Overs	M	Runs	Wkts	Ave.	BB	5wi	10wm
1952	India	15.3	7	37	4	9.25	4-36	—	—
1953	Australia	61	21	165	8	20.62	5-45	1	—
1953/54	West Indies	296.5	88	718	14	51.28	3-76	—	—
1955	South Africa	174	65	353	13	27.15	4-39	—	—
1956	Australia	237.2	115	337	15	22.46	4-41	—	—
1956/57	South Africa	+26	11	38	2	19.00	1-17	—	—
1957	West Indies	114.2	59	163	15	10.86	6-20	2	1
1958	New Zealand	176	93	254	34	7.47	7-35	3	1
1958/59	Australia	+126.2	25	376	5	75.20	4-130	—	—
1958/59	New Zealand	74.5	40	113	13	8.69	6-53	2	1
1961	Australia	107	33	250	3	83.33	2-68	—	—
1961/62	Pakistan	166	71	336	10	33.60	4-70	—	—
1961/62	India	306.3	124	628	22	28.54	6-65	1	—
1962	Pakistan	98	32	241	6	40.16	3-80	—	—
1963	West Indies	91.5	24	230	6	38.33	3-54	—	—
1967/68	West Indies	69	11	212	4	53.00	2-61	—	—
Totals		1,988.1	783	4,451	174	25.58	7-35	9	3
		+152.2	36						

Against each opponent

	Overs	M	Runs	Wkts	Ave.	BB	5wi	10wm
Australia	405.2	169	1,128	31	36.38	5-45	1	—
	+126.2	25						
India	322	131	665	26	25.57	6-65	1	—
New Zealand	250.5	133	367	47	7.80	7-35	5	2
Pakistan	264	103	577	16	36.06	4-70	—	—

	Overs	M	Runs	Wkts	Ave.	BB	5wi	10wm
South Africa	174 +26	65 11	391	15	26.06	4-87	–	–
West Indies	572	182	1,323	39	33.92	6-20	2	1
Totals	1,988.1 +152.2	783 36	4,451	174	25.58	7-35	9	3

On each ground in England

	Overs	M	Runs	Wkts	Ave.	BB	5wi	10wm
Edgbaston	129.1	62	233	11	21.18	3-25	–	–
Headingley	289.3	112	592	29	20.41	7-51	1	1
Lord's	64	29	155	9	17.22	5-17	1	–
Old Trafford	206.3	84	382	16	23.87	7-35	1	–
the Oval	298.5	126	538	34	15.82	6-20	3	1
Trent Bridge	87	36	130	5	26.00	3-61	–	–
Totals	1,075	449	2,030	104	19.51	7-35	6	2

Note: Lock's record overseas was 70 wickets at an average of 34.58

Five wickets in an innings

7-35   *v.* New Zealand at Old Trafford, 1958

7-51   *v.* New Zealand at Headingley, 1958

6-20   *v.* West Indies at the Oval, 1957

6-53   *v.* New Zealand at Christchurch, New Zealand, 1958/59

6-65   *v.* India at Madras, India, 1961/62

5-17   *v.* New Zealand at Lord's, 1958

5-28   *v.* West Indies at the Oval, 1957

5-31   *v.* New Zealand at Christchurch, 1958/59

5-45   *v.* Australia at the Oval, 1953

Ten wickets in a match

11-48   *v.* West Indies at the Oval, 1957

11-65   *v.* New Zealand at Headingley, 1958

11-84   *v.* New Zealand at Christchurch, 1958/59

How batsmen were dismissed

Caught	105	60.3 per cent
Bowled	42	24.1 per cent
Lbw	21	12.0 per cent
Stumped	5	2.8 per cent
Hit wicket	1	0.5 per cent

Batsmen most frequently dismissed

8	R.N. Harvey (Australia)
6	J.R. Reid (New Zealand)
5	G.S. Sobers, F.M.M. Worrell (both West Indies)

Most fielding dismissals from Lock's bowling

11	F.S. Trueman
10	M.C. Cowdrey
9	P.B.H. May
8	G.A.R. Lock
7	P.H. Parfitt

100th Test wicket

J.T. Sparling, c & b Lock, 2 – *v.* New Zealand at Old Trafford, 29 July 1958.

Limited-overs Cricket

Batting and Fielding

Season by season (competitive matches only)

Year	M	I	NO	Runs	HS	Ave.	Ct
1966	1	1	0	1	1	1.00	—
1967	1	1	0	3	3	3.00	—
1969/70	2	2	0	0	0	0.00	2
1970/71	3	1	0	1	1	1.00	—
Totals	7	5	0	5	3	1.00	2

Bowling

Season by season

Year	Overs	M	Runs	Wkts	Ave.	BB	RpO
1966	12	1	52	0	—	—	4.33
1967	12	3	35	0	—	—	2.91
1969/70	+16	0	76	2	38.00	2-37	4.75
1970/71	+12.1	0	87	5	17.40	2-14	7.17
Totals	24	4	250	7	35.71	2-14	3.62
	+28.14	0					5.79

Captaincy

Results in first-class matches

Competition	Played	Won	Lost	Drawn
County Championship	54	17	11	26
Sheffield Shield	35	15	9	11
Other	10	4	3	3
Totals	99	36	23	40

Note: Lock led Leicesterhire for two seasons, in 1966 and 1967; in the latter season the county finished third in the Championship, equalling their previous best of 1953. He led Western Australia for four seasons, from 1967/68; the state side won the Sheffield Shield in this season (for only the second time – their previous title being in 1947/48) and finished in second place in each of the following two.

Results in limited-overs matches

Competition	Played	Won	Lost
Gillette Cup	2	0	2
V&G Cup	5	4	1
Totals	7	4	3

Note: Lock led Western Australia to victory in the V&G Cup in 1970/71.

Miscellaneous Records

Ten or more wickets in a Test for England by lowest average since 1945

4.36	11–48	G.A.R. Lock *v.* West Indies at the Oval, 1957
4.73	19–90	J.C. Laker *v.* Australia at Old Trafford, 1956
5.46	13–71	D.L. Underwood *v.* Pakistan at Lord's, 1974
5.90	11–65	G.A.R. Lock *v.* New Zealand, Headingley, 1958

Most wickets in a Test series against New Zealand

	Season	Tests	Overs	M	Runs	Wkts	Ave.	BB	5wi	10wm
G.A.R. Lock	1958	5	176	93	254	34	7.47	7-35	3	1
S.P. Gupte (I)	1955/56	5	356.4	153	669	34	19.67	7-128	4	–
Waqar Younis (P)	1990/91	3	144.4	51	315	29	10.86	7-76	3	2

Note: In each of the above instances the bowlers were playing at home.

10,000 runs in first-class matches at the lowest average

	Career	I	NO	Runs	HS	Ave.
G.A.R. Lock	1946–70/71	812	161	10,342	89	15.88
R.W. Taylor	1960–88	880	167	12,065	100	16.92

Note: Lock holds the record for the most first-class runs without scoring a century.

2,000 wickets in fewest matches since 1945

438	G.A.R. Lock
460	D. Shackleton
474	J.B. Statham
498	F.S. Trueman

Most wickets in first-class matches in the 1950s

	Wkts	Ave.
G.A.R. Lock	1,639	16.07
J.H. Wardle	1,497	18.04
D. Shackleton	1,497	18.45
J.C. Laker	1,465	16.98
R. Tattersall	1,300	17.68

Note: No bowler has exceeded Lock's figure in any decade since the 1950s.

Best bowling figures in a match for Surrey

16-83	G.A.R. Lock	*v.* Kent at the Rectory Field, Blackheath, 1956
16-119	M.P. Bicknell	*v.* Leicestershire, Guildford, 2000

15-83	T. Richardson	*v.* Warwickshire at the Oval, 1898
15-95	T. Richardson	*v.* Essex at the Oval, 1894
15-97	J.C. Laker	*v.* MCC at Lord's, 1954
15-98	G. Lohmann	*v.* Sussex at Hove, 1889

Most catches in a match for Surrey

8	G.A.R. Lock	*v.* Warwickshire at the Oval, 1957
7	J.F. Parker	*v.* Kent at the Rectory Field, Blackheath, 1952
7	G.A.R. Lock	*v.* Lancashire at Old Trafford, 1953
7	W.S. Surridge	*v.* Leicestershire at the Oval, 1955
7	M.J. Stewart	*v.* Northamptonshire at Northampton, 1957

Surrey's youngest first-class cricketers

| G.A.R. Lock | 17 years 8 days |
| P.I. Pocock | 17 years 279 days |

Comparisons

Highest Test wicket aggregates for England by spin bowlers

	Tests	Balls	Runs	Wkts	Ave.	BpW	BB	5wi	10wm
D.L. Underwood									
1966–81/82	86	21,862	7,674	297	25.83	73.6	8–51	17	6
J.C. Laker									
1947/8–58/59	46	12,027	4,101	193	21.24	62.3	10–53	9	3
G.A.R. Lock									
1952–67/68	49	13,147	4,451	174	25.58	75.5	7–35	9	3
F.J. Titmus									
1955–74/75	53	15,118	4,931	153	32.22	98.8	7–79	7	–
H. Verity									
1931–39	40	11,173	3,510	144	24.37	77.5	8–43	5	2
A.F. Giles									
1998–2006/07	54	12,180	5,806	143	40.60	85.1	5–57	5	–
J.E. Emburey									
1978–93	60	14,227	5,105	138	36.99	103.0	7–78	6	–
W. Rhodes									
1899–1929/30	58	8,231	3,425	127	26.96	64.8	8–68	6	1
P.H. Edmonds									
1975–87	51	12,028	4,273	125	34.18	96.2	7–66	2	–
D.A. Allen									
1959/60–66	39	11,297	3,779	122	30.97	92.5	5–30	4	–
R. Illingworth									
1958–73	61	11,934	3,807	122	31.20	97.8	6–29	3	–

Highest first-class wicket aggregates

		Career	Runs	Wkts	Ave.
W. Rhodes	SLA	1898–1930	69,993	4,187	16.71
A.P. Freeman	LBG	914–36	69,577	3,776	18.42
C.W.L. Parker	SLA	1903–35	63,817	3,278	19.46
J.T. Hearne	MOB	1888–1923	54,352	3,061	17.75

T.W.J. Goddard	RF/OB	1922–52	59,116	2,979	19.84
W.G. Grace	RM	865–1908	51,545	2,876	17.92
A.S. Kennedy	RM	907–36	61,034	2,874	21.23
D. Shackleton	RM	1949–69	53,303	2,857	18.65
G.A.R. Lock	SLA	1946–70/71	54,709	2,844	19.23
F.J. Titmus	OB	1949–82	63,313	2,830	22.37

Youngest bowlers to take 2,000 wickets in first-class matches

W. Rhodes	30 years 233 days
G.A.R. Lock	32 years 133 days
T. Richardson	32 years 299 days

Note: When Lock took his 1,000th first-class wicket he was the fourth youngest to achieve the feat, behind G.A. Lohmann, Rhodes and Richardson.

200 wickets in a season since 1945

		Overs	M	Runs	Wkts	Ave.
T.W.J. Goddard	Gloucs 1947	1,451.2	344	4,119	238	17.30
G.A.R. Lock	Surrey 1955	1,408.4	497	3,109	216	14.39
G.A.R. Lock	Surrey 1957	1,194.1	449	2,550	212	12.02
R. Appleyard	Yorkshire 1951	1,313.2	391	2,829	200	14.14

Note: Lock is thus the last bowler to take 200 wickets in a season. Lock holds the record for most wickets in a season in Pakistan (81 in 1955/56) by a bowler not from that country.

100 wickets in a season on one ground

This feat has been achieved on a total of 15 occasions, the last being by Lock in 1957 when he took 101 wickets at the Oval at a record average of 9.43. The previous lowest average was 11.77, also at the Oval and this was achieved by G. Lohmann in 1888.

Most first-class wickets since 1945

	Career	Runs	Wkts	Ave.
D. Shackleton	1948–69	53,303	2,857	18.65
G.A.R. Lock	1946–70/71	54,709	2,844	19.23
F.J. Titmus	1949–82	63,313	2,830	22.37
D.L. Underwood	1963–87	49,993	2,465	20.28

Best bowling figures in an innings for Surrey

Lock's 10–54 against Kent at Blackheath in 1956 is the third-best innings analysis for Surrey. T. Bushby had figures of 10–43 against Somerset at Taunton in 1921 and T. Richardson took 10–45 against Essex at the Oval in 1894 in a non-Championship fixture. Two other bowlers have also taken ten wickets in an innings for Surrey, J.C. Laker also achieving the feat against the touring Australians in 1956.

100 wickets in a season for Surrey

Lock achieved this feat on a total of nine occasions (eight of them consecutive) and only T. Richardson (ten) has beaten this record. G.A. Lohmann, A.R. Gover and J.C. Laker achieved the feat eight times each.

Most wickets in a career for Surrey

	Career	Runs	Wkts	Ave.
T. Richardson	1892–1904	31,732	1,775	17.87
G.A.R. Lock	1946–63	29,835	1,713	17.41
P.G.H. Fender	1914–35	38,182	1,586	24.07
A.V. Bedser	1939–60	27,918	1,459	19.13

Oldest players to take 50 wickets in a season in first-class matches in Australia

H. Ironmonger	1932/32	49 years 313 days
C.V. Grimmett	1939/40	48 years 49 days
G.A.R. Lock	1968/69	39 years 232 days
A.A. Mailey	1924/25	39 years 60 days

Most wickets in a season in the Sheffield Shield before 1975

	Career	Runs	Wkts	Ave.
L.O. Fleetwood-Smith	1934/35	1,137	60	18.95
W.J. O'Reilly	1939/40	705	52	13.55
G.A.R. Lock	1966/67	1,086	51	21.29
C.V. Grimmett	1934/35	1,043	49	21.28
C.V. Grimmett	1939/40	1,215	49	24.79

Most wickets in a career in the Sheffield Shield before 1975

	Career	M	Runs	Wkts	Ave.	5wi	10wm	BB
C.V. Grimmett	1923/24-39/40	79	12,976	513	25.29	48	13	9-180
G.A.R. Lock	1962/63-70/71	63	7,210	302	23.87	15	2	7-52
A.N. Connolly	1959/60-70/71	71	7,745	297	26.00	12	4	9-67
J.W. Martin	1956/67-67/68	77	8,703	273	31.87	12	0	8-97

Note: At the time of his retirement Lock held the record for most wickets for Western Australia in the Sheffield Shield and also in all first-class matches (326 wickets). These records have since been overtaken by D.K. Lillee, T.M. Alderman and J. Angel.

Most catches in all first-class cricket

1,018	F.E. Woolley	1906-38
887	W.G. Grace	1865-1908
830	G.A.R. Lock	1946-70/71
819	W.R. Hammond	1920-51
813	D.B. Close	1949-86

Most catches by a fielder in a season in first-class matches for Surrey

M.J. Stewart	1957
K.F. Barrington	1957
G.R.J. Roope	1971
G.A.R. Lock	1957
M.J. Stewart	1958

Most catches by a fielder in a career in first-class matches for Surrey

604	M.J. Stewart	1954-72
560	E.G. Hayes	1896-1919
533	G.A.R. Lock	1946-63
513	G.R.J. Roope	1964-82

Caught & bowled dismissals

The number of such dismissals (202) effected by Lock is a world record. 7.10 per cent of his wickets were taken by this method – also a record – shown by comparing his feat with other prolific bowler-fielders as well as other slow left-arm bowlers.

	Catches	c&b	Wkts	c&b as % of wkts
G.A.R. Lock	830	202	2,844	7.10
D.B. Close	813	79	1,171	6.74
F.E. Woolley	1,018	101	2,066	4.88
W. Rhodes	765	190	4,204	4.51
D.L. Underwood	261	107	2,465	4.34

Players with 10,000 runs and 2,500 wickets in first-class cricket

A total of seven players have achieved this feat, the first being W.G. Grace and the last F.J. Titmus. Titmus and Lock are the only players to complete this 'double' since 1945. The other players are G.H. Hirst, A.S. Kennedy, W. Rhodes and M.W. Tate.

A Comparison with J.H.Wardle

Lock and Wardle were rivals throughout the latter's career. Both were slow left-arm bowlers, both made their first-class debuts in 1946 and both had played a similar number of Tests by the time the latter stopped playing first-class cricket in 1958 (apart from one game in 1967/68).

Each of the following two tables shows the respective season or series figures and conclude with the career totals for each player as at 30 September 1958.

First-class cricket

Season		Lock				Wardle		
	M	Wkts	Ave.	5wi	M	Wkts	Ave.	5wi
1946	1	0	–	–	1	0	–	–
1947	2	4	32.00	–	24	86	25.46	4
1947/48	–	–	–	–	6	6	73.50	–
1948	2	11	15.27	2	31	150	19.48	12
1949	25	67	24.95	–	21	103	22.65	12
1950	26	74	23.81	3	33	174	16.71	14
1951	32	105	21.30	5	34	127	19.71	6
1952	32	131	17.07	6	36	177	19.54	18
1953	19	100	15.90	8	31	146	24.24	10
1953/54	9	28	42.07	1	5	18	31.61	1
1954	32	125	16.00	7	32	155	15.80	13
1954/55	–	–	–	–	18	57	20.45	3
1955	33	216	14.39	18	34	195	16.14	13
1955/56	11	81	10.72	10	–	–	–	–
1956	26	155	12.46	15	35	153	16.22	8
1956/57	14	56	14.87	4	14	90	12.25	8
1957	31	212	12.02	21	32	114	20.00	7
1958	29	170	12.08	14	24	91	15.39	5

Summary

	M	Wkts	Ave.	5wi	M	Wkts	Ave.	5wi
Home	290	1,370	15.65	99	368	1671	18.92	122
Away	34	165	17.45	15	43	171	19.17	12
Totals	324	1,535	15.85	114	411	1842	18.95	134

Test cricket

Season	Lock				Wardle			
	Tests	Wkts	Ave.	5wi	Tests	Wkts	Ave.	5wi
1947/48	–	–	–	–	1	0	–	–
1950	–	–	–	–	1	2	52.00	–
1951	–	–	–	–	2	5	34.20	–
1952	2	4	9.25	–	–	–	–	–
1953	2	8	20.62	1	3	13	26.46	–
1953/54	5	14	51.28	–	2	4	26.75	–
1954	–	–	–	–	4	20	8.80	1
1954/55	–	–	–	–	6	15	23.00	1
1955	3	13	27.15	–	3	15	18.20	–
1956	4	15	22.46	–	1	1	59.00	–
1956/57	1	2	19.00	–	4	26	13.80	3
1957	3	15	10.86	2	1	1	53.00	–
1958	5	34	7.47	3	–	–	–	–

Summary

	Tests	Wkts	Ave.	5wi	Tests	Wkts	Ave.	5wi
Home	19	89	14.70	6	21	57	20.70	1
Away	6	16	47.25	0	7	45	20.00	4
Totals	25	105	19.66	6	28	102	20.39	5

… and finally, and sadly

Lock was no-balled for throwing six times in his career. One of these instances was for England against West Indies at Kingston in 1953/54. He was the first bowler to be called for this offence when playing for England and has been subsequently joined only by D.I. Gower who deliberately threw the final ball of the Test against New Zealand at Trent Bridge in 1986.

Laker and Lock

County Championship records

(Matches in which both played)

Season	Matches		O	R	W	Ave.	5wi	10wm
1949	18	Laker	783.3	1,565	97	16.13	7	1
		Lock	494.5	1,014	37	27.40	–	–
1950	19	Laker	988.4	1,759	111	15.84	9	3
		Lock	725	1,304	53	24.60	1	–
1951	19	Laker	922.2	1,982	101	19.62	9	3
		Lock	693.5	1,293	65	19.89	3	–
1952	18	Laker	730.2	1,451	86	16.87	7	–
		Lock	687.1	1,429	85	16.81	3	–
1953	9	Laker	363	752	43	17.48	2	1
		Lock	354	699	62	11.27	6	1
1954	19	Laker	681.2	1,364	96	14.20	10	4
		Lock	689.4	1,195	94	12.71	6	2
1955	20	Laker	649.3	1,431	82	17.45	2	1
		Lock	833.3	1,678	130	12.90	13	4
1956	10	Laker	337.1	794	45	17.64	2	–
		Lock	367	717	57	12.57	5	2
1957	17	Laker	543	1,009	80	12.61	4	–
		Lock	616	1,405	113	12.43	11	4
1958	17	Laker	585.5	1,130	83	13.61	6	2
		Lock	612.3	1,234	95	12.98	6	1
1959	16	Laker	528.2	1,219	46	26.50	4	1
		Lock	616.1	1,461	65	22.47	6	1
Totals	182	**Laker**	7,113	14,456	870	16.61	62	16
		Lock	6,689.4	13,429	856	15.68	60	15

Note: The influence of the 'spin twins' on Surrey's unprecedented seven consecutive Championship titles in the period 1952–58 cannot be overstated. During these seasons of success, Laker and Lock took 44 per cent of the wickets despite bowling only 38 per cent of the overs. When both were playing, Surrey won 71 per cent (78 out of 110) of its games but won only 50 per cent (43/86) when either or both were absent. In the 78 victories there were only four games in which Surrey did not take all 20 wickets, Laker and Lock taking 56 per cent (875 wickets out of a total of 1,548).

Test Record in England

(Matches in which both played)

Venue	Tests		O	R	W	Ave.	5wi	10wm
Edgbaston	2	Laker	92	155	8	19.37	–	–
(1957, '58)		Lock	72.1	111	6	18.50	–	–
Headingley	4	Laker	162.5	247	23	10.73	3	1
(1953, '56,								
'57, '58)		Lock	166.4	276	21	13.14	1	1
Lord's	1	Laker	25	37	5	7.40	–	–
(1958)		Lock	24	29	9	3.22	1	–
Old Trafford	2	Laker	70	97	19	5.10	2	1
(1952, '56)		Lock	78.3	142	5	28.40	–	–
the Oval	6	Laker	208.3	430	26	16.53	1	–
(1952, '53, '55,								
56', '57, '58)		Lock	202.5	319	31	10.29	3	1
Trent Bridge	1	Laker	59.1	87	6	14.50	–	–
(1956)		Lock	58	84	4	21.00	–	–
Totals	16	**Laker**	617.3	1053	87	12.10	7	2
		Lock	602.1	961	76	12.64	4	2

In nine of the above Test matches, the spin combination of Laker and Lock had a combined total of ten or more wickets. These matches are as follows:

Venue	Opposition	Year	Laker	Lock	Total
The Oval	Australia	1953	5-109	6-64	11-173
The Oval	South Africa	1955	7-84	8-101	15-185
Trent Bridge	Australia	1956	6-87	4-84	10-171
Headingley	Australia	1956	11-113	7-81	18-194
Old Trafford	Australia	1956	19-90	1-116	20-206
The Oval	Australia	1956	7-88	3-66	10-154
The Oval	West Indies	1957	5-77	11-48	16-125
Lord's	New Zealand	1958	5-37	9-29	14-66
Headingley	New Zealand	1958	8-44	11-65	19-109

The pair also played together in eight Tests overseas (four in the West Indies in 1954/55, one in South Africa in 1956/57 and three in Australia in 1958/59. On only one occasion did they take ten or more wickets in a match:

SCG, Sydney	Australia	1958/59	7-117	4-153	11-270

This was the only Test of the five-match series that Australia did not win.

Bibliography

John Arlott, *Test Match Diary, 1953,* James Barrie

Peter Arnold & Peter Wynne-Thomas (1989), *An Ashes Anthology – England* v. *Australia,* Christopher Helm

Trevor Bailey & Fred Trueman (1988), *The Spinners' Web,* Willow Books, Harper Collins

Alex Bannister (1954), *Cricket Cauldron,* Stanley Paul

Anthony J. Barker (1998), *The WACA – An Australian Cricket Success Story,* Allen and Unwin

Alec Bedser (1981): *Twin Ambitions,* Stanley Paul; *Cricket Choice,* Pelham

Richie Benaud (1984), *On Reflection,* Willow Books, Harper Collins

Ian Brayshaw, ed., *Cricket West,* Perth Building Society

Ted Dexter, with Ralph Dellor (1996), *Ted Dexter's Little Cricket Book,* Bloomsbury

George Chesterton and Hubert Doggart (1989), *Oxford and Cambridge Cricket,* Willow Books, Harper Collins

Brian E. Hebert and Roger Packham (1990), *Oxted Cricket Club 1890-1990, A Centenary Celebration,* Club

Alan Hill (1988; 1996): *Johnny Wardle – Cricket Conjuror,* David and Charles; *Peter May,* Andre Deutsch

Jim Laker (1979), *A Spell from Laker,* Hamlyn

Tony Lock (1957), *For Surrey and England,* Hodder and Stoughton

Christopher Martin-Jenkins (1984), *Cricket A Way of Life – The Cricketer Illustrated Book of Cricket,* Century Publishing

Ian Peebles (1968), *Straight from the Shoulder,* Hutchinson

Jack Pollard (1988), *Australian Cricket – The Game and the Players,* Angus and Robertson

Gordon Ross (1958), *The Surrey Story,* Stanley Paul

E.W. Swanton (1986; 1954), ed.: *Barclays World of Cricket,* Harper Collins; *West Indian Adventure – with Hutton's MCC team 1953-54,* Museum Press

Kirwan Ward (1972), *Put Lock On,* Robert Hale

Contemporary accounts in the *London Times, London Evening News, Daily Telegraph, News Chronicle, Manchester Guardian, Leicester Mercury, Sussex Daily News, Yorkshire Post, Picture Post, West Australian, Playfair Cricket Monthly, The Cricketer, Surrey CCC Yearbooks* and various editions of *Wisden Cricketers' Almanack* have provided the nucleus of printed sources in this book.

Index